Contemporary Adulthood and the Night-Time Economy

Leisure Studies in a Global Era

Series Editors:

Karl Spracklen, Professor of Leisure Studies, Leeds Metropolitan University, UK

Karen Fox, Professor of Leisure Studies, University of Alberta, Canada

In this book series, we defend leisure as a meaningful, theoretical, framing concept; and critical studies of leisure as a worthwhile intellectual and pedagogical activity. This is what makes this book series distinctive: we want to enhance the discipline of leisure studies and open it up to a richer range of ideas; and, conversely, we want sociology, cultural geographies and other social sciences and humanities to open up to engaging with critical and rigorous arguments from leisure studies. Getting beyond concerns about the grand project of leisure, we will use the series to demonstrate that leisure theory is central to understanding wider debates about identity, postmodernity and globalisation in contemporary societies across the world. The series combines the search for local, qualitatively rich accounts of everyday leisure with the international reach of debates in politics, leisure and social and cultural theory. In doing this, we will show that critical studies of leisure can and should continue to play a central role in understanding society. The scope will be global, striving to be truly international and truly diverse in the range of authors and topics.

Titles include:

Brett Lashua, Karl Spracklen and Stephen Wagg (*editors*)
SOUNDS AND THE CITY
Popular Music, Place and Globalization

Oliver Smith
CONTEMPORARY ADULTHOOD AND THE NIGHT-TIME ECONOMY

Karl Spracklen
WHITENESS AND LEISURE

Robert A. Stebbins
CAREERS IN SERIOUS LEISURE
From Dabbler to Devotee in Search of Fulfilment

Soile Veijola, Jennie Germann Molz, Olli Pyyhtinen, Emily Hockert and Alexander Grit
DISRUPTIVE TOURISM AND ITS UNTIDY GUESTS
Alternative Ontologies for Future Hospitalities

Leisure Studies in a Global Era
Series Standing Order ISBN 978–1–137–31032–3   hardback
978–1–137–31033–0   paperback
(*outside North America only*)

You can receive future titles in this series as they are published by placing a standing order. Please contact your bookseller or, in case of difficulty, write to us at the address below with your name and address, the title of the series and the ISBN quoted above.

Customer Services Department, Macmillan Distribution Ltd, Houndmills, Basingstoke, Hampshire RG21 6XS, England

---

Contemporary Adulthood and the Night-Time Economy

Oliver Smith
Plymouth University, UK

First published 2014 by
PALGRAVE MACMILLAN

Palgrave Macmillan in the UK is an imprint of Macmillan Publishers Limited, registered in England, company number 785998, of Houndmills, Basingstoke, Hampshire RG21 6XS.

Palgrave Macmillan in the US is a division of St Martin's Press LLC, 175 Fifth Avenue, New York, NY 10010.

Palgrave Macmillan is the global academic imprint of the above companies and has companies and representatives throughout the world.

Palgrave® and Macmillan® are registered trademarks in the United States, the United Kingdom, Europe and other countries.

ISBN 978–1–137–34451–9

This book is printed on paper suitable for recycling and made from fully managed and sustained forest sources. Logging, pulping and manufacturing processes are expected to conform to the environmental regulations of the country of origin.

A catalogue record for this book is available from the British Library.

A catalog record for this book is available from the Library of Congress.

Typeset by MPS Limited, Chennai, India.

For Clare and Isaac

Contents

Acknowledgements

Thanks are due to a number of people, some without whom I would have been unable to start this book, and others without whom it would never have been finished. Particular thanks go to Simon Winlow, whose work has been invaluable in helping me define and explore many of the ideas contained herein, and also for taking the time to read and comment on drafts of this book.

Thanks also to a number of friends and colleagues, particularly Rowland Atkinson, Dean Wilson and Chris Pac-Soo, who were integral to either aiding the completion of this book or at least providing a welcome distraction from it.

Thanks to my mum and dad, whose constant support and encouragement has been invaluable.

Thanks of course to my wife, Clare, who accompanied me on field-work (I promise I will never take you to an 80s retro bar again), barely grumbled when I returned home from the field as she was getting up to go to work, and has endured the frustrations of sharing a life with someone writing to a deadline.

I would also like to thank those who tolerated my peculiar interest in their lives during my research. I owe you a pint.

1
Introduction

This book examines how and to what extent the night-time economy (NTE) maintains its allure to committed adult consumers as they leave their twenties behind, and plough inexorably into what would traditionally be termed 'adulthood'. Utilising original qualitative data drawn from an extended group of individuals between the ages of 30 and 40 living in a city in the north of England, I attempt to make sense of the deep emotional and aesthetic attachment many people develop to urban drinking cultures. Of particular interest is the utility of these consumerised leisure markets for youth identities, cultures and social networks and the extent to which these change over time as the individual's circumstances adapt to the changing social requirements of each phase of the life course. On a more abstract level, I am interested in the relationship between the subjective experience of social reality and the overarching influences that shape the social and cultural world. Perhaps young consumers are 'captured' by the ideology of liberal capitalism. Alternatively, the cultures of the NTE may serve as creative and organic structures free from the influence of the dominant ideology. It might even be reasonable to propose that the cultures of the NTE are politically resistant to capitalist hegemony, that the cultural life of the NTE is structured around a 'taking back' of this cultural ground from the dour corporatist agenda. In attempting to explore these possible interpretations, I hope to move beyond the predictable sociological dichotomy of agency and structure and offer a reading of 'youth' lifestyles and consumer desires that skirts around bombastic critique of critical sociology as determinism while avoiding the gaping pitfalls of postmodern relativism and liberal sociology's focus on discursive, liberating, do-it-yourself identities. Drawing upon data taken from a detailed and extended ethnographic study, my hope is to add to the sociological

1

understanding of youth transitions, consumerism and identity and the orderly disorder of the NTE.

Excessive consumption of alcohol has in recent years constituted a significant proportion of current affairs discussion and prompted a huge growth in academic literature, addressing the urban economy and youth cultural practice (Engineer et al., 2003; Hobbs et al., 2003; Hadfield, 2006; Measham, 2008). New, punitive methods of control appear to be announced with startling regularity by policy-makers, despite seeming at odds with the enthusiasm and verve with which the New Labour government pushed for and achieved the relaxing of the nation's licensing laws only a few years previously (see Chatterton and Hollands, 2003; Hadfield, 2006). The shock tactics of 'social marketing', which play on social anxieties and often draw upon a perhaps mythic desire to be socially responsible, have combined with new police and local authority powers to 'crack down' on alcohol consumption outside of regulated spaces. Recent examples include the 2008 banning of alcohol on the London Underground and the increased powers for police and community support officers to confiscate alcohol being consumed in public places, and the 2013 call from the Association of Chief Police Officers for the introduction of privately run 'drunk tanks' in which to deposit those who have transgressed those boundaries of 'acceptable' alcohol use that lie beneath the veneer of hedonism. These policy interventions aim to create the impression that the government is committed to controlling alcohol consumption although only to the extent that their relationship with the alcohol industry remains unharmed. Many of these measures appear to focus disproportionately on the poor, while the drinking behaviours of the wealthy are by implication viewed as unproblematic. Even the widely publicised violence and destruction of the Bullingdon Club[1] are usually meekly framed as little more than 'twittishness' (to use Boris Johnson's phrase). These contradictory themes within government policy inevitably result in a renewed focus on the 'disorderly consumer' and reiterate the government's commitment to its responsibilisation agenda, which most critical commentators believe is hopelessly flawed and ignorant of the broader social, cultural and economic forces that underlie decision-making, not least within the sphere of commodified leisure (Reiner, 2007; Winlow and Hall, 2009).

This book constitutes an important extension to the body of work surrounding alcohol consumption and the NTE. The vast majority of the academic literature that has addressed excessive alcohol use in this specific cultural sphere has focused upon the social behaviours of young people in their teenage years and early twenties (Engineer et al., 2003; Plant and Plant, 2006). This focus is of course entirely reasonable, and while trend data for alcohol consumption among the 16–24 age group suggests a slight decline in the proportion of young people consuming alcohol over the past decade (ONS, 2013), data also suggests that this demographic are more likely to 'binge' when they do drink.

However, the relative absence of interest in these drinkers as they age is perplexing, as it is this generation who were the trail-blazers, the first generation to structure their weekend leisure in relation to the post-industrial urban drinking cultures that came to typify the city centre after dark during the early nineties. The hopes, attitudes and aspirations of this generation of young people are deeply indicative of the fundamental changes that accompanied the almost universal adoption of neoliberalism among the polity and the broader, more opaque influence of postmodernism upon cultural and internal life. After all, they are old enough to remember the last vestiges of organised industrial modernism, and they have become adults in an age in which most of the certainties of that time have been dispensed with. Their generation grew up in the NTE and, as we will see, many now appear incapable of ignoring its allure. Despite looking older than most of the other regulars, they continue onwards and in doing so prompt the development of new niche markets, defined new trends and new products that attempt to speak to the desires of those unwilling to cash in their chips and move on.

Many studies that address youth involvement in the NTE have failed to contribute anything more than a general description of youthful cultural innovation (see, for example, Engineer et al., 2003, who explain the attractions of night-time leisure as little more than an underlying desire of young people to 'have a laugh'). It's now clear that the field must utilise new ideas and new approaches if we are to discover new truths relating to the compelling experience of night-time leisure. Part of this process must involve an acceptance that not everyone who utilises the services of the bars and nightclubs that give the NTE its character are between the ages of 18 and 25. In the standard sociological manner, we must try to explain and understand the key components of this culture and why they are so attractive to such a broad range of people. We need to try and make sense of the diversity we see in night-time leisure venues and trends, while identifying what it is that makes older drinkers keep coming back.

A number of commentators have echoed Côté (2000) in his discussion of the protraction of youth within the life course (see, for example,

Tanner and Arnett, 2009). However, a more thorough unpacking of the actual processes at work that induce the levels of *infantilisation* and *narcissism* suggested by the likes of Barber (2007) and Hall et al. (2008) is certainly necessary. I return to these concepts quite often, but at this stage it is perhaps worth stating quite clearly that I will use them in the precise psychoanalytical sense. I am not in any way offering a conservative critique of youthful or marginalised groups and their cultural characteristics. My goal here is simply to move the debate forwards by drawing on work that usually lies outside of the restrictive boundaries of contemporary sociology. I address this point in more detail later in the book.

Before the economic collapse of 2008, young people had more disposable income and easier access to credit than at any time previously. While their future employment prospects were uncertain, a combination of student loans, Educational Maintenance Allowance and interest-free overdrafts, alongside short-term employment opportunities in retail and service industries (Lloyd, 2013) afforded many the opportunity to engage in unparalleled consumption. They tended to have few, if any traditional responsibilities resting on their shoulders and were subject to a broad range of social pressures that propelled them towards the night-time drinking experience.

However, as we will examine more closely in the following chapters, the first 'generation' of drinkers targeted by changes in local government and laissez-faire policies toward the expansion of the NTE are now in their thirties. As such, the individuals who form the basis of this research are inconsistent with the 'drinking arc' narrative (Maggs and Schulenberg, 2004; Seaman and Ikegwuonu, 2010) which suggests that growing 'maturity' can be linked to a marked moderation in consumption. Indeed, there appears to be a general assumption of young consumers that 'they'll grow out of it' (Wright, 1999: 38). Data tends to support the argument that excessive drinking behaviours are lingering further into adulthood for a much greater proportion of the population than we might assume (Smith and Foxcroft, 2009). The Office for National Statistics (2013a) reports that 25% of men, and 20% of women between the ages of 25 and 44 drank 'heavily' on at least one day in the previous week, compared to 22% of men and 17% of women aged 16–24.

The giant conglomerates responsible for the rise to prominence of most of the major pub and bar chains across the United Kingdom (the most notable of which are perhaps All Bar One, The Living Room, Pitcher & Piano, The Slug and Lettuce, and Walkabout) appear to have recognised this fact and tailored spaces and experiences in order to cater for their customers' changing and assiduously cultivated tastes, while the behemoth of global capitalism's consumer ideology plays its part by ensuring that they remain convinced that all manner of personal pleasures, alongside tangible and intangible social benefits, are to be found in the NTE. These bars offer an experiential adventure firmly grounded in consumer signification. Patrons *believe* they are purchasing the experience of exclusivity and indulgent, rarefied hedonism while being surrounded by a group of like-minded, informed and critical consumers, all of whom reaffirm each other's belief that they are consuming tastefully and that the highly priced drinks are somehow 'worth it'. Beyond the sale of alcohol, the bar is aiming to retain an amorphous sense of 'cool' (see Frank, 1998; Heath and Potter, 2006), which becomes commodified and distinguishes it within a highly competitive marketplace. In this context, consumers are encouraged to develop an appreciation for the taste and sign value of alcoholic beverages. The cultural context of consumer exclusivity means that the cheapness and alcoholic strength of the drinks is not foregrounded, and can appear quite tawdry to this self-identified metropolitan elite. Consequently, these older consumers are targeted with a range of cocktails rather than ready-to-drink alcopops, a vast selection of wines and an array of olives and sun-dried tomatoes that serve as up-market bar snacks. Lighting, seating, bar-backs, menus and music are often conscientiously designed to appeal to older drinkers. The goal is to encourage customers to identify with the bar in a process of mutual recognition, and ideally a magical intertwining of bar and clientele should take place. The decor, music and ambience should fit neatly with the tastes, dispositions and aspirations of those who return and find comfort and affirmation in its sights and sounds. For those keen to experience the more immediate, visceral delights of the NTE, and for those who believe the wine bar circuit to be populated by poseurs, there is little inducement to enter. Inevitably, there is another bar, another club, another pub that somehow fits, and all are encouraged to believe that their tastes have primacy, that their approach to intoxication is the right one, and that other denizens of the night fail to consume in the correct manner.

Some pubs and bars appear to be predominantly populated by couples or groups of couples – a clear signal that traditional markers of 'adulthood' and responsibility are no barrier to fulfilling immersion within the NTE. Of course, as Beck (1992) and Bauman (1998a) have been keen to point out, relationships are increasingly fraught with risk and uncertainty, compelling many individuals to seek and defend their own subjective interests. As we will see, some men and women appear drawn towards seeking sexual conquests in ever-greater numbers, and while this may not be entirely new, it is certainly a demonstrable characteristic of some of the dedicated night-time consumers entering the twilight of their youth. Others attempt to put a string of failed relationships behind them as they continue to seek 'the one' endlessly promised by myriad cultural and marketing devices; the NTE caters for all of these and more.

Some researchers have focused only upon the surface details of this process and portray consumers as essentially defining their own drinking experience through creativity and innovation (Jayne et al., 2010). Of course, what is missing from this kind of analysis is a detailed appreciation of the ability of the market to adapt and thrive on consumer diversity. These commentators appear unwilling to countenance the possibility that the surface diversity they champion may not be a clear indication of the innate ability of the consumer to control and determine his or her own cultural engagement. This surface diversity may actually reflect the very energy the contemporary marketplace needs to renew itself. Of course, consumer capitalism needs to maintain the illusion of diversity and constant innovation if it is to avoid the bland consumer universality that would sound its death knell. The range of pubs and bars often reflects nothing more than deliberately cultivated niche markets, beneath which lies nothing more innovative than profit accumulation enabled by the skilful manipulation of consumer desire. This is not to say that the consumer is merely a manipulated cipher occupying a desolate neoliberal landscape in which all individuality and creativity have been crushed by evil corporations. Instead, I want to develop an analysis that attempts to rethink the relationship between the subject and the objective environment of the NTE. I want to think about the pressures placed upon this population and the needs, desires and motivations of my research sample, and I want to move away from the baseless optimism and progressivism that constitutes much that has been written about youth cultures and contemporary forms of leisure.

The emergence of a NTE that caters for its customers as they progress through their life course has to date been largely ignored within academic literature. For most authors it seems to be assumed that young people will simply 'give up' the reckless preoccupations of youth as they age and adopt the characteristics of the socially embedded and respectable 'adult' (see Matza, 1990). However, examination of the meanings and associations the over-thirties apply to and extract from their continued involvement in urban drinking cultures is certainly worthy of attention. In an effort to explore the social, cultural and economic processes that perpetuate the allure of the NTE, and to understand how the traditional responsibilities of adulthood are evaded or mediated, I will attempt to illuminate the life-worlds of a sample of people who are experiencing a crucial biographical progression that is now fraught with risk, uncertainty and the promise of self-fulfilment through the pursuit of hedonistic pleasures. I will investigate the meanings they draw from the cultural context of alcohol consumption and explore the troubling contention that 'traditional' adulthood is being eroded by a powerful historical trend that is destabilising identity, cultivating narcissism, social competition and instrumentality and essentially infantilising a generation.

Chapter outline

After a brief history of the study area, I will offer a description and defence of the research methods I have used to gather the data that forms the foundation of this book. Chapter 2 outlines the social and economic backdrop against which we have witnessed the staggering growth of commodified leisure and, more pertinently, the NTE. The decline of heavy industrial production in the West prompted a profound change in the nature of British society. Our 'real' economy is now driven by the selling of goods and services to one another, and this rather stark fact should be understood within the context of the recent crises of fictitious capital (see, for example, Keen, 2010; Dumeil and Levy, 2013) which many believed had become Britain's passport to ever-increasing wealth and prosperity. Leisure time, and its relative importance to the individual underwent a period of growth (see Rojek, 1989), although there is some indication that the ascension of leisure was short-lived. Today an argument could be made that the affective labour of social media, and the constant stream of email to mobile devices is in fact contributing to a contraction of real leisure time and a blurring of the boundaries between work and leisure. What we can say for sure is that consumerism and conspicuous consumption was becoming increasingly embedded within mass culture. From within a maelstrom of social and economic change and the rapid erosion of traditional forms of social structure, numerous forms of commodified leisure were to arise, of which the alcohol industry is perhaps the most conspicuous, growing into a financial behemoth integral to the nation's economy.

Chapter 3 looks more closely at the specific conditions that have given rise to the night-time leisure economy as we understand it today.

It places specific cultures of alcohol consumption – the determined drunkenness commonly referred to as 'binge drinking' against the commodified experience offered by the night-time high street, and the core socioeconomic changes outlined in the previous chapter. It seems unlikely that authentic modes of liberation are to be found in the NTE, which makes it all the more important that we attempt to understand the attraction of these spaces to consumers. How can we explain the enduring allure of these spaces to an ostensibly adult cohort, and what is the relationship between committed engagement with the NTE and other facets of life, adulthood and employment?

Chapter 4 explores how marketing and branding within the NTE represent a triumph of the symbolic over the material, a reflection of consumer society more broadly. The marketisation of the NTE ensures that all preferences and ages are catered for. These tend to be assiduously managed spaces, each competing for market share within their particular niche.

Chapter 5 engages with the process of becoming 'adult' under contemporary global capitalism. Changes in the way that individuals make their transitions to adulthood, changing perceptions of 'youth' and the drive towards the infantilisation of consumer populations (Barber, 2007; Hall et al., 2008) all contribute to the powerful allure of the NTE. Each of these social trends will be explored in detail in this chapter.

Chapter 6 contextualises some of the wider themes that are present within this piece of work with a more in-depth consideration of the drinking biographies of two of my participants, Rob and Andrea. Both these participants acted as 'gatekeepers' (see Whyte, 1959) to aspects of the NTE that I would otherwise have been unable to enter unobtrusively, and have thus contributed to this work significantly. Their inclusion, and an appreciation of their individual drinking biographies, serves as a valuable aid for unpacking and understanding a number of concepts that surface repeatedly over the following pages.

Chapter 7 explores the desires and motivations that are tangled up with continued and unabated participation within the NTE. For many of the respondents, this involved a level of commitment that is not necessarily reflected in all other aspects of their lives. This chapter will explore the reasons why these individuals retain such an attachment to the excessive consumption of alcohol that is bound up with their continued dedication to the NTE. Answering this question, however, tends to bring up more questions than answers – respondents often reported that a bad night out was not uncommon, and found it hard to articulate what was so great about a particular night, event or bar, conundrums that beg to be unravelled. Also apparent is the fear of *cultural inconsequentiality* that is persistently and malevolently looming over many of these individuals, a fear that is matched by the last vestiges of traditional invocations of guilt that are attached to the perception of familial and relationship roles. Within this chapter it is possible to identify the growing centrality of instrumentality to the core identity. As the traditional foundations of identity are challenged by prevailing social circumstances, the individual is increasingly compelled to search out, defend or advance his or her own self-interest (Lasch, 1979; Bauman, 2000; Winlow and Hall, 2006). This is not a self-interest that can be conveniently distilled into an expression of mere anti-social selfishness. Rather, this self-interest, the focus on the needs and desires of the self now structures social experience. Those who display these characteristics are 'fitting in' and 'being social' by a wealth of other means, that will be explored in due course.

Chapter 8 explores the creation and maintenance of identity within the NTE by utilising a combination of participant observation and unstructured interviews with regular participants within the night-time drinking strip. My respondents are all over the age of 30 and often occupy fairly mainstream work positions and family lives. In the standard sense then, they are adults, not children, and the transition to adulthood, such as it is, appears to be complete. However, this has not meant the rejection of youthful pursuits and the adoption of a social bearing that emphasises decorum and respectability. Through this chapter we are able to come to some understanding of how these individuals contextualise their alcohol consumption within the broader picture of their self-identity, how they conceive of their alcohol consumption in comparison to younger, less experienced and apparently less sophisticated consumers and where they see their drinking behaviours developing in the future. Respondents reminisce fondly about the distant drinking experiences of their formative years, while comparing themselves favourably with today's young drinkers. They also indicate that they believe they are consuming in a far more sophisticated fashion than they did in their youth. The ways in which these individuals articulate their past, present and future alcohol consumption is analysed against the backdrop of the social and economic processes discussed elsewhere, which may have a much stronger influence on alcohol consumption than many consumers would like to believe.

Chapter 9 examines the mediation of conflicting spheres of life as they come into contact with each other. Specifically, this chapter is concerned with to what extent dedicated consumers within the NTE manage to negotiate paid employment and the maintenance of friendship networks alongside committed participation in alcohol-based leisure activities. While some respondents appeared to successfully compartmentalise the conflicting aspects of their life-worlds, in general the fear of *cultural inconsequentiality* – the deep anxiety that accompanies the danger of not being invited out, of not fitting in, impacted other aspects of their lives and work identities. Some respondents clearly placed a greater degree of importance on their lives outside of work, their 'second lives' (Presdee, 2000) which took precedence over their working lives. For these respondents, work was to be endured, rather than enjoyed and their 'real' selves were to be found at the bar, on the dance floor or nursing Lucozade and a bacon sandwich on a Saturday morning.

The book concludes with a chapter that attempts to pull these many disparate threads together to create a nuanced picture of the lived experience of these committed adult consumers within post-industrial Britain.

In the chapters that follow I will attempt to depict the ways in which the macro-level social and economic pressures that have been identified as bearing down on young people within the United Kingdom (UK) (see Winlow and Hall, 2006) not only show no signs of weakening but are compounded, exacerbated and prolonged as individuals travel through the life course. It is important to acknowledge that my respondents do not find themselves on the margins of society. While they come from a variety of class backgrounds, they can all be described as socially *in*cluded, generally or usually employed and, aside from the occasional procurement and consumption of illegal drugs, they are not involved to any great extent with criminal markets. In these respects, they represent the 30 to 40-year-old British mainstream and, as such, the very core of 'middle England'. While my study is 'particular' in as much as it draws upon a highly localised and rather small sample, my rather grand hope is that it is 'generalisable' to the extent that a lot of the structural pressures and ephemeral seductions to which the sample members are subject manifest themselves throughout the British mainstream to varying degrees. Other researchers have applied a similar theoretical approach to marginalised populations (Hall et al., 2008) but there is still much work to be done in extending our knowledge of the intricacies of hedonism and seduction, consumerised leisure, individualism and social competition alongside the transformation of identity and biography. I hope this can make a small contribution to this process and perhaps act as a point of departure for further studies that might address the contemporary life-worlds of this specific age group.

Methodological note

Vikton

The city of Vikton[2] is a natural location for this study. Perhaps most importantly, it is the city in which I grew up, and from the outset I was confident that I possessed a thorough and comprehensive geographical knowledge of the area and its history. Furthermore, this degree of local knowledge would surely prove invaluable in terms of saving time and effort in getting to know a new or unfamiliar city with the degree of intimacy necessary with which to conduct ethnographic work.

When I mentioned to colleagues my intentions to conduct alcohol-related research in Vikton, they often suggested that I may get less dramatic results than if I were to conduct my research in one of the larger conurbations such as Manchester, Leeds or Newcastle. Aside from a comparative lack of familiarity with these cities, I felt confident that the development of the NTE in Vikton, while perhaps a little smaller and more contained, was not too far removed from that of many other cities across the country. I suggested to my colleagues that they join me on a night of observational research down the 'Miracle Mile', a Mecca for single-sex groups, cheap drinks and loud music, before queuing for a kebab and taxi in the melee that constitutes the city centre in the early hours of Saturday morning. As many other authors have noted (Chatterton and Hollands, 2001, 2003; Hobbs et al., 2003; Hadfield, 2006) there is an unavoidable element of uniformity that transcends local specificity, and the night-time drinking experience in Vikton possesses many of the same dynamics as other cities. Indeed, in my experience, the city centre was able to rival any other British city as the stage for drama that would keep the producers of hyperbolic documentaries on the less reputable satellite television channels in material for many months.

Vikton is a relatively small city, and lacks any great diversity in terms of ethnicity. It could be described as rather compact, and today is predominantly sustained by tourism, leisure and services, with much of the tourist information boasting proudly of its museums, churches, pubs and theatres, while gift shops are crammed full of items celebrating the lives of the city's famous sons and daughters.

Vikton shares a number of historical characteristics with many of the larger cities in the north of England, holding dear a rich industrial past. As employers began to relocate outside the city, due to the wane of manufacturing across the country, the city centre became in need of, and received an injection of incentives in order to generate renewed business interests. Vikton was not alone in this venture, as during the mid to late 1990s many municipal authorities in Britain shared the common ambition to create the '24-hour city'. The shared aim was that of bringing vibrancy to central urban areas across an elongated time span, a utopian vision of the night-time streets of the UK profiting under a European model of relaxation, cosmopolitanism and urbanity (O'Connor and Wynne, 1996; Montgomery, 1998; Zukin, 1998). These aims were in accordance with land use planning guidance of the time, which encouraged local authorities to promote a mixture of retail, leisure and residential usage in urban centres:

> One of the main reasons people give for shunning town centres at night is fear about their security and safety: one of the main reasons for that fear is the fact that there are very few people about. Breaking that vicious circle is key to bringing life back to town centres ... adopting planning policies that encourage a wide and varied range of uses ... may well extend, for instance, to enabling arrangements that help promote the night economy. (DoE, 1994: 14)

As a consequence, a stroll along the river reveals where old warehouses have been pulled down to make way for a night-time leisure courtyard, around which are centred a cinema and associated café bar, Pitcher & Piano and Revolution chain bars, and a couple of restaurants. Wooden decking provides drinkers and diners with a facility to enjoy a river view over the once bustling waterway that now merely hosts scenic cruises and a flotilla of pleasure craft. Similarly, former banks have been transformed into Vertical Drinking Establishments,[3] and entire streets have been colonised by a mixture of corporate and independent licensed premises (see Chatterton and Hollands, 2003). During the day, tourists and shopping crowds will struggle to identify the magnitude of this shift in local government policy and economic activity. After dark, it's impossible to miss.

Confident that there was indeed an exciting and unique research opportunity quite literally on my doorstep, I began to re-read a number of key ethnographic texts in the search for methodological inspiration, and decided to hit the town:

I look out of the window and assess the weather. It's drizzling. Not really raining, but I know that I'm going to get wet walking into town. I consider ordering a taxi, but reason that there will be a long wait – it is Friday night, and there are probably a couple of thousand people who are even less keen to get wet than me. Also, I only live 10 minutes' walk away. The possibility of cancelling crosses my mind, but it isn't really an option – I've already confirmed the meeting place by text. Besides, I am a social scientist, about to embark on ethnographic research within one of the most exciting social environments of the post-industrial age – the night-time leisure economy. I zip up my jacket, close the door behind me and head for the pub.

It is 7 p.m., and we are meeting in what might be termed a 'real ale pub', a microcosm of the NTE, yet one which appears to signal diversity, tradition and independence in the face of mass homogenisation. It is located down a side alley, just off the main strip; a sanctuary to some from the chain pubs and theme bars that lie only a few metres away. The bar is made of dark wood, and the hand-pull pumps display beers from local breweries with names such as Roosters Yankee, Yorkshire Terrier and Daleside Dalesman. Toward the far end of the bar are two large brass frames, with taps offering more generic fare; Foster's, Strongbow, Kronenbourg and John Smith's Extra Smooth. The bar staff are wearing simple black polo shirts with the name of the pub embroidered onto the left breast. In the corner to my right, the landlord is deep in discussion with two men who appear to be in their fifties, drinking halves of bitter. They are busily scribbling notes in a notebook, while discussing the various merits of the brew. Perhaps they are sociologists, but I think it is more likely that they are members of CAMRA, the Campaign for Real Ale, a voluntary organisation with over 100,000 members, which acts as a consumer group promoting 'good quality bars and pubs' (CAMRA, 2014). While I am standing at the bar, my contact walks in, accompanied by two other lads that I don't know. We shake hands, exchange pleasantries and mutter something about the weather, and I offer to get a round in. Everyone asks for lager, and I order four pints of Foster's, feeling a little shameful at plumping for the generic option, in the face of an array of real ales. However, I reason that it is wise to remain on the same type of drink for as long as possible, and bitters at the other destinations we are likely to visit are probably going to be of a much lower quality.

We move over to a free table, and I glance at the other customers: there are approximately 20 in total. The pub is divided into two main rooms, one of which has the bar in it, stone floors, a piano and a quiz machine that looks incongruous beneath a shelf of Victorian plates and quart pots. The grinning face of the *Deal or No Deal* quiz host Noel Edmonds sporadically leers out across the pub, and I am grateful when three men in their forties walk over and deposit money in the machine, obscuring my view. The other room is carpeted, the pattern indecipherable in a line from the front door toward the bar where countless pairs of feet have ground dirt and debris into the ageing fibres. There is an old iron stove (or at least a replica of one) in the fireplace and framed 'historic' photographs of the local area. A couple who appear to be in their mid thirties are sitting in the corner, with a dog of indeterminate breed lying at their feet. I make the assumption that this is not simply a starting point to a debauched night out for them. I don't think the dog would get past the bouncers, custodians of the night-time drinking arenas, as he isn't wearing shoes. In the middle of the room are a group of men of varying ages. They are in shirtsleeves and loosened ties, with jackets slung on the back of their chairs. Snippets of their conversation reveal them to be work colleagues from a large office just up the street. Their drinks are a mixture of lager, bitter and Guinness. There are the two men at the end of the bar that I had noted earlier, and another group of lads that appear to have the same intentions as my comrades and me. They are talking excitedly, and drinking a variety of lager and alcopops.

The first pint of the night doesn't last long, and we are soon back out on the street. It doesn't seem to be raining as hard, or perhaps I am just sheltering under the umbrella-like effect of the beer. We turn right and toward the centre of town, continuing our conversations from the pub on topics such as the inconvenience of work and how our teams are progressing in the FA Cup. As we pass a budget hotel a bizarre chorus line of girls erupts onto the street. It looks like pink is certainly the colour of the evening, accompanied by fairy wings and tinselly halos. We all turn and watch as they make a beeline for the eighties theme bar across the road. Everyone is looking to enjoy themselves in their different ways, and the NTE extends the promise of pleasure and indulgence that draws people inexorably towards it.

Previous studies of drinking cultures and the NTE, whether funded by research councils such as the Alcohol Education and Research Council (AERC), government offices such as the Home Office or the Office of the Deputy Prime Minister (ODPM), industry groups or lobbyists such as the Portman Group have tended to rely heavily on quantitative analysis, deliberating over statistics in search of trends and longitudinal change within the drinking habits of a nation.[4] As many commentators have observed, reliance on statistics within the social sciences can lead to a number of pronounced problems (see Coleman and Moynihan, 1996; Young, 2004). While the production of statistics serves to provide a baseline for discussion, they are often little more than an indication that more detailed work needs to be carried out in the field. Rather than contribute to the growing numbers of statistics around the subject of the NTE, this study takes a critical theoretical stance collating a rich and diverse dataset through observation and interviews with a relatively small number of participants.

The core research questions around this piece of work, as well as my own predilection toward the research techniques of numerous academics (Whyte, 1959; Liebow, 1967; Ditton, 1977) made the methodological decisions reasonable easy. My aim is to gain a 'clear, firsthand picture' (Liebow, 1967: 10) of people in their thirties regularly consuming within the NTE, and achieve a level of understanding that would simply not be possible without the inclusion of ethnographic fieldwork. While quantitative research may be a valuable approach for some research issues, it would not be suitable for this project. Statistics are unable to communicate any sense of human subjectivity, about what it actually *feels* like to operate in specific social and cultural environments. The static nature of quantitative research, with its emphasis on relationships between variables, is not suited to dealing with issues that evolve over time and as a result of interconnected relationships between subjects. Similarly, the likelihood of being able to uncover actors' meanings and the chances of concepts emerging from data collection is enhanced through the use of qualitative methods (Bryman, 2004). In simple terms, I wanted the data I gathered to reflect the lived realities of the contemporary – I was keen to collect data that indicated emotional engagement and personal feelings, delving beyond statistical analysis in order to reveal what it means to be a regular and long-term participant in the alluring and seemingly bacchanalian drinking cultures of post-industrial Britain.

Of course, ethnography as a method of data collection is not perfect. Detractors have suggested that it lacks an impact in terms of policy-making and practice and is consequently irrelevant within the 'real' world of politics and policy (see Hammersley, 1992). However, qualitative and ethnographic sociology has frequently contributed to government policy (Cloward and Ohlin, 1960; Willmott and Young, 1973). It is clear that the judicious use of ethnographic methods in the collection and interpretation of data offers us not only the opportunity to advance our knowledge of human behaviour but also, to paraphrase Marx, the chance to change it.

Access

The issue of access is not one that poses a particular problem within my area of study, and consequently I was not to suffer the 'rude surprise' identified by Feldman et al. (2003: vii) as catching many potential social researchers unawares upon commencement of their research project. In terms of data, much could be achieved by simply sitting at a table in a bar or pub, while heads were unlikely to be turned by the sight of a man writing notes at a bar, just as observers in a covert study of patients' lives in mental hospitals discovered that they could take notes in full view, as staff simply interpreted this as a further sign of their mental illness (Rosenhan, 1974). Therefore having a 'front' was unnecessary (Ditton, 1977). In fact at times, this 'lone man at a bar' persona proved to be somewhat beneficial as curious drinkers or bar staff would engage me in often illuminating conversation enabling me to clarify many of the observations that I was making.

As a participant researcher, the danger associated with note-taking was the possibility that this practice could raise eyebrows or perhaps 'chill the scene' (Polsky, 1971: 127). This problem was countered by adopting techniques deployed previously by Williams (1990) whereby notes and key words would be hastily jotted down immediately after each night out, to be written up in full the following day. The only other reasonable option to this would be to follow in the footsteps of Ditton (1977) and secure myself within the lavatory to write down my observations as they occurred. I discounted this possibility however, as while portraying a certain degree of know-how within the arena of illicit drug use could be useful in terms of access and credibility, I wanted to draw the line at becoming widely known within the city which is my home and workplace as either a cokehead or an incontinent.

The research environment

As a 30-year-old sociologist with a fondness for a pint, I felt reasonably confident that I had a fairly solid understanding of the social environment within which I would be conducting my research. My appearance, demeanour, and knowledge of popular culture past and present enabled me to participate within a world that may appear alien to a researcher either much younger or much older than me. It is perhaps too simple to suggest that I was successful in fitting in. Rather, I stuck out in the youth dominated night-time leisure economy, but only to the same extent as my respondents. I experienced first-hand their desire to find a place that caters to their needs. Put simply, in sticking out, I blended in.

As I have described earlier in this chapter, I chose to centre my studies on a city of which I have knowledge, and a pre-existing network of friends and acquaintances that would be happy to allow me to join them on a night out, and introduce me to people that they knew. The use of relevant skills and knowledge already in my possession was also a great enabler in terms of integrating myself into the groups of people I was studying, in a way similar to that of Winlow (2001) in his engagement with hypermasculine cohorts in the north-east of England, and Holdaway (1982) in his covert study of the police.

Throughout the course of the research, I conducted unstructured interviews and/or wrote up fieldwork notes that focused on over 30 of the individuals who made up my primary research cohort. Some of the respondents had been known to me for several years previously as acquaintances, enabling me access to areas of their lives and the lives of their friends that might otherwise have been lost as a result of being too much of an 'outsider'. For example, Rob and Evan, whom the reader will encounter in the chapters that follow, were indispensable in terms of enabling me to access a much larger network of respondents. While some researchers have faced significant impediments in mobilising existing social networks (see, for example, Cassell, 1988), my access to and utilisation of established friendships was both fortuitous and remarkably straightforward. As a result, I accompanied respondents on stag weekends, I attended a couple of weddings and I was present through childbirth (in the pub, not the labour ward) and a broad range of other life events experienced by those I'd drawn close to. I believe that integration and acceptance into the life-worlds of the individuals whose experiences, attitudes and beliefs are so important to this piece of work, and the wealth of data this allowed me to collect, justifies my rather restricted sample size. Additionally, while the sample size may constitute a rather narrow band in terms of race, sexuality and socioeconomic background, I make no apology in following Hobbs and May (1993) and Corrigan (1979) in their assertion that in order to write about the experience of social exclusion, racial or gender inequalities, it is greatly beneficial to have experienced it first-hand and from the point of view of the marginalised subject. Nevertheless, while a number of respondents within my piece of work are female, gender was not a barrier to detailed interviews and ethnographic field notes. The women I interviewed were often as willing to admit to participating within the NTE in pursuit of the same hedonistic desires as were the men, while their attention and commitment to a consumerist ethos did not appear to be perceivably different to that of their male counterparts. Female respondents did tend to shroud talk of their alcohol consumption in terms of social drinking to a greater extent than did the males, but on the whole, I have declined to look at gender comparisons, and have discussed both sexes as similarly ensconced within the circuits of consumer culture, and subject to many of the same pressures and anxieties of global capitalism.

Covert observation was employed throughout the course of the research, especially on occasions where I was unfamiliar with the surroundings or the people I was with were no more than acquaintances of people I knew. Covert research was also a feature in situations where I was more interested in the overall dynamic of a particular venue. Listening to the after-work crowd at the bar for example, overhearing exchanges between bar staff and customers, dynamics between different groups of drinkers and so on, allowed me to pick up snippets of information that subtly informed my approach and analysis.

The data collection process

Talking to respondents about their participation within the NTE is not an arduous task, and researcher participation can therefore be limited to maintaining conversation rather than directing it through a structured interview. This allowed me to avoid methodological pitfalls such as the inclusion of leading questions or cornering the respondent. The fact that participants were happy to recount tales from their drinking biographies, compare their drinking habits now and wax lyrical on countless related topics led to a largely painless data collection process. Furthermore, this process of data collection, relying so heavily upon participant observation and ad hoc unstructured interview data, allowed me to confirm the accounts that I had been offered during the arranged interviews. Observational methods also enabled me to confirm or deny hypotheses, as well as develop a more detailed appreciation of interaction. Submersing myself in the culture I was studying enabled me to avoid making simple errors within the interview context, as well as allowing me to discover the answers to many questions myself, without having to recourse to asking my respondents. The repetition of my participation in nights out, celebrations, birthdays, weddings and so on necessarily led to me becoming deeply attuned to the operation of the culture I was studying, becoming an expert not through the asking of questions about the thing, but by becoming a part of the thing itself, feeling its compulsions and acting on its injunctions. I was feeling firsthand the excitement and expectation surrounding a 'big night out', suffering the hangovers and the damaged bank accounts alongside my respondents. Bolstered by my knowledge of sociological theory and an awareness that there was perhaps more to this culture of hedonistic excess than met the eye enabled me to offer a much more detailed analysis of these people and these places than would have been the case were I to simply confront individuals with a barrage of carefully constructed questions. Without this deep knowledge and appreciation, the application of *verstehen*, there exists a real risk that my analysis would fail to progress beyond simply recounting and validating the sterile observations of my respondents, who actually know very little about the meanings of things or how to account for their actions.

Due in part to the nature of the material being discussed, but also for the sake of convenience, organised semi-structured interviews tended to take place within the environs of the pub. While of course this could be a frustrating or time-consuming process as meetings were cancelled by participants with little notice or sometimes no notice at all, I tended to find that the familiar and informal surroundings contributed positively to the data collection process as subjects would relax and talk freely over a few drinks. Indeed on more than one occasion, an interview would turn into a night out with no warning, as thinking gave way to drinking.

Ethics

Issues around ethics have received much interest in recent years (see Coomber, 2002; Van den Hoonaard, 2002; Crow et al., 2006). Social research ethics appear to be largely regarded as similar to medical research ethics (see Beauchamp and Childress, 2001), which are focused on rights-based or deontological approaches, which make much of autonomy, non-maleficence, beneficence and justice. However, there is some debate around to what extent these approaches transfer to the social sciences, not least due to the fact that ethical dilemmas within social research tend to be very context-specific. Furthermore, adhering to a set of very specific ethical rules around research methods can have an adverse effect on the very issue that is to be studied, to the extent that in many cases, particularly around ethnography, it can be impossible to conduct effective research at all (see Punch, 2002). Wiles et al. (2006: 3.1) appear to favour a more self-regulatory approach, stating that the guidelines of the British Sociological Association (BSA), the Social Research Association and the British Education Research Association:

> are intentionally vague, and leave researchers able to interpret them in ways that fit the needs of the specific research they are undertaking and their own orientation to research ethics (2006: 3.1)

Indeed, the BSA statement of ethical practice (2002) states:

> The Association encourages members to use the statement [of ethical practice] to help educate themselves and their colleagues to behave ethically. ... [it] does not, therefore, provide a set of recipes for resolving ethical choices or dilemmas, but recognises that it will be necessary to make such choices on the basis of principles and values, and the (often conflicting) interests of those involved (cited in Wiles et al., 2006: 3.1)

and it is in the spirit of this statement that I found my own ethical position.

While some commentators (see Bulmer, 1982: 3) contend that covert research is never justified in that it reduces the researcher to the status of a spy or agent provocateur, this is (needless to say) not a position that I sympathise with, and like Bell and Newby (1977: 59) I believe that it would be at once ridiculous, not to mention cripplingly disruptive to warn all with whom I came into contact that I was conducting research. As far as I was concerned, I was confident in the belief that my bit-part in their night out will have had little or no impact, and in instances where respondents' data was to be used verbatim, a pseudonym was assigned in the interests of anonymity. Nevertheless, I did not experience plain sailing in this regard, as exemplified by my interaction with Louise.

Louise is a 34-year-old office worker, who gave me a number of interviews on her participation within the NTE. During the course of one of these interviews we talked about her aspirations for the next five years, where she would ideally be, and then what she thought a more realistic interpretation might be, given her current socioeconomic position, attachment to the NTE and present relationship status. As it turned out, she appeared to come to the conclusion that many of her goals, including having children, getting married to her boyfriend, engaging in protracted holidays as a means of exploring as much of the world as possible, were stymied by an apparent reluctance on the part of her boyfriend. According to Louise, he showed little interest in travelling, and buying a house together was the absolute limit of his level of commitment. He was content to sit 'in a rut' and 'blow all his money' on going out on the weekend, rather than saving for holidays or other expressions of consumer acquisition. I left the interview with a cassette tape bulging with data that confirmed much in the way of instrumental relationships, fetishistic desire in the consumer economy and pressure to adhere to the traditional life course while maintaining an identity that exudes individualism, youth and 'cool'. I thought little more of Louise, until our paths crossed on the high street. 'How's it going?' I enquired. 'Not great', she admitted, as her eyes began to glisten. 'Since we were talking, I realised that me and Paul really don't have a future, and he can't give me what I want, so I've just moved out, back to my mum and dad's, and I feel like I've lost everything.' I stood there for what felt like an age in silence. Was this indirectly my fault? If my line of questioning hadn't pushed her into considering the likelihood of her aspirations being met under the influence of contemporary global capitalism, would she still be happily dwelling in her two-bedroom terraced house on the outskirts of Vikton? 'Well', I ventured. No courses or books on ethnographic data collection had prepared me for this. 'These things usually turn out for the best'.[5]

Heading up the 'Miracle Mile', a notorious drinking strip that draws stag and hen parties from across the land, I found myself subject to a dress code. This dress code was imposed both formally by the guardians of the night-time leisure scene, bouncers or doormen, who would take a look at my feet and announce 'no trainers mate', but also informally, by the groups of brand-aware individuals with whom I was spending the evening. On one occasion I had arranged to meet a group of male drinkers on a weekend night out. The first stop was a pub named The Academy, and I was introduced to several people I had never met before, but was hoping might prove useful participants in my study. The very next bar, however, was implementing a strict door policy, which prevented me from entering on account of wearing a t-shirt and trainers. I now faced a predicament. Although the lads I was accompanying offered to go to a different bar so we could carry on drinking, I was unwilling to be the cause of any degree of resentment that might lead to them being unreceptive to the questions I was planning on slipping into conversation as the night progressed. Furthermore, my primary objective was to observe their behaviour on a normal night out – having to change their plans because of a social researcher with no dress sense was likely to skew the data I collected. The natural environment of these individuals when participating in the NTE is the Vertical Drinking Establishment, with its associated expensive bottled beer, loud music and dearth of available seating, and this is where I wanted to observe. I made plans to call Julian, my contact, during the week to arrange another opportunity and headed to a pub with a less strict door policy for a solitary pint before heading home. That weekend, I visited the Designer Outlet shopping centre, and bought a shirt and shoes, top quality brands for an extremely affordable price. I was ready to submerge myself in the environment of Julian and his mates. This was my first experience of the cultivated exclusivity that through mechanisms of emphasising designer clothes, and demanding cultural competence alerted me to the fact that I was witnessing the niche marketing of the NTE rather than any real or culturally significant diversity. A similar experience befell Dick Hobbs, during his research for *Doing the Business*, his ethnography into criminal entrepreneurship in the East End of London. When it came to looking the part, Hobbs explains:

> In pubs and clubs I had to blend in sartorially; I could not be obtrusive. As a consequence I now possess a formidable array of casual shirts with an assortment of logos on the left breast. This awareness of my appearance, and acknowledgement of the importance of image-management held me in good stead for the next stage of my work ... In the most part I spoke, acted, drank and generally behaved as though I was not doing research. Indeed I often had to remind myself that I was not in the pub to enjoy myself, but to conduct an academic enquiry, and repeatedly woke up the following morning with an incredible hangover facing the dilemma of whether to bring it up or write it up. (1988: 6)

2
Socioeconomic Change, Work and Leisure

This chapter aims to examine the contextual factors that contribute to the experiences of those consuming within the night-time economy (NTE). The past four decades have borne witness to unprecedented levels of socioeconomic change within Britain and beyond. The crumbling of traditional forms of industrial employment, the shift toward an economy based on leisure and consumer and financial services rather than production combined with the myriad complexities, risks and challenges facing those growing up, learning, working and surviving under conditions of late modernity are comparable in magnitude and significance to the agricultural and industrial revolutions of the eighteenth and nineteenth centuries (Hobsbawm, 1976, 1996). At the time of writing, we find ourselves half a decade into the worst financial crisis in living memory, an event that exacerbates the consequences, experiences and anxieties that constitute life under liberal capitalism. Despite the apparent wholesale collapse of the neoliberal project, the absence of any alternative way of organising the global economy appears to have cemented liberal capitalism as the 'least-worst' option. For the majority, the apparent indestructibility of the neoliberal project contributes to a feeling of impotence, characterised by political apathy and inertia, alongside an acceptance of capitalist realism (see Fisher, 2009).

Over the coming pages, we will explore the shifts in the socioeconomic terrain that have culminated in the dominance of liberal capitalism as a way of organising the economy. We will endeavour to understand the socioeconomic consequences of the dismantling of a system based on Keynesian state interventions to stimulate demand and maintain full employment, and its replacement by neoliberal economic policy, based on the fantasy of free trade.

The shift from industrialism to consumerism had dire consequences for labour markets and work cultures within Britain. The relatively structured regime of industrialism all but dissolved during the 1980s due to widespread downsizing among Western workforces and the rise to prominence of the flexible and insecure arena of service employment (see Byrne, 1995, 2005). Cities and towns that had previously been built around production were remoulded as spheres of leisure and consumption. A process of 'pacification by cappuccino' (Zukin, 1995) ensued as part of a broader rebranding exercise, as local councils, in cahoots with many of the now ubiquitous high street brand names attempted to maximise potential profits by offering the city as a fashionable and desirable centre of cultural and consumerist activity (Harvey, 2006; Minton, 2009). As the daytime high street underwent a process of recommercialisation, the net effect was one of homogenisation. City centres were effectively replicated across the country, dominated by recognisable brands ensconced within glittering new shopping precincts and reinvigorated high streets (Ewen, 2001; Hobbs et al., 2003). Over time, this process would be replicated within the night-time leisure industry, as high streets and drinking strips became dominated by a handful of corporate-owned theme bars and Vertical Drinking Establishments, whose presence on the streets of cities served as core indicators of an area's prosperity, success and desirability (see Chatterton and Hollands, 2001; Hobbs et al., 2003; Hadfield, 2006).

The shift of the city centre to its present position as a hub of leisure activities exemplifies the bond between leisure and the continued progression and expansion of capitalism, a concept that seems at odds with those from the liberal left who tend to view leisure as synonymous with freedom, providing us with a social arena within which we are free to mould and remould identity (see Jayne et al., 2006, 2008).

These very distinct cultural transformations within the spheres of work and leisure have been instrumental in creating a generation who identify with the pursuit of hedonistic pleasure to a far greater extent than any previously. This is a process that is crucially enabled by what Slavoj Žižek has identified as the 'injunction to enjoy' (2002, 2008). Here, Žižek convincingly argues that there has been a historical shift in our cultural superego. The guilt that is traditionally associated with a superego that uses its power to plague the individual with incessant demands to subscribe to cultural rules has changed quite significantly in orientation. The power of the superego's guilt function is evoked instead to push the subject towards the shallow and increasingly commodified pleasures of contemporary culture. These days guilt is borne by the subject when it fails to take advantage of opportunities to advance its interests or to experience more of late capitalism's hypnotic semiological life. Failure to enjoy, to take advantage of the continued benevolence of the culture industries, leads to anxiety and feelings of cultural irrelevancy, which results in older consumers becoming increasingly infantilised and bonded to consumer culture (Barber, 2007). The NTE – with its viscerality, liminal excess and promises of sex and violence – provides many with a smorgasbord of cultural enjoyment. This chapter attempts to illustrate how these key changes are linked to a number of social and economic upheavals that have come to represent epochal change and are indelibly bound up with changing notions of lifestyle, identity and individualisation.

Fordism to post-Fordism

Most simply summarised as the age of 'intensive accumulation' with 'monopolistic regulation' of the economy (Amin, 1994), and labelled variously by sociologists as 'early modernity' (Bauman, 2000) or 'industrial modernity' (see, for example, Winlow, 2001), Fordism consisted of the implementation of organisational and technological innovation driven by the dynamic of mass production (Harvey, 1989). As a form of business organisation, Fordism was reliant on the intensification of work and the detailed division of labour. This led to the establishment and consolidation of a gender order that placed a high degree of value upon hard, physical work, juxtaposing the male 'breadwinner' alongside women, who were expected to play subservient roles within the patriarchal family unit (Willis, 1997; Bourke, 1994). The clear, definable roles and the interests of the capitalist economy were bolstered by the Church, through their support of the hegemony of the bourgeois class (Weber, 1930; Boltanski and Chiapello, 2007). This 'spirit of capitalism' was a social ethic; a binding structure of attitudes and behaviours closely identified with ascetic Protestantism and its associated religious sects. The individual was encouraged to remain in the station and calling which God had determined, and 'restrain his worldly activity within the limits imposed by his established station in life' (Weber, 1930: 81–85). It made use of 'Psychological sanctions which, originating in religious belief ... gave a direction to practical conduct and held the individual to it' (Weber, 1930: 197). This combination of economic factors, augmented by the involvement of the Church, drove the concept and reality of 'work' deep into the core of the working classes. Aside from the obvious financial necessity to work, there existed a number of internalised and perpetual cultural forces and deeply ingrained dispositions that compelled the vast majority of working class males toward a form of adulthood defined in relation to the work experience and other key aspects of what was a relatively stable social structure. In simple terms, biographical processes unfolded with a relatively clear demarcation between youth and adulthood, and a broad range of symbols associated with each life stage. Similarly, this obvious social structure allowed individuals to develop a relatively fixed and secure sense of self in relation to the objective world that surrounded them. The industrial capitalist economy was sustained by the fact that sons would tend to follow their fathers into industry, thereby assimilating occupational roles and biographies (Willis, 1977) and socially reproducing the established social hierarchy (Bourdieu, 1984). Similarly, financial necessity and cultural pressure funnelled women into marriage and assimilation of their mother's familial role. Bourdieu and Passeron (1990) point out that the motherhood role serves to embed within children their acquiescence to fulfil and perpetuate class-based gender roles. In this way, the continuation of the industrial economy was assured through guaranteed labour within the specific roles in a continuing replication of previous generations.

From the 1970s onwards, the Fordist model of economic and social production began to crumble as a range of interrelated crises beset the industrialised West. Notable here are the rapid emergence of new technologies and the opening up of world markets (Amin, 1994; Harvey, 2007), but other factors are important. For example, the productivity of the immediate post-war period began to wane during the 1970s, and relatively politicised trade unions had won important concessions from the capitalist class and sought further pay rises and benefits. The application of new information technologies to manufacturing and service processes led to intrinsic changes around the distribution of labour within industries and organisations, rendering swathes of routine clerical, managerial and manual jobs obsolete, while at the same time raising the amount of skill required by key level workers (Castells, 2000). Although social mobility existed to a greater or lesser extent within the Fordist regime, as exemplified through the embourgeoisement of the more affluent workers (Goldthorpe et al., 1968), there was a clearly defined class system that remained in place. Of course we should not view this period through rose-tinted glasses – it is important to acknowledge that in many ways this was a system characterised by inequality, tension and injustice (Cohen, 1972; Ferree and Hall, 1996). However, it was equally characterised by a level of certainty and stability that allowed those within it to embark upon journeys through their own biographies that were continually contextualised by a series of relatively comprehensible cultural processes, meanings and values, bolstering a sense of identity within clearly defined social groups (Bauman, 1992, 2001). Even those individuals who were able to take advantage of the new levels of social mobility realised by the early bourgeois revolutions were able to assimilate within similarly comprehensible class cultures (Winlow and Hall, 2006). By the late 1970s and early 1980s, there was a discernible shift away from the labour-intensive manufacturing processes of Fordism, toward a new era of global consumerism, characterised by the ideological shift embodied by Ronald Reagan in the US, and Margaret Thatcher in Britain. Over the ensuing years, the commitment to manufacturing, provision of a welfare safety net and full employment would be cast aside in favour of consumerism, 'free' markets, economic rationalisation and the cult of the atomised, ambitious entrepreneur. It is to this neoliberal political environment that our attention must now turn in order to contextualise the changing face of urban consumerism.

Neoliberalism

State forms and international relations were aggressively restructured following the Second World War in a series of moves designed to prevent a return to the economic slump of the 1930s, a catastrophe that threatened the very essence of the capitalist order, as well as to discourage the inter-state geopolitical rivalries that had acted as a precursor to war (Harvey, 1989). It was argued that both communism and capitalism in their unadulterated forms were unsustainable, and the solution lay in a blended construction of state, market and democratic institutions (see Dahl and Lindblom, 1953). This was achieved through the Bretton Woods agreements, and the creation of institutions such as the World Bank and the International Monetary Fund (IMF). There was consensus that economic growth, full employment and welfare should all come under the remit of the state, and state powers should be used alongside or even instead of market processes in order to maintain this focus (Hobsbawm 1996; Dumeil and Levy, 2013). Keynesian fiscal and monetary policies were engaged in order to dampen extremes within the business cycle and to contribute toward the maintenance of full employment. States actively intervened in industrial policy and took responsibility for creating a number of welfare systems such as healthcare and education. This 'embedded liberalism' successfully returned high rates of economic growth in Britain and beyond throughout the

1950s and 1960s. However as the 1970s approached, embedded liberalism was beginning to crumble on both the international and domestic stage. Rising levels of inflation and unemployment heralded the start of a period of 'stagflation' that would last most of the decade, with Britain requiring the intervention of the IMF in 1975 as tax revenues plummeted and social expenditure continued to rise. Fixed exchange rates were abandoned and the Western world sought alternatives to Keynesian fiscal policy. In 1972, the CIA-backed coup in Chile allowed economists to set up a South American laboratory for the neoliberal ideas emanating from Chicago, while closer to home, further crises provided the impetus and opportunity for widespread adoption of economic reforms or 'shocks' (Klein, 2007). In May 1979 Margaret Thatcher was elected as Prime Minister, intent on reforming the economy. Due in part to her strong connections with the Institute of Economic Affairs, a neoliberal think-tank, she was confident in the belief that Keynesianism had to be abandoned in favour of monetarist 'supply side' solutions in order to cure the British economy of the stagflation that had blighted it for the past decade. In real terms this represented a U-turn in fiscal and social policies, and her determination to dismantle the institutions and political structures of the social democratic state soon became clear, as she embarked on a collision course with the trade unions, attacking all forms of social solidarity that served as a stumbling block to competitive flexibility. In short, this consisted of reducing and reversing the commitments of the welfare state in favour of 'workfarist' social policies, the privatisation of public enterprises such as social housing, reducing taxes and encouraging entrepreneurial initiative, culminating in her famous declaration that there was 'no such thing as society, only individual men and women' (Keen, 2010). Thatcher embarked on a crusade to privatise all the sectors of the economy that were in public ownership at the cost of jobs and wages, as part of her broader aim to increase personal and corporate responsibility within the political culture of the nation alongside the encouragement of initiative and entrepreneurialism. Consequently British Aerospace, British Telecom, British Airways, British Rail and reams of other state enterprises were sold off in an enormous deluge of privatisations. According to Harvey, Thatcher was able to forge consent for these changes as well as the dismantling of the welfare state through the cultivation of a middle class that:

> relished the joys of home ownership, private property, individualism and the liberation of entrepreneurial opportunities. With working class solidarities waning under pressure and job structures radically

changing through deindustrialisation, middle class values spread more widely to encompass many of those who had once had a firm working class identity. (2007: 62)

From these processes emerged a clearly identifiable neoliberal subjectivity, characterised by individualism, entrepreneurialism and most simply exemplified today through a plethora of reality TV shows, where a particular form of delight is gleaned from the failure of others (see Presdee, 2000). Freedom becomes synonymous with self-interest, and the individual is redefined as a consumer, a client or as an entrepreneur, obligated to work, responsible for their own training, development and education.

Consumer culture was able to flourish following the opening of Britain to freer trade, while the proliferation of financial institutions aided by massive deregulation was responsible for the birth of a debt culture into British life formerly characterised by deferred gratification and saving. Although some on the liberal left may claim a wealth of greater freedoms as a result of these changes (see Featherstone 1987; Miles, 1998), the opposite is more likely to be true. Freedom is lauded as perhaps the prevailing virtue of neoliberalism, although it is a form of freedom heavily codified and edited within a particular framework. The freedom offered by neoliberalism is:

> not the realization of any political, human or cultural telos, but rather the positing of autonomous self-governed entities all coming naturally equipped with some version of 'rationality' and motives of ineffable self-interest, striving to improve their lot in life by engaging in market exchange. (Mirowski, 2013: 61)

Popular perception of working life in previous eras might assume a miserable existence eked out in rigid and enforced discipline. Indeed, those critical scholars keen to adopt the dominant Foucauldian model might suggest that capitalism requires the *soul* of the worker in order to advance its interest. More truthfully, capitalism simply required them to be reasonably pliable and recognise the accepted need to fulfil a number of pre-set roles, such as that of providing for their family. Furthermore, it appears that, in comparison to the worker-consumers of today, the modern factory worker was relatively 'free' in his time away from the workplace. Clearly there is a close relationship between work and economy and structures of pleasure and taste (Bourdieu, 1984), but in simple terms, once his work was done and immediate needs met, the industrial working class man was relatively free to shape and be shaped by forms of collective culture that existed within these communities. In contemporary society the needs of capital long ago seeped over traditional demarcations and began to pollute elements of social life that were previously free from its influence (Hall and Winlow, 2005). Despite the rhetoric of freedom and choice that echoes throughout global culture, there seems to be good reason to suggest that we are less free than at any time in our recent history. As Žižek (2002) has acknowledged, in the absence of any genuinely alternative ideological project it seems that we 'feel' free because we lack the very language to articulate our 'unfreedom'. As we shall see, for many worker-consumers this paradox has a palpable impact upon identities, biographies and leisure practices.

The period of comparative prosperity and high employment that ensued following the end of the Second World War coincided with an economic shift into a consumerist phase creating opportunities to garner capital and security on an unprecedented level from within the working classes (Cross 2002; Hall and Winlow, 2005), enabling access to housing and consumer markets that had been simply unobtainable previously (Hobsbawm, 1996; Young, 1999).

This 'golden age' (Hobsbawm, 1996) of stability began to disintegrate during the 1970s and throughout the 1980s. Following the shock of this historical transformation, that many on the right believed was an act of 'creative destruction' there began a period of painful industrial disputes, urban riots and the impoverishment of once relatively functional industrial areas (Byrne, 2005; Macdonald and Marsh, 2005), while the economy became increasingly reliant upon service and leisure sector employment (see Lloyd, 2012, 2013). This process was at least partly predicted by Daniel Bell (1973), who forecast the rise in importance of technical expertise and education within the world of work. Traditional working life trajectories began to fragment as part-time and non-standard (such as that organised by an employment agency) work became more common, alongside increased demand for technical skills and 'flexible specialisations' (Furlong and Kelly, 2005). Stuart Hall (1988: 24) identified the key elements of post-Fordism as:

> A shift to the new 'information technologies'; more flexible, decentralised forms of labour process and work organisation; decline of the old manufacturing base and the growth of the 'sunrise', computer-based industries; the hiving off or contracting out of functions and services; a greater emphasis on choice and product differentiation, on marketing, packaging and design, on the 'targeting' of consumers

by lifestyle, taste and culture rather than by categories of social class; a decline in the proportion of skilled, male, manual working class, the rise of the service and white collar classes and the 'feminization' of the workforce; an economy dominated by multinationals, with their new international division of labour and their greater autonomy from nation state control; and the 'globalisation' of the new financial markets, linked by the communications revolution.

Although Stuart Hall was not alone in pinpointing flexibility as a key factor within post-Fordism, other commentators prefer to emphasise the increased levels of insecurity and risk encountered by the individual (Beck, 1992; Bauman, 1998b). Rather than predictable and collectivised transitions, which were integral to social reproduction, the majority began to experience a succession of different forms of transitory and insecure employment (Standing, 2011). Contemporary labour markets appeared to be taking on some of the characteristics more usually associated with those of third world countries, through a process of Brazilianisation, as 'bastions of full employment' (Beck, 2000: 1) increasingly took on the characteristics of precarity and uncertainty more commonly associated with emerging economies of the Global South. Furthermore, employment within an economy that served to satisfy basic needs through the conception and production of innovative products in increasingly efficient and convenient ways was replaced by employment within an economy that produces commodities and lifestyles laden with cultural signifiers that serve to convince consumers that their quality of life is constantly improving (Baudrillard, 1983).

Although it could be argued that greater opportunities for further education and training are now available (see Brown and Hesketh, 2004), the existing social disadvantages remain and are compounded by the likelihood of long periods of unemployment and lateral movement between equally poor employment (Lloyd, 2013). Today, as a university education no longer guarantees well-paid or even full-time employment, graduates find themselves thrown into the mire of unfulfilling work and mounting debt, encountering risk and insecurity on a daily basis (Standing, 2011). Many, including university graduates, find themselves shackled by zero-hour contracts, whereby employees are expected to maintain a perpetual state of enthusiasm and readiness for work in the hope that more shifts are put their way (Southwood, 2010). Recent revelations that hugely profitable firms such as Sports Direct, Amazon and Tesco have been using these contracts as a way of boosting productivity and efficiency highlight the pervasive nature of neo-capitalist employment practice. In addition to the endemic instability of work and the overtly exploitative nature of much of the employment market, some sociologists have identified further onto-logical shocks visited upon vast swathes of individuals (Berardi, 2009, Marazzi, 2011). It is within this context that a number of my respond-ents find themselves, as will be explored in more detail below. Suffice to say that when the precarity of the employment market is combined with increasing levels of cultural fluidity, erosion of adult identity and elongation of the life course, we begin to see a potentially devastating amalgam of social, economic and psychosocial influences on dedicated adult consumers within the NTE. A thorough understanding of these processes may also go some way toward explaining and describing the changes we have witnessed within the alcohol industry and city centre night-time leisure spaces over recent years.

The financial crisis of 2008 prompted a number of commentators to predict the demise of the neoliberal project. It seemed inconceivable that an economic system responsible for waves of austerity, swingeing cuts, and the worst crisis to face the financial sector in living memory could survive unscathed. And yet, in 2013, we can only wonder along with Colin Crouch (2011) upon the strange 'non-death' of neoliberal-ism. Part of the explanation for its apparent indestructibility lies in the very cultural embeddedness of neoliberal doctrine. The mantra of 'There is no alternative' is broadly accepted as truth, internalised through what Mirowski (2013) terms 'everyday neoliberalism'. Consider, for example, the changes to the employment market outlined above. Cederström and Fleming (2012) illustrate the way in which the incorporation of life into the neoliberal world of work has condemned the worker to a state of 'living death'. The injunction to 'be ourselves' in customer-facing McJobs, while concurrently adhering to a litany of corporate values, vision and mission statements epitomises the degree to which neoliberalism is melded with everyday life. We are exhorted to perpetu-ally conduct ourselves as if a tiny corporation, constantly marketing, expanding and diversifying in order to gain or maintain employment, while failure to succeed in the job market results in the suggestion that there is something wrong with our attitude, our bearing or our soft skills (Ehrenreich, 2010). We are encouraged to outsource all aspects of life that do not meaningfully contribute to life under neo-capitalism, to go under the knife to conform to ideals of beauty, to forge and then discard identities as we manoeuvre through the consumer circuits of consumption and taste. It is clear that in the contemporary ideological climate, there is no fixed identity, no permanent 'us', only a project of personal betterment with no end in sight (Cederström and Fleming, 2012). Elsewhere, neoliberalism is woven into the way in which we perceive ourselves, providing the categories and aspirations which suggest social mobility and class distinction.

When we witness these aberrations through our news media, when we learn of the latest scandal involving bankers or MPs, our responses are again depoliticised and toothless. The figureheads of neoliberal excess may be lampooned on television, mocked in *Private Eye*, but this serves simply to prove that the system works, allowing for dissent in a way that other ideologies would crush. Eventually, a different political party may get into power, although the policies are largely the same and previous policy is rarely rescinded. The man in charge may wear a different colour tie, or even a skirt, but they will have studied at the same universities, learning the same economic theory from the same professors who form part of Mirowski's (2013) 'Russian Doll' of the Neoliberal Thought Collective. Furthermore, individuals are captured by the mechanisms of debt that have historically proved vital to the onward march of capitalism (Graeber, 2010). Students attending university in England today can expect to take out student loans to the value of £9k a year for the duration of their degree, simply to pay for tuition. This extortionate induction into debt peonage is largely accepted, an exemplar of Fisher's (2009) capitalist realism, although the effects are far reaching. The neoliberal university is by its nature a marketised environment. Students are purchasing a degree, which subsequently alters their orientation toward the institution, the discipline they are studying and the faculty. Disciplines whose market value is limited, but from where dissent and radicalism have traditionally sprung, find themselves undersubscribed, and in some cases closing their doors to students altogether. Beyond university, individuals find themselves again indebted through mortgages and extortionate rents, which demand compliance, malleability and unquestioning adherence to neoliberal doctrine. Of course, even the most indoctrinated of us cannot help but be moved to action upon witnessing the pain and suffering caused on a global scale by the machinations of global capitalism. However, the solution to these problems can be found without thinking too deeply or altering our ideological standpoint. Simply donating to charity through pay cheques or a simple tap on the screen of our phone can reassure us that we have made a difference. Or we can ensure that we buy fair trade coffee, purchase Bono's product RED, and ignore the messy negative externalities that are linked to these processes (see Dienst, 2011). Far from threatening consumer capitalism, however, the existence of charity, fair trade and 'green' branding are simply niche markets that serve the added purpose of legitimising neoliberalism, providing an acceptable and purportedly ethical face to this particular form of capitalism. It is within this context that we must view the experiences of the committed adult consumer, ensconced within the consumer symbolisation of the NTE and question whether any genuine identity gains or authentic experience is possible within this arena.

Social class

During the industrial modern period the limited geographical and social mobility experienced by individuals resulted in relationships (both on a community and personal level) that appear to have been rather 'deeper' and more stable than today's 'liquid' relationships (Bauman, 2000). However, the disintegration of traditional peer bonds is not necessarily mourned by those who appear to be without them. Today, in many respects, it could be argued that it is wiser to be without enduring social bonds. The complications, restrictions and responsibilities that are associated with friendship in the truest sense of the word do not sit comfortably with the pressures and fluidity of consumer society (Beck and Beck-Gernsheim, 1995). On a related point, it is increasingly possible to detect a growing disconnect between contemporary young people and history, with familial, communal and even national history assuming a greatly diminished importance in the face of the malleable identities promised by the seductions of consumer capitalism (Jameson, 1998). Additionally, a constant connection to the matrix of social media (see Fisher, 2009) contributes to the evaporation of a grounded sense of who we are and where we come from as we become increasingly attuned to the ethics of the market and accept and embrace the idea of the self-created persona. This disconnect from history can be further witnessed in the fetishisation of retro, and nostalgia, not least within the arena of night-time leisure, which will be explored within a later chapter. The ubiquity of social networking enables friendships to be maintained on a very basic level, with individuals perhaps having little more in common than shared experiences within the NTE. This has the effect of grounding friendship in little more than a base use-value that elicits only a grudging acceptance of reciprocity (Bauman, 2001; Rosen, 2007). The traditional Symbolic Order, the social world of communication, rules and conventions that allows us to understand the world we inhabit, falls away to reveal a more fractious, insecure and instrumental social setting upon which contemporary young people must attempt to build a life.

The removal of these 'certainties', alongside the rise of postmodern reflexivity, suggests the possibility that individuals making their way through their biographies are finding acceptance of the Symbolic Order increasingly problematic. Unpredictability undoubtedly contributes to the sense of social anxiety evident among young people today (Fisher, 2009). Work, during this period of industrial capitalism, was more than a means of acquiring money – it lay at the very core of self-identity and shaped cultural practice. This is not to say that elements of economic instrumentalism were entirely missing from workplace settings, and in a more complex way a barely conscious form of cultural instrumentalism was to be found in the desire to secure a sense of self within working class community, identifying individuals within a clear structural hierarchy and securing a sense of value, place and psychological security (Bourdieu and Passeron 1990; Bourdieu, 1984). Social mobility was limited as a result of the clear categorisation signalled by a tangle of symbolic and cultural capital and competencies that were difficult to acquire or reproduce (Bourdieu, 1984; Winlow and Hall, 2006). The dominant ideology of the time did not require each individual to be aggressively acquisitive, and consequently the desperate scramble for upward social mobility was less a part of social relations. From the 1950s onwards the rigid industrial structure appears to have loosened up (see, for example, Lipset and Bendix, 1992). However, the apparent intransience of class itself began to appear vulnerable when capitalism itself began to evolve (Pakulski and Walters, 1996; Harvey, 2007).

The depictions of community above have relied heavily on exemplars and academic literature that centre on the experiences of the working class. This is to a large extent down to necessity, as there is a dearth of studies upon the emergence and creation of a distinctive middle class culture, although it is fair to surmise that reduced levels of aggressive accumulation, increased levels of communitas and the existence of deferred gratification would have been applicable beyond the boundaries of the working classes. However, as the vast majority of the participants within this piece of work could not by virtue of their education and upbringing be reasonably categorised as working class, some attempt at quantifying a middle class culture is necessary.

The squeezed middle

Traditionally, the middle classes were integral to the functioning of towns and cities, holding positions of power on councils and committees (see Morris, 1990). Their economic circumstances and associated lifestyles were characterised by a degree of cultural and political individualism that did not lend itself to collective action outside of the interests of business interests or professional privileges, although they would have made use of the informal social networks that were prevalent within the middle classes (Stacey, 1960). Throughout the twentieth century the class cohesion of the middle classes was relatively low, forming a clearly bounded class in relation to the working class, but internally divided due to the difficulties involved with moving from propertied to employed and self-employed positions (see Johnson, 1972). There was, however, a shared culture that appreciated the importance of education, deferred gratification, inward-looking family units, conservatism and restraint. This minimal cohesion continued to disintegrate throughout the second half of the twentieth century, and managerial, professional and propertied sections of the middle classes became increasingly distinct from each other (see Savage et al., 1992). In short, the term 'middle class' has become increasingly devalued, with John Prescott's famous claim that 'we are all middle class now' neatly encapsulating the bulging middle class that sits uncomfortably between the very rich and the very poor. While Prescott was in effect claiming that liberal capitalism had led to a fairer and more socially mobile society, this suggestion seems little short of preposterous, as contemporary society currently includes a significant proportion of socially excluded as well as exploited workers who exist on flexible or temporary contracts (Southwood, 2010; Carlstrom and Fleming 2012). Underlying Prescott's statement is the fact that the term 'middle class' has been reduced in usefulness, no longer really existing as a concrete identity or cohesive cultural group. Instead, the middle class as a label has come to encapsulate all those who do not possess the cultural characteristics of the traditional working class. The end of relative certainties as delineated earlier in the chapter has affected these groups in a similar way to the way in which it affected the traditional working classes, creating an aurora of anxiety in the face of the very real threat of downward mobility. The reproduction of the cultural values of education, hard work and deferred gratification are battling against a riptide of competitive acquisition and promises of immediate gratification, and the increasing levels of graduate unemployment or underemployment is a stark reminder of the lack of solidity offered by the former bastions of the middle class. While to some extent we can speak objectively of a middle class in terms of increased life chances, any remnants of it indicating the 'middle' are rapidly diminishing. With studies suggesting that 'middle class' as a self-descriptor is just as likely to be used by manual workers as by non-manual workers, and almost a third of bank managers referring to themselves as working class (see Tweedie, 2006), it is clear that as far as individuals refer to themselves, there has been a move away from the middle ground of British society, and demarcations are increasingly blurred. To try and counter the inadequacy of the term, Savage et al. (2013) have attempted to recategorise the middle class into three distinct groups. This new model suggests that in addition to an established middle class, we would do well to speak of a class of technical experts and a class of 'new affluent' workers. Meanwhile, the working class has been divided int a 'traditional working class', 'emergent service workers' and the new 'precariat', characterised by low levels of social, cultural and economic capital. While Savage et al. are probably correct to suggest that class categorisation should no longer rigidly adhere to occupation, the implication that the notion of precarity is exclusive to those at the bottom is misleading. Few in the middle class have the financial resources to be able to maintain mortgage repayments, support families, and service countless other commitments for long in the event of losing their job. And in an era that has seen swingeing cuts in many of the occupations filled by the middle classes, that in previous years would have been unthinkable, combined with reduced pensions, and legislation which makes it increasingly easy for employers to dismiss their workers, alongside a reduction in free legal representation, there are few in society who should not view themselves as precarious in one way or another. Pay for the 'squeezed middle' has fallen in real terms on an annual basis since 2009 (Office for National Statistics, 2013c) and public discourse has taken an aggressive turn between private and public sector workers, young and old. This accentuates the absence of a class interest, which has been replaced by a determined individualism, and *negative solidarity* (Adorno, 1990), based in crude dichotomies politically representative of the old maxim 'divide and rule'. While it is easy to identify a group of very wealthy people at the top, and a group of very poor people at the bottom, the only thing that we can say with certainty about those in between is that they constitute a writhing mass of humanity, each trying desperately to defend their interests, push upwards, or fight against the current dragging them down.

A neatly defined structure no longer exists, as all are beset by profound anxiety, with cultural capital serving to provide vital handholds.

Understanding work and leisure

Theories of leisure have been roundly criticised by a number of commentators. Van Moorst (1982), for example, dismisses such theories as a series of superficial concepts and spurious distinctions. One particularly important point of contention is the role of work within the understanding of leisure. Roberts defines leisure as the 'relatively freely chosen non-work area of life' suggesting that 'to understand leisure in modern society, it must be seen, in part at least, as the obverse of work' (Roberts, 1978: 3). Similarly, Kelly (1990: 9) claims 'leisure is generally understood as chosen activity that is not work'. These descriptions, however, do not satisfactorily explain the kinds of work maintained within the NTE – bouncers, bar staff, waiting staff and so on, who are occupying roles imbued with social standing and significance, while consuming alcohol, flirting, joking and to all intents and purposes engaging in leisure-like behaviour (see Hobbs et al., 2003 for discussion on the meanings and significance associated with 'bouncing'). Furthermore, the distinction between work and leisure is increasingly muddled. A host of social media, such as Facebook and Twitter, all rely on the assiduous attention lavished upon them by an army of unpaid volunteer-consumers who provide the content on which the company's value is based (Marazzi, 2011).

Many of the claims about leisure subscribe to the overarching ideology of 'freedom granted by consumerism' (see Fiske, 1991). Individuals are granted unfettered freedom to spend their 'free time' in myriad ways, bounded only by the imagination of the individual, in a process seen as integral to the process of 'becoming' (Cheek and Burch, 1976). In real terms, however, this notion of freedom is illusory. Contemporary leisure can in no way be considered malleable to our own needs and desires, as leisure is simply one more consumer item, albeit fragmented and compartmentalised. Therefore we are compelled to consume leisure items that are served up by, and act to serve the needs of consumer capitalism and what is rendered appealing by the culture industry.

The immediate, involving nature of the consumerised drinking experience seems to crackle with creativity and the resistance of the traditional carnival, but underneath the tumult lies capitalism's enduring exchange relation and a profit motive perfectly capable of intruding upon the inner life of the subject to shape human desire. Indeed, some of my respondents seemed to grow aware of this as time passed. They could sense the uniformity that lay just underneath the surface diversity, but, in the absence of something radically different, they continued to return to the NTE with waning hopes of finding something new and rewarding or of rediscovering their original passion for the vivid spectacle of alcohol-soaked excess. Indeed, put bluntly, it appears that consumerism within the NTE (as elsewhere) fails to deliver on its promise:

It actually promises universality of happiness. Everybody is free to choose, and, if everybody is let into the shop, then everybody is equally happy. That is one duplicity. Another duplicity is the limitation of its pretence that you resolve the issue of freedom completely once you offer a consumer freedom. So it is a reduction of freedom to consumerism. That is the other duplicity. People are led into forgetting that there could also be other ways of self-assertion than simply buying a better outfit. (Bauman, 1992: 255)

As we will see in the next chapter, to consign a critique of capitalism to the intellectual garbage heap is absurd. Any reasonable attempt to understand the production of cultural forms must address the onward march of the profit motive and its increasingly incisive ideology.

Marxist approaches to leisure have come under criticism from some quarters (see Moorhouse in Rojek, 1999), primarily for an unwillingness to recognise that paid work has the potential to be for most people a source of satisfaction, purpose, creativity, preferring to couch it in terms of routinisation, alienation and drudgery. However, while a relatively small number of individuals fortunate enough to be considered through their mode of employment as members of the creative classes may well feel that paid labour is indeed a rewarding and positive qualitative experience, this is not the impression given by my participants, and nor does it seem the experience of workers elsewhere (see Cederström and Fleming, 2012; Lloyd, 2012). Indeed, one might argue that the majority of people are starkly aware of the pointless nature of much of their paid employment, reminiscent of the notion of 'non-stop inertia' recounted by Southwood (2010).

It is becoming increasingly impossible to divorce our social understanding of work and of the work role from the logic of capitalist ideology. Capitalism and its associated ideology has the power to penetrate our dreams and shape our desires. Through what Žižek (2008) terms 'symbolic efficiency', work can only be viewed as rewarding once it is considered so by a society that is increasingly concerned with status.

Symbolic efficiency dictates that core elements of our identity can only be considered 'real' if they are acknowledged by the Big Other – Lacan's term for the mass of social institutions, laws and customs into which an individual is socialised. For example, while I might be a fine musician, it is not believed by me or anyone else until that fact is recognised through the Big Other, until I get a recording contract, attain thousands of followers on Twitter, or play a sell-out gig. The same could be said to be true of work identity. We cannot find work satisfying without this satisfaction being ratified and acknowledged by the Big Other. Indeed, the overriding view is neatly summed up by the following comment, made by Rob, a 33-year-old client relations manager for a multinational financial company, who will be further introduced in more detail in the following chapter:

> I spent most of my twenties in a series of crap jobs and rented rooms. But even now, yeah, I've got a 'proper' job, but I still feel like I hate it, I'm still living in a rented house and I'm just looking forward to going out at the weekend or for Champions League [televised football] during the week and just getting pissed.

The jobs Rob talks about are 'crap' by definition, being non-unionised, insecure and short term, characteristics that, rather than instilling an element of competition to the job marketplace, driving individuals forward to constantly improve and strive for the top, instead strip the worker of the opportunity to construct and maintain an image of themselves that is socially useful, or a source of pride and identity. The only certainty within the job market in its present incarnation is insecurity, and a swathe of literature concerned with the contemporary workplace indicates a workforce that is only too aware of its comparative place in history, that is the first generation in almost 100 years likely to be worse off than their parents (Wright, 2013). Here a state of precarity is becoming normalised, and work increasingly devoid of positive symbolism (Winlow and Hall, 2013). It is against this background that we are witnessing the death of the social, alongside which we experience the relentless promotion of consumerist fantasy, while lives appear to be increasingly structured around the accumulation of new products and experiences.

3
Binge Britain

The British media has, over the past few years, developed something of an obsession with the drinking habits of the nation's youth. Graphic television programmes document the debauched nightlife of some of the UK's major cities and towns, while the pages of broadsheet and tabloid newspapers are littered with tales of excess and litanies of concern over the 'new British disease'. It is therefore hardly surprising that the issue has attracted increased interest within the academic fields of sociology, social policy, anthropology, health economics and social psychology. Academic, media and public interest have centred predominantly on the binge drinking behaviour of young people in the UK. Aside from concern surrounding underage drinking, many column inches, parliamentary discussions and pages of journals have been dedicated to the drinking behaviours of 18–24 year olds. Alcohol consumption among young people within this age bracket has been linked with crime and disorder, with violent incidences being exacerbated by a number of environmental factors such as noisiness, crowding, poorly maintained premises, inadequate seating and door policy as well as irresponsible serving practices (Hadfield, 2006).

Much data points toward the fact that drinking alcohol and getting drunk has become an accepted, if not integral part of social interaction within British culture. The majority of adults drink alcohol regularly (Office for National Statistics (ONS), 2013a), and while the economic crisis, combined with cheap supermarket deals on alcohol, may have contributed to an increase in domestic consumption (British Beer and Pub Association (BBPA, 2013), profit reports from major corporations in the night-time economy (NTE) indicate drinking at home is not necessarily to the absolute detriment of the high street balance sheet. Indeed, research indicates that many consumers blend domestic and

41

NTE through the process of pre-loading (Barton and Husk, 2012). ONS (2013a) data indicates that 18% of adults reported drinking 'very heavily' on at least one occasion over the previous week, a type of alcohol consumption commonly referred to as a binge. In simple terms, binge drinking consists of high levels of consumption of alcoholic beverages over a relatively short period of time. Extant literature also frequently focuses on drawing links between high consumption drinking patterns and health concerns or social harms (Moore et al., 1994; Engineer et al., 2003), invoking a variety of diverse and sometimes clumsy terminologies, such as 'Risky Single Occasion Drinking' (RSOD), 'episodic' and 'sessional' drinking (Murgraff et al., 1999). All of these terms refer to the practice of embarking on a drinking session with the intention or outcome of becoming drunk.

The governmental line on 'binge drinking' is still largely defined in terms introduced under New Labour (Prime Minister's Strategy Unit, 2004), where a 'binge' is enshrined as drinking twice the UK recommended daily amount of alcohol for low risk consumption in one day – eight units or more for males, and six units or more for females. A unit equates to approximately a single measure of spirits, half a pint of normal strength beer, lager or cider or a small glass of wine. The alcohol strategy introduced by the Coalition government (2012, 2013), refers to 'irresponsibility', stating that alcohol accounts for 1 million alcohol-related violent crimes, and 1.2 million alcohol-related hospital admissions in 2010–2011. The economic cost of these drinking behaviours is highlighted, and calculated at £21 billion per year, a figure that is broken down into costs to the NHS (£3.5bn), alcohol-related crime (£11bn), and lost productivity due to alcohol consumption (£7.3bn). Although these figures are undeniably high, it must of course be noted that they are largely offset by the claims of the BBPA that the beer and pub industry contributed an estimated total of £19.5bn to the UK economy in 2010/11, while HM Revenue & Customs (HMRC) received around £10bn from alcohol duties in the year 2012/13.

The term 'binge drinking' is at best contested and at worst misleading. English speakers have developed countless numbers of terms for drinking alcohol and getting drunk, while the term 'drink' has come to mean 'alcoholic beverage' in a number of contexts. Rather than become embroiled in debates between medical and social definitions, I will regard binge drinking in its most simple terms, being to drink alcohol with the express purpose of getting drunk.

Whether or not 'binge drinking' is a new cultural phenomenon is the source of continued debate (see Harrison, 1994; Measham and Brain

2005). Certainly, leafing through the pages of any national newspaper (not just the tabloids) any time over the past few years, we would be forgiven for making the assumption that Britain is in the grip of an entirely 'new culture of intoxication' (Measham and Brain, 2005). Those wishing to challenge this argument often suggest that press campaigns to exaggerate and demonise youth leisure have a historical basis dating back to the Victorian hooligans and earlier. The stirring of public concern over bingeing culture is apparent in the Hogarthian-era depictions of *Gin Lane* and the punchbowl in *A Midnight Modern Conversation* much as they are in the 1980s portrayal of lager louts, or the 1990s demonisation of ecstasy in the wake of the death of Leah Betts (Murji, 1998). It seems reasonable then to couch binge drinking in terms of Stanley Cohen's (1972) 'moral panic'. However, it is advisable to be wary of the term. Key to the notion of moral panic is the assertion of a threat to mainstream values posed by the supposed crisis, and a positioning of the 'folk devil' as non-conformist. With regard to binge drinking, who could reasonably claim that the arena of the NTE does anything other than reproduce and reaffirm mainstream norms, through the rewards placed upon competition, individualism and entrepreneurism? Those who binge are not non-conformist then, but steadfastly conformist, obediently, even meekly making use of the consumer objects proffered by the culture industries. As many researchers have shown (see, for example, Briggs, 2013), the cultures of the NTE are not bursting at the seams with proto-political forms of resistance and rebellion. For the most part these are corporatised spaces that draw upon the traditional symbolism of the carnival in order to attract consumers to clubs and bars. There is no inversion of traditional hierarchy, and certainly no mocking of the dominant ideology.

There also lies another problem with the simple deployment of the moral panic thesis. To dismiss public and media concern over issues of social disorder, violence and other problems surrounding heavy drinking and intoxication as 'just a moral panic' is short-sighted, as these undoubtedly constitute genuine social and individual harms that cannot be sidelined in favour of a simple criticism of media interests. We should bear in mind that the NTE displays incredibly high levels of crime and violence, and is one of the primary sites of sexual assault and rape, especially for young women, with 41% of female victims believing their assailant to be under the influence of alcohol during a serious sexual assault (ONS, 2013b). We should also note that the motivations for drunkenness are not always positive and life-affirming. Youthful consumers of the NTE experience also drink to forget the multifaceted problems they face, and problem drinking behaviours amongst the young are continuing to rise. Are we to continue to dismiss these things as merely youthful hijinks? It would be little short of negligent to steadfastly refuse to investigate the motivations of those who find their leisure in the NTE, only to lapse into the tired refrain of the 'the kids are alright' and 'boys will be boys'. It is paramount that the social sciences reject the affirmative analysis of culture as resistance against the oppressive power of the state and its fundamental desire to ostracise youth, and begin to think critically about the pressures, anxieties and insecurities that bear down on young people within post-industrial Britain.

The fact remains that the neoliberal state has no desire whatsoever to crack down on the drinking behaviours of 'marginalised groups' as they are displayed in the NTE (and here it is worth reiterating my earlier claim that a significant proportion of NTE consumers are not marginalised at all and in fact represent the symbolic centre ground of 'middle England'). The history of the post-industrial NTE displays quite clearly that the state's primary concern is to enable the drinks industry – and a broad range of ancillary industries in the NTE – to grow. If there is public disquiet about violence, drunkenness and other lamentable behaviours in the city after dark, then the strategy is to responsibilise consumers and punish only those who overstep the rather hazy boundaries that define what is and what is not acceptable in this hyper-commodified cultural sphere. It is salutary to note that, cast as we are in a period of economic crisis and social disruption, supposedly critical sociologists and criminologists continue to return to out-of-date ideas in the hope of understanding developing social and cultural forms. This is not the 1970s. Capitalism, class, consumption and the social order have all changed radically since Cohen and Young were formulating the one-size-fits-all structure of the 'moral panic'. The key focus as we move forward must be how to make sense of the world as it is now. We need to offer an explanation for the enduring attachment many adult drinkers have to this ostensibly 'youthful' leisure environment, and attempt to describe and understand what is going on in the lives of these drinkers that makes them wary of the obligations of adulthood, and what it is that beckons them back to the city centre for yet another big night out.

Rather than simply deploying the 'moral panic' argument, we need to understand that transitions to 'adulthood' today involve a range of vague but undoubtedly profound anxieties and insecurities, which when linked to the competitive acquisition synonymous with the commercialised hedonism of leisure spaces leads us to consider important concepts around the structural contexts of identity formation. Rather than becoming hung up on the social and political reactions to the unsavoury elements of the NTE, sociologists need to be scrutinising the behaviours themselves, their meanings, motivations and underlying causations.

The attraction of hedonistic excess within the NTE appears to be a complex amalgam of both push and pull factors. Undoubtedly, it has the potential to help individuals momentarily escape the social pressures they face. It promises the benefits of collective inebriation in a world characterised by frail bonds and weakened personal ties, and holds the potential to fulfil (if only vicariously for most) the visceral needs of sex and violence. For all the criticism of the NTE within these pages and in the words of other social commentators (see Winlow, 2001; Chatterton and Hollands 2003; Hobbs et al., 2003; Hall et al., 2008), the night-time leisure scene (for all its niche marketing and hyperreality) can provide a heavily involving and gratifying consumer spectacle that allows issues such as debt, relationships, work, careers and housing to fade into the background. Amid the tumult of a big night out exists a more or less unconscious commitment to the excess and hedonism that appear to be the key elements of consumer identity (see Measham, 2004; Measham and Brain, 2005). Drunkenness suggests a desperate desire on the part of these consumers to punctuate the dull normality of work and consumerism, akin to what Badiou (2007) refers to as a 'Passion for the Real'. The Real here does not simply refer to what we understand as 'reality', which is experienced through symbolism and language. Instead, the Real relates to pre-symbolic subjective psychological experience, an intoxicating mixture of conflicting stimuli and drives that cannot be defined through language. The closest we can get to understanding it is to try to empathise with a baby, overwhelmed by raw experiences that cannot be put into words. Badiou (2007) suggests that individuals are increasingly developing this 'passion for the Real', yearning to experience the Real in contrast to the sterility and mundanity of everyday life. As Žižek (2002: 10) describes:

> On today's market, we find a whole series of products deprived of their malignant properties: coffee without caffeine, cream without fat ... the contemporary redefinition of politics as the art of expert administration, that is, as politics without politics, up to today's tolerant liberal multiculturalism as an experience of the Other deprived of its Otherness.

Elements of the Real are therefore sought and found through a variety of different avenues, through mechanisms such as rejecting safety features that serve to sterilise life experiences or transgressing minor laws and social mores. All we know is that we want to push beyond the banality of the contemporary consumer spectacle (see Debord, 1983) and experience a genuine sense of engagement. It seems reasonable to suggest that living in an increasingly artificially constructed universe creates an 'irresistible urge to return to the Real' (Žižek, 2002: 19) and the more artificial our culture becomes, the stronger the desire to regain some kind of foothold in 'real reality' (ibid.). Indeed, we want to experience genuine existential passion, but find ourselves trapped in a complex double bind, forced to find traces of the Real *within* our artificial world (see Žižek, 2002). The Real therefore always exists as the thing that cannot be described, that resists symbolisation and exists beyond language (see Fink, 1995). A further point to make here is that as Badiou and Žižek both realise, the 'passion for the Real' only leads to further experience within the Symbolic. Even the most dedicated hedonists within the NTE, those whose commitment is spelled out in vomiting, bloody high definition by reality television producers are not experiencing Reality in the Lacanian sense, and it is this pervading sense of lack which prompts the drive to experience a genuine *event* that inspires awe.

With respect to the NTE, the mystery and frustration brought about by the unattainability of the Real is represented by the all-pervasive culture of celebrity – professional footballers, musicians, actors all playing out lives dripping with the essence of the Real – conspicuous consumption of the markers of social distinction – consumer goods, flash cars, flashier clothes, strings of sexual conquests that are filtered down to the coalface of consumer culture through lurid media headlines and exposé.[1] Cruelly, the denizens of the NTE are destined for failure in their quest to emulate the apparent satisfaction of those on their gilded pedestal, and instead the individual is condemned to return again and again in the hope that this time their satisfactions will be realised. Under previous forms of capitalism, enjoyment was limited by what Freud termed 'the pleasure principle'; the law that dictates to the individual to enjoy as little as possible, the transgression of which leads directly to pain, since there is only a finite amount of pleasure that an individual can bear. However, the reorientation of the superego as discussed above has led to a directive to take enjoyment to beyond its limits, with desire no longer repressed but nurtured, encouraged and defended from all that might seek to prevent or postpone enjoyment, pleasure and gratification.

The Lacanian 'cuts' in the Symbolic are cauterised and the individual finds reason, desire and essence in the hyperreality proffered forth by consumer culture governed by the twin elements of the Imaginary and the Real. Untold pleasure is rendered unobtainable not by processes of repression, but by the experience of jouissance,[2] which can only be negated by returning to the beginning of the cycle of desire, pleasure and jouissance through the fetishisation of commodities rendered, packaged and spoon-fed through consumer culture. It seems likely that the NTE is at once a showcase, frontier and frontline battlefield for the disintegration of the standard psychosocial processes and the rise to prominence of new, psychoeconomic processes.

What these consumers desire is to distance themselves from artifice and wholeheartedly embrace a world free from normative social control (Presdee, 2000), a world that stands in contrast to the mundane, the workaday monotony of work under late capitalism. But the harsh reality is that what they are served is commodified and devoid of real transgression. In a hyperreal world in which transgression is a commodified cultural norm, the consumer cannot experience the thrill of overstepping the boundary into illegitimacy. Excessive alcohol consumption within the NTE provides the most simple, legal and accessible route into something that looks like where they want to be, even though they know, in a barely conscious way, that real 'liberation' is not on offer and that they are being carried along an experiential conveyor belt only to find that at the end of their journey their pockets are empty and they didn't really enjoy the experience quite as much as they thought they would.

The growth of the NTE

Pubs, bars and restaurants have undergone significant changes in recent years as they have been caught up in the rising tides of what has become known as the NTE. As recently as the late 1980s, city centres, although undoubtedly impacted by consumerism, were already viewed as failing to maximise their potential:

> Bleak, windswept, grey concrete wastelands, discarded litter blowing along the gutters, threatening groups of bomber-jacketed youths lounging in shop doorways, down alleys, or rampaging spray-can-in-hand across graffiti splattered walls. Boarded up shops, an abandoned supermarket trolley, a dog meandering across an anonymous, brutal urban landscape. (Gardner and Sheppard, 1989: 126)

While the above account is doubtless hyperbolic, it is useful in highlighting the transformation of British cities over the past 20 years. High streets that by day provide brightly lit shop windows with open doors drawing consumers into a utopia of consumer desirables transform over the course of minutes to blank-faced shutters, the streets clearing of all human life. In the past, the streets would have remained desolate for the remainder of the evening, the night punctuated only by the gentle hum of an electric street cleaner or milk float as morning approached and the high street readied itself for another day of busy activity. Today, as we plough individual furrows into the twenty-first century, the period of quiet at the end of the trading day is barely discernible, as the NTE is kick-started by the after-work crowd. During the course of my fieldwork I observed lawyers and legal secretaries from a nearby law firm drawn by the lure of cocktails and glasses of rosé wine, to a bar overlooking the river, while a pianist plays middle-of-the-road interpretations of recent classics. Alcohol serves as the 'vital lubricant that aids the propulsion of ... people into this carnivalesque and consumer-oriented world' (Hobbs et al., 2003: 36). The bar itself is housed within a once defunct and dilapidated warehouse, reminding us of the way in which cities across the nation were recast as sites of leisure and consumption rather than work and production, through a larger rebranding exercise which promoted themselves as sites of cultro-economic activity (see Zukin, 1995; Harvey, 2006).

The NTE is part of a wider phenomenon that has been experiencing a boom in recent years, namely that of the urban entertainment economy, a complex web of businesses including casinos, strip clubs, night clubs, restaurants, bars and pubs. Corporate control, predicated upon neoliberal ideology and the relentless pursuit of profit is commercialising public space to the detriment of historic or alternative local development, while the more traditional community pubs and bars synonymous with Fordist forms of collective consumption in working class industrial cities are displaced (Chatterton and Hollands, 2003). Pubs are reported to be closing at the rate of 26 a week (Jones, 2013), although these closures appear to be clustering around independent pubs, and community pubs, rather than those in city centres. The trend has been for ownership and control of spaces constituting the NTE moving away from individual entrepreneurs, small breweries or even national companies, toward a decreasing number of global corporations, although a recent growth in small, independent breweries has occurred. In a reflection of the post-Fordist restructuring of the labour markets discussed earlier, aspects of decentralisation and flexible specialisation, standardisation and market domination are identifiable within the rise of the NTE (Kumar, 1995: 44–5). According to Reuters (2010), the 'top four' brewers account for over half of the global beer market, while the trade in hops is controlled in the main by only four privately owned companies (Barth-Haas Group, 2012). Indeed, the financial pages of the broadsheet newspapers are often carrying news of the latest merger or acquisition among firms involved with the production and sale of alcoholic beverages. The recent takeover of Scottish and Newcastle by Carlsberg and Heineken means that all the biggest beer brewers within the UK are foreign-owned multinational companies (BBC, 2008). The largest brewer in the UK, AB-InBev, is also the world's largest brewer, employing 114,000 people in 23 countries, and styles itself as a 'truly global brewer', with a 'portfolio' of 200 beers (ab-inbev.co.uk, 2013).

Continued governmental approval and enthusiasm for the continued granting of licences despite warnings from the police, health services and various other sources may well be explained by the fact that the NTE is integral to government coffers. At the peak of growth in the area, capital investment in the NTE was estimated at £1 billion a year with the turnover of the pub and club industry constituting 3% of GDP (Gross Domestic Product) (Home Office, 2000). The government also recoups vast amounts of money from tax on alcohol. Additionally, the sector employs around 650,000 in the production and retail of alcohol, and a further 1.1 million people in the wider economy. Again, at its peak the alcohol industry was responsible for creating 'one in five of all new jobs' (Home Office, 2000). These jobs, however, tend to be far from secure, being for the most part poorly paid, transitory and non-unionised, with many establishments offering work on zero-hour contracts, which guarantee no fixed number of hours, and require flexibility through last-minute offers of shifts.

From the early 1990s onwards the competition between leisure companies for development sites became a serious business, a phenomenon born out of a distinct and dire need for the alcohol industry to rescue their product from a clearly discernible slump in both popularity and fashion. The emergence of rave culture was responsible for diminishing attendance at licensed premises, as a generation of young people 'eschewed alcohol and licensed premises in favour of illegal drugs, soft drinks and spontaneous partying in warehouses, motorway service stations and the rural wilderness' (Hadfield, 2006: 58). Indeed, the alcohol industry 'began to worry that the shift may be irrevocable, a nascent nation of teetotallers fuelled by pills, powders and puff, drinking only Lucozade and Evian water' (Collin and Godfrey, 1998: 273).

Increasing police powers based in The Criminal Justice and Public Order Act 1994 alongside a smattering of other laws enacted between 1990 and 1997 contributed to taming rave culture, whereupon it underwent somewhat of a metamorphosis, being channelled into licensed premises, commercialised and centred around alcohol, rather than the bottled water and drugs that went hand in hand with rave culture. The alcohol industry wasted no time in welcoming these prodigal consumers back into the drinking fold with an array of ready-to-drink alcopops, laden with conspicuous 'cool' branding and additives such as guarana offering a 'natural high' , in an attempt to co-opt or encapsulate the spirit of psychopharmacology associated with rave (see Measham 2004; Measham and Brain 2005; Hadfield 2006).

The changes within the global economy discussed earlier in the chapter also had considerable effect on the local state. The 'return to the urban centre' (O'Connor and Wynne, 1995) was instigated by the belief that the revitalisation of the former industrial cores of British cities would act as a catalyst for economic regeneration, leading to a shift in the very function of the role of the local state toward involvement via property development, deregulation and the encouragement of inward investment (Jessop, 1997). The rapid and unabated expansion and evolution of the NTE should therefore be articulated as reactionary governmental policy designed to counter macro-level processes occurring since the early 1970s.

The adoption of neoliberal economic policies resulted in the decline of many of the traditional sources of employment in manufacturing industries in favour of the provision of services. The very real effect this process had on the towns and cities of the UK was a shift from urban spaces that were rooted in production, to ones rooted ever more firmly in consumption. By the early 1990s this was evident in a number of towns and cities across the land. Within these urban areas (Manchester, Leeds and Newcastle being notable examples), aggressive city centre initiatives that heavily promoted cultural elements of the NTE were being pursued. Around the same time, cultural and leisure activities became recognised as integral to reinvigorating these city centre spaces, and the NTE was soon being promoted as central to the image of modern 'European' cities within the UK (O'Connor and Wynne, 1996). Many of these cities had skylines characterised by silhouettes indicative of Fordist economic policy – towering chimneys and red brick warehouses crowding the banks of a dirty, stagnant canal – graveyards for traffic cones and the rusting carcasses of abandoned shopping trolleys. Just as industrialisation forged these characteristic sights, so too post-industrialism has moulded the cityscape. Today the modern and neon-light bright Quayside and The Gate in Newcastle, or the Gay Village in Manchester reverberate with throngs of drinker-consumers and repetitive bass rather than the industrial machinery of a bygone age.

These sites of hedonistic consumption are far from organic places. They are created environments, wilfully distorting reality, and sharing more in common with Disneyworld than the pubs and alehouses of previous generations (see Bryman, 1995). Within the proliferation of theme pubs – the Irish bars, the nostalgia bars, the 'real ale' pubs, we can clearly see a degree of hyperreality (Baudrillard, 1994). The original has been copied and copied again to such an extent that any semblance of the real has been lost, and it no longer matters what was initially the subject of the copy due to the fact that the reality of the original has been asphyxiated beneath layer upon layer of fabrication. They are, more often than not 'non-places', to use Marc Auge's (2009) term, lacking authenticity and for many being a place of transience, of passing through. A 'real' Irish pub (that is a pub actually located in Ireland) may be viewed by the external commentator as a poor specimen for its lack of what is commonly perceived to be the mainstay features of an 'Irish bar', the wit and proverbs adorning the walls in Gaelic script, or the shamrock etched on the surface of a pint of Guinness.

The steps taken by local government were geared toward capitalist ends, seeking to facilitate local economic growth, development and entertainment within the NTE and quickly assumed centre stage within the economic restructuring processes (Chatterton and Hollands, 2003). The idea of the '24-hour city' rapidly became a desirable end-goal for any of the key stakeholders wishing to rid the night-time of its more traditional connotations as a shadowy 'other', riddled with marginal activity, crime and liminal pleasures (Lovatt, 1996). However, the utopian dream of a continental café-style culture remains elusive in the face of hedonistic excess and the media demon of 'binge drinking' on the streets of cities and towns across the UK.

The NTE has served as an important bargaining chip for politically engaging the British youth, or perhaps more accurately ensnaring their vote. 'New' Labour were shameless in this regard, placing the NTE near the top of their political agenda in their 1997 general election campaign. Their infamous 'Cldnt gve a XXXX 4 lst ordrs' text message indicated their confidence in the NTE to develop and revitalise the hospitality and leisure industries under the auspices of following a (mythically utopian) European model. Despite the warnings and protestations of economists, sociologists and numerous academics from other disciplines that reductions in supply-side controls and legislation would lead to increases in alcohol-related harm, the government and (unsurprisingly) the drinks industry remained adamant that liberalisation of the alcohol retail markets would reap positive results for all those concerned (Plant et al., 1997; Babor, 2010).

City centres now house the high street brands and shopping experiences that emphasise conspicuous consumption, and the NTE has become the forum for enacting identities that have been purchased within the daylight hours. It has been widely argued that pressure to consume is most directly applied to the young (Featherstone, 1987; Miles, 2000). However, as youth, and its association with vitality, freedom and vigour are increasingly packaged and commodified, consumer experience appears to be increasingly desirable to a significant proportion of individuals who are heading through their thirties and beyond. This appears to be a journey that for many is accompanied by the less desirable aspects associated with youth such as lack of permanent and stable employment, exclusion from property markets and fear or rejection of long-term relationships (see Winlow and Hall, 2006).

For these older drinkers, who, due to the disintegration of traditional modernist biographies are both unable and unwilling to tread the traditional Fordist path, the presence of the NTE provides an all too easy seduction. Purchasing a 'good time' and the promise of the carnivalesque (see Bakhtin, 1984; Presdee, 2000) appears to offer a unique opportunity to 'become', to create identities and forge group memberships or friendships on shared experiences. The NTE provides limitless opportunities to obtain a sense of status or peer approval that is more elusive within daytime or midweek hours. It is a primary purpose of this book to examine the meanings drawn from these lived experiences and contextualise them against the backdrop of the post-industrial economy.

It is apparent that the social and economic changes that have been at the heart of an array of global transformations have been responsible for myriad changes on both a national and local level within the UK. The flexibility, complexity, risk and challenges that have become synonymous with life within a neoliberal, consumer-driven economy have profound implications for the individual, who must negotiate an individualised, contingent and risky biography, further complicated by community dissolution and the growing importance of consumerism to the creation of identity (Bauman, 2007). Processes that appear to be contributing to infantilisation and erosion of adulthood are highly visible within the NTE (see, for example, Winlow and Hall, 2009), which is to where our attention turns in the next section, as we explore the ways in which individuals consume alcohol within the NTE, and investigate how and to what extent meaning is derived from this prolonged immersion within environs that have previously been the domain of youth.

The marketplace of the NTE

If you were to visit this city centre chain bar on a weekend night, it is unlikely that you would find a vacant booth or table, let alone an ergonomic leather seat on which to perch while sipping your drink. You would more likely find yourself elbow to elbow, three deep at the bar while the group of women flanking you go about the excruciating process of analysing the cocktail menu and wine list, while the flat screen TV above the bar beams 'fashion TV', a 24-hour style and fashion channel focusing on the catwalks of Milan and Monte Carlo into the faces of those trying to catch the eye of the bartender. This looped TV show represents aspirational programming at its least subtle and serves as a suggestion to customers that they should be as slim as the stems on their martini glasses to frequent this temple to chic and style. I am sitting on a stylish and unsurprisingly uncomfortable stool at the bar however, on a Monday afternoon. Behind me a group of river-viewing diners lingering over their late lunch are the only other customers. I am sipping on a glass of Coke with ice. A lot of ice. A previous visit to this bar under less temperate circumstances had caught my interest due to the layout of the bar, my attention drawn to the layers of overt symbolism to attract those who conform to the industry's perception of drinkers with more refined tastes. Noticeably absent are the traditional hand-pulled beer pumps. In their place are two sets – at opposite ends of the bar – of four slender, graceful polished steel and unbranded taps. They dispense lager, 'export' lager, Guinness and a 'Smooth' bitter, but an impression is created that these beverages are tolerated rather than celebrated. The back of the bar is the real showpiece. A wall of mahogany and mirrors, soft lighting and ten or twelve different types of glassware state that this is a sophisticated establishment for consumers of distinction. Wine bottles are displayed proudly in bespoke recesses, enabling customers to make a conspicuous choice. The name of the grape and country of origin, along with some basic tasting notes are carefully inscribed on a chalkboard below each bottle. This detail suggests the wine has been chosen specifically by an expert, rather than chosen at random from a supplier's list. The single malt whiskies are behind a lockable glass door, giving the impression that they are a precious commodity, while a selection of designer vodkas are displayed, softly lit from beneath to give an ethereal effect. To the right-hand side of the bar are nine lockable cabinets. A sign above indicates that they are 'spirit lockers'. A brushed steel plate adorns each, upon which a name is engraved. Some investigative work reveals that these are allocated to VIP customers (regulars, in less salubrious surroundings) who can store a bottle of their preferred drink, if it is not stocked by the bar. So long as they purchase the bottle at a premium price, and consume it within a set amount of time, they have the privilege bestowed upon them of retaining the spirit locker to house a further bottle. I suspect that the reasons for acquiring such a locker go beyond the simple desire for a particular brand of alcohol over and above the baffling array already on display, and instead is bound up with conferring a sense of distinction, a tool to assist in positioning the individual as a preferred customer, above the herd of ignorant consumers clamouring at the bar for their generic gin and tonic or bottled lager. Owning a locker confirms status as one of a band of individuals who know what to buy and how to flaunt it.

The variety of glassware on display assures the customer that this is a place that knows its alcohol, and reassures them that they will be purchasing not simply a beverage, but an *experience*. The same can be said for the collection of exotic spirits. Eschewing the familiar rack of optic dispensers, the bottles are crowded together on progressively elevated platforms, like football supporters on old-style terraces. On a busy night, as bottles are withdrawn and replaced, upended and emptied, a spectacle is created that adds a sense of the theatrical to the otherwise rather uniform leisure experience of the customers. Many of the ubiquitous brands are absent from the ranks of bottles, and are instead squirrelled out of sight as the 'house spirits' on the 'speed rail' from which the simple vodka and Coke or gin and tonic would be produced on a busy night. This is perhaps neatly representative of the chasm that exists between the advertised and the real in the NTE. The more luxurious and expensive drinks are integral to seducing the consumer, while their purchase, and requesting them confidently when ordering drinks enables the consumer to display his or her good taste to those who are either unwilling or unable to pay the premium prices or perhaps are not adequately attuned to the nuances of the finer things in life. During more quiet times, staff are enthused and engage with customers on the merits of different drinks. This is a quiet time, and I am drawn toward the cocktail list. Slickly produced in a luxurious booklet format, the list reads like a novel, with the reader introduced to a plethora of exotic characters. I hear how my Godfather cocktail utilises vodka that is somehow related to the fields on which the last remaining buffalo in Poland roam. I'm not convinced I believe the barman (despite or perhaps because of the fact that he refers to himself as a mixologist) but I like the story and I already think the cocktail tastes better for it despite the fact it has yet to touch my lips. And so it should at the best part of ten quid. I taste the cocktail and have to admit, it is good.

The transition from an economy based in production to one reliant on consumption, and the related growth in consumer symbolism (see, for example, Baudrillard, 1984) has been explored in an earlier chapter. However, it is here that we start to consider exactly what this means for consumption of alcohol within the arena of the NTE. For the purposes of this section, alcohol consumption refers not to frequency and quantity of alcohol consumed (for discussions of this nature see Plant and Plant, 2006; Babor, 2010), but instead is concerned with the significant restructuring of the night-time cityscape and the resultant transformations within British drinking cultures and the consumer society. It has become clear that the NTE is bound up with the economic logic of liberal capitalism (Hobbs et al., 2003; Winlow and Hall, 2006) while the cultural behaviours displayed within it are indicative of broader shifts within identity and sociability.

Gaining a conceptual understanding of consumption is made difficult by the fact that successive left-liberal interpretations have enveloped the concept in baseless optimism, framing studies in consumption as supplying us with evidence that people freely use, communicate and construct their collective identities with mass-produced and mass-mediated commodities (see Hebdige, 1979; Fiske, 1991). These studies are used to support the contention that commodities are symbolically recontextualised and materially adapted to provide liberating spaces for self-expression and cultural resistance to dominant social realities. De Certeau is particularly vehement in his defence of the creative and empowering possibilities of everyday cultural action, perceiving the relationship between production and consumption:

> In reality a rationalised, expansionist, centralised, spectacular and clamorous production is confronted by an entirely different kind of production, called 'consumption' and characterised by its ruses, its fragmentation ... its poaching, its clandestine nature, its tireless but quiet activity, in short by its quasi-invisibility, since it shows itself not in its own products, but in an art of using those imposed upon it. (1984: 31)

De Certeau positions consumption as analogous to a 'guerrilla war' in which the powers of the economic and political system are challenged through the creative use of consumption within their everyday lives, stressing the supposed dynamic and culturally enabling nature of consumption.

Similar Panglossian echoes are to be found in the positioning of consumer goods to that of a liberating and empowering resource. Fiske, for example, talks of cultural subversion surrounding the tearing of jeans and the 'misuse' of shopping malls by teenagers, citing these and other examples as proof that capitalism is unable to impose a popular culture which is coherent with the ideology behind the production of its commodities, claiming that:

> Popular culture is made by the people, not by the culture industry. All the cultural industries can do is to produce a repertoire of texts or cultural resources for the various formations of the people to use or reject in the ongoing process of producing their popular culture. (1989: 24)

Through Fiske's lens, popular culture is viewed as a celebrated, subversive space in which cultural forms and artefacts are used, modified and customised by the consumer in order to satisfy their diverse subcultural needs. However, the slavish optimism of this viewpoint fails to appreciate the false choices that abound within his argument. Taking the ripped jeans of Fiske's example as a point of departure, it is clear that the individual is still denied the choice between buying jeans or not. She has 'no choice but to choose' (Giddens, 1991). Indeed, how are we to conceive of the ripping of clothing as a subversive act? The corporate giants who have commissioned the manufacture of these items, most likely exploiting offshore foreign labour are not going to be unduly concerned, and in fact, any suggestion of an attempt of resistance at the point of consumption will be negated through ingestion into their own brand strategy, evidenced by the pre-ripped, pre-faded jeans on offer in high street shop windows.

This is not to say that consumption does not involve the use of consumer goods for communication, but this communication is distorted by the underlying logic of capitalism and the quest for profit. Marx (1975) argues that within market societies, commodities are capable of masking or even replacing relationships between people. His concern relates to the fact that the processes of capitalism drove a wedge between labour and consumption. That workers sell their labour power for the mass manufacture of commodities for sale into the market occurred at the expense of the creation of products that satiated immediate desires, needs and identities. Changes in the labour process drove mental and physical work further and further apart leading workers to consume the products of others, and also to produce for the consumption of others, with the goal and end product of cramming commodities into the marketplace to serve the profit-driven needs of owners and investors (Hall and Winlow, 2008). This leads to a dual level of alienation; on the one hand, workers are alienated from the products of their labour, while on the other, as consumers, they are alienated from the social meaning of their accrued products:

> The object that labour produces, its product, stands opposed to it as something alien, as a power independent of the producer. The product of labour is labour embodied and made material in an object, it is the objectification of labour. The realisation of labour is its objectification. In the sphere of political economy this realisation of labour appears as a loss of reality for the worker, objectification as loss of and bondage to the object and appropriation as estrangement, as alienation. (Marx 1975: 324)

The relentless search for profit is directly related to a perpetually increasing range of products, which can only find a market through control over and manipulation of the consumer, a process hidden by the 'mask' of the commodity. Through packaging, promotions and advertising, goods are masked in such a way that they are to manipulate the relations between things, and the wants and needs of individuals simultaneously, while the negative externalities of production and consumption, the exploitation and ecological implications are offshored, kept at arm's length and out of sight. The dominance of exchange-value within the marketplace savagely diminishes the association with the original use-value of the good, freeing it to take on a secondary use-value through a range of cultural associations and illusions, a mechanism of 'commodity aesthetics' (Adorno, 1978). Suffice to say, the sphere of consumption has reached such a level of hyperreality (Baudrillard, 1983) that the idea as well as the act of participating within consumer markets – of making purchases – serves as a motivation for a vast number of individuals to go out and do paid work.

The symbolic associations with goods affects consumers in their accessing of clothing, cars, furniture as well as alcoholic drinks and the procurement of pleasure within the leisure economy. Individuals believe they are constructing identities through their use of symbols within the circuits of consumption, and it is to the commodified experiences found here that the symbolic characteristics of pleasure have been successfully attached. In short, people try to become the thing they desire to be through the consumption of items that they believe will help to sustain that image or identity. Baudrillard (1970) draws attention to the fundamental shift from needs to desires, stating that consumption is not based upon the satisfaction of a set of pre-existing base needs, lodged deep within the biological framework of humans. Consequently, he rejects connotations of consumption to simple material objects, and speaks of a consumption of signs and symbols, which accounts for a sense of emptiness experienced by the consumer once they have attained an object that they have longed for. The anticipation of consuming therefore is more enjoyable than the act of consumption itself, an idea clearly reflected in the anticipation and deflation that is experienced by a number of my respondents with regard to participation within the NTE:

> There are no limits to consumption. If it was that which it is naively taken to be, an absorption, a devouring, then we should achieve satisfaction. But we know that this is not the case: we want to consume more and more. This compulsion to consume is not the consequence of some psychological determinant etc., nor is it simply the power of emulation. If consumption appears to be irrepressible, this is because it is a total idealist practice which has no longer anything to do (beyond a certain point) with the satisfaction of needs, nor with the reality principle ... Hence, the desire to 'moderate' consumption, or to establish a normalising network of needs, is absurd moralism. (Baudrillard, 1988: 24–25)

A swathe of sociological rhetoric has been carved from the assertion that individuals are free to mould and remould their identities at will. The core theme of the individual exercising self-control over their personal destiny is an attractive one and to a greater or lesser extent reflects the self-image that many people hold of themselves and like to think that they project. Of course, it would be wrong to insinuate that individuals are bereft of any capacity for autonomous action, it is just that the level of autonomy is limited – to the extent that in absolute terms it could be said to mean very little. This myth of 'freedom' has developed from a set of arguments which maintain that interaction with the symbolic and material resources of consumer culture is integral to the choosing of self-identity – therefore consumer culture directly enhances the core freedom of the individual. Despite Giddens' assertion (1991) that 'lifestyle choice is increasingly important in the constitution of self-identity' we must be careful not to overemphasise the importance of 'rational' self-creation. Rather, as Lodziak (1995) reminds us, we should consider the more pressing problems associated with the maintenance of meaningful and satisfying identities. The continual assertion that it is now possible to 'choose' our own self-identities and creatively display them using consumerised lifestyle accoutrements neglects structural factors and omits critical discourses that connect the pressure of social expectation with developing forms of ontological insecurity.

Furthermore, to argue that material consumption contributes in some way to an enhanced experience of freedom misses a core point. The extent to which individuals are able to participate in this arena is dependent on a financial income, obtained through relinquishing freedom in order to work. With labour markets characterised by transience, insecurity and alienation the level of freedom available to the individual appears to be negligible, despite the increased array of (essentially meaningless) choice that is available within the consumer market (see Adorno, 1978). As Lasch puts it:

> Unless the idea of choice carries with it the possibility of making a difference, of changing the course of events, of setting in motion a chain of events that may prove irreversible, it negates the freedom it claims to uphold. Freedom comes down to the freedom to choose between Brand X and Brand Y, between interchangeable lovers, interchangeable jobs, interchangeable neighbourhoods. (1985: 38)

At first glance we may assume that the increase in the number and variety of goods that are available is indicative of more choice for the consumer, and as such more freedom – however this simplistic view does not take into account the consequentiality of choice. In the case of the vast majority of decisions within the consumer market – the NTE included – the difference between consumer items and their subsequent consequence is negligible. After all, what difference does it really make which flavour or brand of alcopop one chooses, or indeed whether one chooses lager or cider.

To equate consumer choice with freedom is to misunderstand the illusory devices of consumer capitalism. Much of the left-liberal thinking on consumerism accentuates and emphasises the degree to which individuals possess the capacity for autonomous action under late capitalism (Featherstone, 1987; Fiske, 1989). The core view emanating from cultural studies appears to be one offering the most simplistic interpretation of Cartesian subjectivity, intimating that the transition from Fordism to post-Fordism had the effect of liberating individuals from tradition and narrow role prescriptions, giving them the freedom to attribute meaning to items that are consumed, while the meaning becomes part of the self-identity. People, according to this view, are unconditionally free to decide and choose who they are and what they become, actively assembling and reshaping their identity through the process of consumption. The plethora of inconsequential choices facing the consumer in themselves contributes to a negation of freedom rather than a promotion of it. The very fact that we have no choice but to choose (see Giddens, 1991) suggests that making choices has become mandatory – which of course is, to say the least, a peculiar form of freedom. Therefore, to ally consumer choice so closely to freedom is a gross misrepresentation. The choice is simply to choose from one of a set array of options, rather than the unfettered freedom that is implied through much of the literature and rhetoric. As Bauman points out:

> Individual choices are in all circumstances confined by two sets of constraints ... One set is determined by the agenda of choice: the range of alternatives which are actually on offer. All choice means 'choosing among', and seldom is the set of items to be chosen from a matter for the chooser to decide ... [the second set of constraints] is determined by the code of choosing: the rules that tell the individual on what ground the preferences should be given to some items rather than others and when to consider the choice as proper and when as inappropriate. (1999: 72–73)

The agenda of choice alluded to by Bauman above is undeniably the range of options controlled by big business – in terms of the NTE the pubcos[3] and other industry stakeholders – who are able to access levels of freedom that are denied to the consumer. By association, this rejects the supposition of 'consumer-led production', the assertion that outputs of production are 'shaped by the noises coming from the street' (Mort, 1989: 167). It is these processes that the next chapter will explore in more detail, aligning notions of choice and identity to more specific examples of branding and marketing evident within the NTE.

4
Consuming the City

The practice of marketing has long been held within the contemporary setting as being (along with consumption) intrinsically linked to the formation of identity, and consumers within the night-time economy (NTE) in particular are viewed as being especially susceptible to, or placing the most value upon the consumption-driven signals of identity. At least, as far as the NTE is concerned, it seems reasonable to suggest that marketing materials and artefacts have become 'miasma in the ethereal identities and microcultures of ... youth in ways that naturalise, normalise and encourage alcohol consumption' (McCreanor et al., 2005: 26). The layers of branding and marketisation are overtly displayed within an arena that serves to reward ostentation and standing out from the crowd.

The relationship between alcohol consumption and fashion is strong. Enter any of the Vertical Drinking Establishments such as The Slug and Lettuce, Pitcher & Piano or All Bar One on any high street in the UK and it is clear that there is much more going on than the satiation of the singular desire to quench a thirst. Whether part of the after-work crowd or later in the evening, consumption is far from inconspicuous, and it is impossible to see anonymous pint pots of ale being drunk – bottles are highly visible, and spirits asked for by name, while 'export' lagers are drunk from the bottle or from ostentatious vessels branded with frosted typography or bold, golden swirls and flourishes.

I am standing with a group of four males on a mezzanine floor of a riverside bar. A quick glance at the shirt of one of the staff collecting glasses at a nearby table confirms that it is the Pitcher & Piano, but it could easily be The Slug and Lettuce or any one of the other bars ubiquitous to city centres across the country. Taking in the hundred or so individuals crammed into the space beneath me, I am struck by the conspicuous presence of the global culture industry (Lash and Lury, 2007).

From my vantage point I see myriad designer labels and branded clothing, emblazoned across any available space of valuable cloth real-estate. I see women with handbags, some of which are branded with insignia that I can identify from up here; others are perhaps more subtle in that regard, but their size and obnoxious leatheriness places them as either expensive designer items, or at least purporting to be. Obviously, I lack the cultural attuning necessary to be able to tell the difference. Turning my attention to the drinks in the hands of the people below, I find that I am able to identify the particular brand of draught alcohol that people are holding from the shapes of the vessels they are served in. Guinness is easy enough to spot, not least because the drink itself is easy to identify, a sharp black, contrasting with the centimetre or so of white 'head'. Beck's is served in a tall glass, the circumference of which is slightly bevelled to give it a squared-off look and feel, while Peroni, a premium Italian lager, is served in a fluted tall glass that cries elegance and sophistication to those in the know. Stella Artois, an unremarkable beer of Belgian heritage but long-since brewed domestically, is served in perhaps the most ostentatious glass of the beers I can see. It is in fact more of a chalice, or oversized wineglass, with a short, sturdy stem and gold detailing that runs around the rim of the glass. A long-running advertising campaign promoted Stella Artois as 'Reassuringly Expensive', and it is clear that this theme is associated with the glassware, despite the fact that this tagline appears to have been shelved in the face of the recent financial crisis.

The role of alcohol consumption within the wider arena of consumerism raises a number of interesting issues, as, aside from the negative health connotations, alcohol can be an important tool in assisting consumers to obtain social approval and broadcast the manner in which they prefer to be perceived by others (Parker, 1998). Consumption of different types and brands of alcohol (at least within public spaces) serves as a mechanism for communicating group membership and differentiation from other social segments, while aligning with others (see Measham and Brain, 2005). Indeed, the very vessels for alcoholic beverages have become an integral part of the experience for consumers. Gone are the days when the patrons were offered a choice between a straight glass and the traditional pint-mug. Lagers and beers are heavily branded, with the more ostentatious glasses conferring a degree of the connoisseur upon the drinker, as exemplified by Mark, a 33-year-old architect:

> Have you seen those new Stella glasses? They're a bit ridiculous – it's like you're drinking out of a vase or something, but I guess that's

kind of the point. They used to have loads at mine and Louisa's local, but they all walked. I was in there the other night and got served in a normal boring glass, which pissed me off a bit. I mean, at five quid a pint, you want people to know what you are drinking don't you? I should have just ordered Carling or something.

Alcohol undoubtedly plays an important role in the creation of branded identities for a significant proportion of individuals within the UK. The Puritan ethos of hard work and deferred gratification and its associated identity politics are a thing of the past as once-strong bonds of capitalist productivity and strongly defined morality loosen and dissolve. Identity has become increasingly linked to 'lifestyles' that are interwoven with commercial brands and products. With reference to alcohol, different incarnations of similar products are imbued with myriad messages that are broadcast to others, and drinks and drinking venues come into fashion and fall out of favour. Inhabitants of the NTE are all too aware of the transitory nature of these fashions as pubs and bars are loaded with value that far exceeds their functionality as a venue for social activity. Baudrillard states that the social determinants of meaning have been eclipsed with the result that the signs and symbols of fashionable display circulate without logic:

> The acceleration of the simple play of signifiers in fashion becomes striking, to the point of enchanting us – the enchantment and the vertigo of the loss of every system of reference … There is no longer any determinacy internal to the signs of fashion, hence they become free to commute and permutate without limit. (1983: 87)

Baudrillard explains how fashionable items derive their prestige not from the function they perform, but from the way they do it. Indeed, 'fashion aims for a theatrical sociality and delights in itself' (1983: 94).

Alcoholic drinks are generally assumed to be one of a number of branded products that people use to signal identity and belonging (Measham and Brain, 2005). The birth and rapid expansion of the network society have opened up a number of new channels such as events, mobile phones, websites, music and television – as well as diverse modalities such as advertising, product placement, branding and sponsorship, utilised by alcohol marketing to influence the formation of youth identity (McCreanor et al., 2005). Alcohol marketing has been recognised as being at the forefront of what has been termed 'postmodern marketing' (Brown, 1993) utilising Information and

Communication Technologies, and the ubiquitous social networking sites to propagate their message through less traditional means. Viral advertising campaigns, for example, are devised in order to market products through subversion, while the tone of adverts may be self-deprecating and self-aware (Jackson et al., 2000; Jernigan and O'Hara, 2004). The Bacardi brand is particularly active on the social networking site Twitter, relentlessly linking aspirational images, insipid motivational slogans and extolling the insertion of their particular brand of rum into celebrations of the mundane, such as the arrival of Monday, or the release of a new video game console. This alignment with the zeitgeist can be viewed as problematic for a number of reasons, not least the age-inappropriate overlaps that frequently occur.

The advertising campaigns for WKD, a ready-to-drink (RTD) bottled beverage, appear to be targeted at males in their late twenties and thirties. Adverts typically show either a prank or joke at the expense of either one of the group of 'lads' or their wives or girlfriends, utilising the tagline 'Have you got a WKD side?' The core message is quite clear. The answer to the question the advert poses is clearly supposed to be an unequivocal 'yes'. Despite getting older and taking on the responsibilities of a committed relationship, the ageing male is supposed to retain a child-like fascination with pranks and jokes as this implicitly demonstrates a broad range of positive cultural characteristics. Yes, the advert tells us, you may be getting older, but this does not mean you have to relinquish your sense of humour or the bonhomie of male company. The interesting, popular and 'successful' male recognises that one should not take life too seriously and that having fun with friends is a vital part of 'the good life'. This basic ideological message is then neatly packaged into a short film and connected to a particular brand. This central message of retaining the interests of youth is also clearly exhibited in other areas of the NTE and its associated markets such as fashion and music.

Herd (2005) illustrates the prevalence of alcohol references within rap music songs between 1979 and 1997, with a strong increase in the lyrical placement of alcoholic brand names after the early 1990s as well as an increasing focus on using alcohol to signify glamour and wealth. Although her findings are limited to the genre of rap music, there are no shortages of similar examples within the music charts any given week. Consequently we are urged to Eat, Sleep, Rave, Repeat (Fatboy Slim, 2013) and to 'keep partying like it's your job' (David Guetta, 2013). Elsewhere the 'striver–skiver' dichotomy favoured by David Cameron's coalition government is accentuated within the context of success within consumer markets and the NTE. Britney Spears (2013), for example, assures us that the good life is available, marked out by fast cars and branded champagne, as long as we are prepared to 'work, bitch'.

Within the alcohol industry itself, there has been an overall shift away from small breweries and independent venues to the distinct corporatisation of all aspects of the industry. While some (Held et al., 1999) may view this as part of the process of globalisation, it is worth noting due to the specific impact these processes have had on structuring the contemporary alcohol industry. Within the UK market, traditional large brewers such as Scottish and Newcastle, Bass or Whitbread evolved beyond their simple brewing roots to become part of national or multi-national entertainment conglomerates, with retail departments capable of running a wide variety of venues from premium-branded bar venues, health spas and hotels, to unbranded, tenanted pubs. Whitbread, for example, style themselves as a 'family of brands' (Whitbread.co.uk., 2013), which consists of Costa Coffee, Beefeater Grill, and Premier Inn.

Additionally, the market is increasingly dominated by the voraciously acquisitive pubcos such as the Punch Group and Pubmaster or J D Wetherspoon, companies often backed by European banks or venture capitalists (such as GI Partners), who pounce as former brewers continue to sell off their pub estates (Zukin, 1995; Chatterton and Hollands, 2003; Hadfield, 2006). They possess the capital necessary to transform prime location city-centre buildings into new licensed premises, creating swathes of urban nightlife in which competition is fierce, and wealth a devastating advantage in the bid for market share (Zukin, 1995; Chatterton and Hollands, 2004). Punch Taverns, for example, is one of the largest pub and bar operators in the UK, controlling somewhere in the region of 4,000 tenanted, leased or managed pubs (Punch Taverns website, 2013). Within the nightclub market, those operators unable to adapt and diversify to the changing marketplace initiated by a relaxing of the licensing laws, and subsequent blurring of the bar/nightclub market, went to the wall.

The economic downturn of the latter part of the past decade has had a discernible impact on this industry. According to the British Beer and Pub Association (BBPA), the second half of 2009 saw an average of 22 free houses closed a week, compared to 12 tenanted and five managed pubs (BBPA, 2010). These statistics, combined with a contraction in the beer market overall, are contributing to a frenetic marketing campaign asserting that 'Pubs are Great'. It seems somewhat fitting that an industry founded on the provision of liquid pleasures is, then, in such a state of unstable fluidity.

Bucking this trend to some extent is the identifiable rise in the production and availability of real ale and craft beer. According to CAMRA (2013), there are 840 brewers in Britain, the majority of which would be classed as micro-breweries, able to operate under the UK progressive Beer Duty threshold of 5,000 hectolitres a year, a taxation mechanism introduced in 2002.

Branding and marketing

While branding is nothing new to the alcohol industry (consider the once ubiquitous Bass red triangle was the first registered trademark in the UK), it has metastasised, becoming integral to the expansion strategies of modern licensed premises operators, representative of the triumph of the symbolic over the material, synonymous with consumer society. Emphasis on brand development has both the purpose and effect of shaping new consumer identities within the NTE through differential approaches to licensing arrangements, and varying attitudes towards dress codes and gender relations. A stroll around any British town or city will reveal branded venues specifically aimed at students (for example, It's a Scream, Varsity), young professionals (All Bar One, The Living Room), or sports fans (Walkabout).

This practice of reproduction and theming draws criticism from a number of sources, not least the 'traditionalists' who yearn for a yesteryear of authenticity and realism. There are also a number of 'consumer groups' who often purport to defend the interests of the consumer, keen to encourage a genuine diversity of 'leisure options', and traditional publicans, with one eye on declining revenues and market share, who argue that the damage to the traditional British pub and its clientele is irreversible (Chatterton and Hollands, 2004). However, their voices are weak in the cathedrals of night-time consumer leisure. The relentless branding blends seamlessly with the broader ubiquity of branding in everyday life. Consumers are on the whole unconcerned at the fact that corporations are drawing upon key symbolism in order to attract our attention and capture custom. Put simply, it is nothing new. Huge swathes of consumer culture are firmly rooted within this kind of fabrication to the extent that we are able to conclude that we are in fact living branded lives, through the cars we drive, the clothes we wear, the music we listen to (see Holt, 2004; Barber, 2007). Branding is doubtless central to the success of licensed premises within the contemporary NTE, being the major conduit through which to add value to a product. This is Naomi Klein's (2000) point – although many companies can make a pair of trainers for $20, only those with an established brand may sell them for $200. In this way, leisure consumers are drawn toward localised incarnations of branded leisure outlets, safe in the knowledge that they are guaranteed a uniform experience with discernible and paradoxical overtones of exclusivity. For the majority of people I spoke to, the pre-packaged uniformity and the almost tangible sense of staged artificiality and spectacle (Debord, 1983) did not appear to inspire a fully conscious desire to return to the Real (Badiou, 2002). Conversely, it seemed that consumers were expressing closeness to the brand image, whose artificiality offered some degree of comfort. The product and the associated experience thus seem to some extent guaranteed by its image. Respondents often displayed a knowledge and awareness of the logic of capital underlying these places and accepted them for what they were, nevertheless valuing the goods and services that were made available by their existence on the high street. In this way, many of the individuals I talked to were displaying something similar to what Mark Fisher terms 'reflexive impotence' whereby knowledge of a situation becomes irrelevant due to the further knowledge of their inability to do anything that might change it (Fisher, 2009). Of course these individuals could simply avoid the NTE, but in the face of no viable alternative, this would likely render them culturally obsolete, a potential fate that forms a core source of anxiety.

In order to remain 'cool', bars and clubs within the NTE must draw on current lifestyle symbols, experiences and expectations, and depending on which market niche these branded venues identify as home turf, enforce dress codes that reflect the stylistic expectations the bar has for its clients and which its clients have for others who are accessing their social space. Some brands in particular, such as All Bar One or The Slug and Lettuce, are able to utilise the 'aspirational advertising' aspect of alcohol consumption, by linking their combinations of products sold and venue to a number of pre-packaged formulae, promising success, youth, glamour and the kind of social distinction that aims to inspire envy (see Hall et al., 2008). While younger consumers may be forgiven their naivety to some extent in buying into the promise of bounded liminality and hedonistic excess, one might expect its hold to weaken on consumers as they age. As the dedicated nightlife consumer ages and adopts a more discriminating taste, the raucous hedonism of the youthful drinking strip may start to lose its appeal. They begin to yearn for the finer things in life – stylish and aesthetically pleasing decor, a more muted, laid-back ambiance that suggests a studied coolness coupled with natural class, held together by a soundtrack that does not pander to musical fads or the pop charts. All of these needs are now adequately catered for in Britain's urban night-time economies. However, these 'alternative' drinking spaces, in which the coarse and vulgar have been filtered out, do not represent a direct response to the shifting desires of increasingly discerning customers. Indeed, it is likely that this niche market, adopting the rhetoric of 'discerning, adult customers' and creating calculated distance from the problematic mainstream of the NTE has actually played an important role in creating the very desires that it caters for, through encouraging consumers to pursue social distinction through 'alternative' leisure options.

It is important not to lose sight of the fact that alcohol, the key commodity on sale within our NTE, is one of the most strongly marketed of all products within the broader consumer economy (see Measham and Brain, 2005). As with other literature within the area, much of the work conducted by social scientists has concentrated heavily on the influence of alcohol marketing on young people, with little consideration given to established, older drinkers. These consumers represent a particular challenge for the marketing moguls. As they age and take on an increasing number of traditional adult roles, the NTE finds itself competing for access to an increasingly thinly spread pay packet. In a relationship? Weekend breaks are expected and expensive, meals out as a couple eat into time and resources that could be spent out on the 'lash'. Got children? Increasing demands for an array of consumables make weekend drinking evermore a luxury. Add to this the cynicism that comes with age, the belief that we are immune to the tricks of marketing, that we see through the thinly veiled marketing messages. We install Adblocker software, and set our TVs to skip commercial breaks. We are, however, still seen as valuable potential consumers of consumer products, and advertising will find a way, perhaps most innovatively, and certainly most insidiously through the utilisation of murketing. Murketing blurs the line between branded products and experiences and everyday life, and is most clearly evident in the promotion of goods and experiences which desperately want to appear authentic or non-conformist. The murketing strategies around malt whisky provide an example of this within the drinks industry. Malt whisky offers consumers an authentic drinking experience rooted in romantic visions of misty Scottish vistas, and the assertion of small distillery heritage (Spracklen, 2011). In reality, the majority of the malt whisky to be found in bars and pubs is owned by major players in the drinks industry. Caol Ila, for example, is owned by Diageo, a fact only ascertained through accessing the website of the parent company. It is murketing that keeps this association hidden, as Diageo know that their product is more desirable for its claims to authenticity and tradition. Hence, consumers are allowed to feel as though they are 'opting out' of the crass consumerism offered by the majority of the drinks industry, while in reality being as embroiled as their detested opposite, drinking lager in a theme bar.

Drinking and symbolic capital

The existence of alcohol as symbolic capital was highly evident among the subjects of this piece of research, as the data introduced over the coming pages will attest. Symbolic capital cannot be viewed as a specific form of capital in the same way as economic, social or cultural capital may be, but instead is 'what every form of capital becomes when it obtains an explicit or practical recognition' (Bourdieu, 2000: 242). Once capital is perceived as a positive sign, it has the effect of making those in possession 'visible, admired and invited', and granting them the justification for membership of the group as well as having the right to 'recognise – or to state with success what merits being known and recognised' (ibid.).

Among younger drinkers, drinking experience is stated as the main form of symbolic capital, as a certain amount of prestige is designated to those who have started drinking earliest, been to the greatest number of parties and have the largest network of friends through drinking at parties (Jarvinen and Gundelach, 2007). The evidence that will be presented over the coming pages, based on observational work and unstructured interviews with drinkers in their thirties, while uncovering little to suggest that any prestige is given as a result of taking up drinking at a young age, did reflect a certain degree of prestige attributed to individuals who drink a lot, and/or often. However this picture is complicated by the fact that there appears a line beyond which negative connotations are applied to behaviour. Behaviour that takes the individual beyond this line may earn them the brand of 'fuck-up' or 'crank'. Symbolic capital appears to be linked to an individual maintaining an active role within the NTE, drinking, perhaps consuming drugs, or participating in violence, while at the same time holding down a job, relationships, or family. Individuals who to a greater or lesser extent survive while (in their eyes) embracing countercultural ideology are also afforded more by way of prestige. This was borne out within the lived experiences of a number of my respondents, perhaps nowhere more clearly than with Ian and Spider, two individuals in their late thirties who in many ways epitomise dedication to the NTE. Ian, who earns a living playing in bands and DJing is perhaps envied by some of his peers, who may well be earning more in real terms. This contrasts with Spider, who, lurching from one bar job to another, supplants his income through dealing drugs. While it is likely that Spider deals drugs in part for the perceived prestige it may earn him (Coomber and Moyes, 2013), he was rarely spoken of in positive terms by members of the cohort I interviewed. While they were happy to purchase or receive free product from him, he was certainly perceived as peripheral and not to be trusted. During fieldwork, I noticed that while tolerated by the group on a night out, his presence was coincidental, never planned, and generally quite fleeting as he would soon be off to another bar, with no plans made to rejoin the group later, and no visible sorrow shown at the fact he was leaving.

Contemporary theories of consumption and youth identity are important in fostering an understanding of the ways in which alcohol and associated products are both consumed and marketed. The use-value of commodities, including alcohol, has been eclipsed by aesthetic considerations that generate symbolic value (Lyon, 1999). The market is frequently viewed as fluid and networked, while the self is continuously moulded and reformed through the negotiation of various and variable identities. Giddens (1991) speaks of 'lifestyles' as describing the reflexive relationship between structures of society and the agency of the individual, while Miles (2000: 26) posits that lifestyles are 'lived cultures in which individuals actively express their identities but do so in direct relation to their position as regards the dominant culture'. Through symbolic consumption, Miles claims that young people are able to assert meaning and significance within their lives, creating microcultures that shape their identities and status in relation to others, experiencing stability within a snowstorm of constant and rapid social change through the creation of consumer identities, in effect 'establishing lifestyles that make the world a manageable place' (2000: 142). As has been discussed earlier in this chapter, Miles is guilty of both simplifying and idealising the notion that free agentic action is easily obtainable within the post-industrial society, while there is perhaps a tighter connection between agents and their structural positions.

If the central tenet here is concerned with the way that a proportion of 'adults' are failing to loosen their cultural and aesthetic attachment to the culture of intoxication, then it is important to try and identify just what it is that makes regularly consuming alcohol within the NTE so very attractive. Perhaps these adults are trying to replicate the leisure choices of the 18–24 age group whose exploits fuel the fires of right-wing reactionaries and their left-wing antagonists in popular media outlets, or alternatively simply maintaining a lifestyle that they are unable or unwilling to relinquish. While these explanations will be interrogated in due course, an excursion to a busy student pub reveals some of the complexity around the issue of niche marketing and identity.

Walking past the bouncers, up tiled steps slick with the rainwater being trailed in by the evening's punters, it is immediately obvious that we are in one of the city's more popular student pubs. Beneath the constant hubbub it is possible to make out a generic guitar driven tune. It might be the Kaiser Chiefs, but could be almost anything. Interaction takes place mostly in groups – some around tables, which hug the perimeter of the pub, but many are in huddles with members standing, holding bottles of lurid alcopops, or pints of lager. Empty bottles and pint glasses litter almost every available surface, and tables are awash with spilled drinks. Having taken advantage of the relaxing of the licensing laws regarding opening hours, this pub is open until 2 a.m. every night of the week, providing an alternative to the nightclub just up the street for those who wish to keep drinking into the early hours of the morning. On a table of around 12 students no more than 5 metres from where I am standing, a young woman lowers her head to the table, and soundlessly pukes a mostly clear, slightly viscous liquid that washes lazily across the table and drips down onto the floor. As her friend puts her arm around her and leads her the few uncertain steps to the washroom, activity around the rest of the table continues unabated. One member of the group absently shepherds the vomit onto the floor with the aid of a beer mat, which he subsequently discards on the floor. A few minutes later, I am approached at the bar by a student I recognise as being from one of my tutorial groups. I ask how his night is going. It seems to be going well. 'What are you doing in here?' he enquires. 'It doesn't seem like your kind of place.' 'No,' I reply. 'It isn't.'

The practice of 'going out' lies beyond the parameters of routinised time and place, and is set apart from the student's responsibility for self-improvement and career-building and the lectures, seminars and tutorials of the working week. The space within the walls of the venue described above operates in relation to a 'liminal masquerade' (Turner, 1975: 243). The pub owner has worked to create a sense of communitas around what for the majority of customers will be a ritual event, which aims to be extemporaneous, instinctive and brimming with vitality. In the excerpt above, I intimated that the bar I found myself in was not my kind of place. Reflecting upon this, I appreciate the fact that the bar is not dissimilar to the places where I spent a number of my formative drinking experiences. However I am acutely aware that the surface pleasures of the loud and dirty student drinking den with its cheap alcohol offers and sticky floors, stripped-down washrooms with graffiti and broken fittings no longer seems to hold any appeal for me. A combination of age and experience has perhaps drawn me away from places like this, but, crucially, not from pubs altogether. In a way demonstrated by a number of the respondents within this piece of work, as far as my leisure life is concerned, I am happy to revel in the conceit that I have transcended this world, now able to access a higher plane. When confronted with echelons of the NTE that fail to provide for my new-found distinction, I am left feeling somewhat out of place and isolated. It seems as though the feeling of 'out of placeness' comes from the existence of communitas (Bourdieu, 1984) among the majority of drinkers who prioritise cheap alcohol, 'cool' music and becoming raucously and conspicuously intoxicated with their friends above and beyond more inclusive and intelligible conversation, comfort and relaxation. As Malbon states:

> This communal ethic, the pleasure of being with others, is born both from the sharing of space (a territory) and the proximity of that act of sharing, and from the establishment and maintenance of some sense of unity or membership. (1998: 273)

Looking around the bar, this sense of communal ethic is clearly visible – on one level through observing the styles and fashions that are utilised by individuals within the bar to create some baseless form of pseudo-individualism (see Hall et al., 2008), but also through the aesthetics of the bar itself, from the drinks discounts offered to students, to the offers of cheap meal deals.

Back in the pub, the cocktail menu is cheap, brightly coloured and offers drinks named after cultural icons. No description is necessary, as a sense of 'knowing' is created among regular frequenters of the establishment. And besides, the taste is less important than the alcohol content. Some of the cocktails are served out of a 'frosty' drink dispenser, a transparent vat within which you can make out the viscous, brightly coloured alcoholic slush being churned. That, combined with the bright colours and artificial flavours of many of the drinks that people appear to be drinking leads me to conclude that many of the alcoholic beverages on sale are certainly childish in their overall presentation, an assertion compounded by a glance along the flavoured vodka rack. Here vodka has been flavoured with a number of taste sensations that have more in common with the pick 'n' mix in the local sweet shop than an establishment required by law to cater only for adult consumers.

Drinking to get drunk is clearly the aim for the majority of these drinkers, while drinking in order to 'combat stress' or to 'take their mind off things', which were common reasons given as motivations for alcohol consumption within previous studies on 18–24 year olds (see Engineer et al., 2003) seemed – at least on the surface – curiously absent. Conversations with several of the young people within this establishment served to compound this assertion:

> I'm out with a bunch of us from [University campus halls of residence]. We've had a few pre-drinks in the kitchen, then headed straight here before going into [local night club, hosting student night]. We just have a laugh really, get pissed and dance later on (Aaron, 18, student).

> Getting pissed is just all part of the fun, isn't it? Plus if you all go out and get really, really drunk, then it's good value, cos you get to relive the night again the next day. Someone's always done something stupid you can laugh at them for (Zoe, 18, student).

The desire to get drunk as exemplified by the student drinkers above, and often viewed as an integral part of other young people's drinking biographies (see Szmigin et al., 2008; Griffin et al., 2009), does not appear to have significantly waned as far as my respondents are concerned. While opportunities for excessive alcohol consumption within the arena of the NTE may diminish as traditional demarcations of traditional adulthood seep into their daily lives, the desire to participate in these specific circuits of consumption appears to remain – which is where my attention will turn over the coming pages.

Excessive consumption of the type witnessed during the course of this research has historically been regarded as moral weakness, sinfulness or pathology among the lower classes, or as a sign of status among the elite classes (see Babor, 2010; Holt, 2006). Within the post-Fordist era, however, such insatiable desire for self-gratification has not only been normalised and positively sanctioned, but is integral to the stability of the socioeconomic order (Baudrillard, 1984; Bauman, 1998b). Ritualistic participation within the NTE exemplifies the essence of contemporary consumption, in that it appears to be 'an activity which involves an apparently endless pursuit of want' (Campbell, 1989: 37). In order to survive and prosper, the NTE must produce and cater for 'neophilic' consumers, so termed for their love of new commodities and experiences (ibid.). Importantly, many of the subjects of this study were at the start of their drinking biographies when the first wave of RTD prepackaged alcopop-type drinks flooded onto the market, as Ben, a call centre worker in his mid thirties recalls:

> Yeah, when Hooch and Two Dogs came on the market ... We couldn't get enough of it. We were drinking it like it was lemonade. We used to mix Hooch or whatever with vodka, like a really alcoholic vodka and lemonade, Or a Blastaway, with Diamond White and Castaway.

Consumers within the NTE exemplify Bauman's term 'sensation gatherers'; impulsive, dissatisfied, narcissistic and spontaneous. With its emphasis on the 'new' and the 'now' (Virilio, 2005) the NTE is representative of consumption having precedence over accumulation (Baudrillard, 1970), whereby the idea of saving or postponement of anything becomes redundant in the face of the present becoming overwhelmingly intense and desirable.

While continually creating the new and the now keeps participants within the NTE stimulated and engaged by the consumption of liminal pleasures, an interesting development has been the rise in the numbers of theme pubs that line the high streets. While the ubiquitous Irish pub with its pithy Irish wit adorning the walls in stylised Celtic typography promises authentic surroundings in which to truly appreciate a perfect pint of Guinness (or perhaps Carlsberg, glass of Australian wine or even a bottle of WKD), other establishments offer to transport us temporally, taking us back to a decade gone by, enabling us to (re)experience the 1970s or 1980s.[1]

I am standing outside a building that is of no little historical value. The building used to be a public house. The windows, which some years previously were shrouded by dark, velvet curtains heavy with the texture and scent of the smoke of countless cigarettes, are now spilling forward a harsh neon light. Fluorescent tubes are shaped and twisted, pulsating intermittently to produce a crude approximation of a disco dancer. Metal barricades divide the pavement immediately outside. Later these will serve to segregate the hordes of drunken revellers waiting to get in from the hordes of drunken revellers filtering past on their way to a different bar, a nightclub, late night food or taxis. It is early, however, only 7.30, and there is no need for me to queue as I pass the door staff and make my way into the bar. The bar is Reflex, part of a chain of over 40 establishments each promising 'the ultimate 80s party'.

I am one of only five or six people in the bar at this time. There is the unmistakeable sickly smell in the air of stale alcohol, a smell synonymous with a certain type of establishment, where drinks are spilt often and floors cleaned less so. The bar itself occupies a central position directly in front of me as I enter, its glittered surface winking lewdly, and has an array of chrome beer dispensers along its length, each of which proclaims proudly which global corporate brand name it is allied to. Stella Artois, Foster's and Strongbow all feature. The back of the bar is heavily mirrored, with a heavy predominance and promotion of Corky's Vodka Shots. The brightly coloured bottles stand three deep at the bar in order to make the transition from empty to full bottle as quick as possible. The bottles contain a variety of coloured, almost glutinous liquid, the hues highlighted by the lighting from behind and underneath the bottles. The possible flavours to tempt the drinker are plentiful, and include apple sour, blueberry, cappuccino, cherry, chocolate orange, cola cube, cream egg, mint cream, strawberry and cream, toffee and white chocolate. According to their website, Corky's shots are 'a true game changer … creating never before seen theatre of serve, boosting interest and excitement' (globalbrands.co.uk, 2014). This, however, is not enough to convince me, and I order a bottle of Beck's. Above the regiment of Corky's Shots run a fairly standard selection of spirits, some of which are available as a double measure for an extra pound, indicated by a garish star in neon card and glitter. In addition to alcohol, the bar offers a number of items for sale that could be considered loosely in keeping with its 1980s theme. This includes oversized and glittery sunglasses, wigs, candy necklaces, 'Madonna-style' conical brassieres, and Reflex-branded sweatbands and T-shirts. Bar staff wear bright coloured T-shirts, laden with 80s references to the cult film *The Goonies* and Liverpool band Frankie goes to Hollywood, whose 'Relax' motif is ubiquitous as far as any homage to the decade is concerned.

The 80s theme is rammed down the throats of the drinkers everywhere I look; rather than being designed along an 80s theme, the place takes on more of the character of a poorly thought-out museum. From the ceiling hang glitterballs, oversized Rubik's Cubes, and television sets playing videos that sometimes match the tune being played by the vocal DJ. A cardboard David Hasselhoff, leaning on his iconic car, looms over the revolving dance floor, while brightly coloured posters inform us of the drink deals on offer tonight. The fonts used on posters and on the TV screens have been liberated from classic 80s cultural heavyweights such as *The A-Team* and the Tom Cruise film *Cocktail*. Ascending the stairs to the lavatory I am accompanied by a barrage of familiar faces from the 1980s, leering out from the walls, before being faced with the option of entering a door titled 'East End Boys' or 'West End Girls', a nod in the direction of The Pet Shop Boys' 1985 hit. Inside the gents, the music from downstairs is piped through, complete with the DJ's less than intelligent or intelligible commentary. Above the trough urinal is a mural in graffiti art style, as perhaps you might see sprayed on the side of a New York subway train in an Eddie Murphy film. Closer inspection reveals that the 'art' is in fact little more than a short section of print, duplicated several times along the length of the wall. Finding something real or authentic in this establishment is impossible, with everything presented as a cut-price parody of a corporate perception of a moment in time.

Back in Reflex, it is starting to fill up, and by 9 p.m. there is a long queue of people waiting outside to get in. A rough estimate of the average age of the clientele would be around the late thirties. There are some couples, and some mixed-sex groups, but the majority are same-sex groups.

At one end of the building sits the revolving dance floor. Earlier in the evening it had been inhabited only by a handful of women in their late twenties, while a group of lads of a similar age stood or danced with more than a hint of irony nearby. Now, however, it is labouring under the weight of perhaps 20 people – what looks like a hen party and several smaller groups of males who appear to be weighing up their chances with the women dressed in black, sporting fluorescent pink sashes, name tags and cowboy hats. One of the hen party – a robust woman pushing the far end of her thirties is dancing with a younger, skinny lad on a platform replete with 'pole', elevated about four feet above and to the side of the revolving dance floor. Gripping the chrome pole, she sticks out her ample posterior and gyrates into the grinning lad, unaware of the fact that he is raising his bottle of blue WKD to his mates who are standing on the periphery of the dance area and all but collapsing with laughter.

Describing the atmosphere in the bar is not an easy task, not least because it is so subjective. However, being sober and ensconced within the role of covert researcher, I was acutely aware of the underlying tension that was present and building throughout the evening. The linear layout of the bar ensured that a constant stream of traffic flowed past me, either on the way to the restrooms, the bar or to and from the dance floor. Accidental collisions seemed to be met with challenging stares, and the queue at the bar would be better termed a scrum. Sex and violence are both on the menu tonight, and every girl is appraised by the eyes of the men they pass. More often than not, a short skirt or pair of hot pants on any girl in her twenties are stimuli for bawdy, leering comments, everyday sexism brought into stark relief. As couples of the opposite sex interact, conversation appears to be eschewed in favour of screaming the lyrics of the 80s chart-topper currently being played over the sound system into each other's sweaty, red face. To my right, a group of young women enter the bar, one of whom wears an oversized badge proclaiming today to be her 21st birthday. Raucous, unpleasant laughter erupts from a group of lads in their late thirties. Simulating a sexual act with nothing but fresh air, a man in a short-sleeved shirt bedecked with the name 'Henley's' in large, capitalised towelling letters declares that he in fact would like to wish her 'a happy fucking birthday'.

Although some people have stayed in the bar for the duration of the time I have been there, most people tend to stay for one or two drinks before moving on to the next bar in the drinking 'circuit', so I am unsurprised to hear some of the more popular songs being played several times while I am conducting my research. The music is a relentless barrage of (as one would expect) hits from the 80s, punctuated by the DJ alerting patrons to the special offers on drinks, or informing everyone that it is in fact Beverly's 41st birthday today, or that we are unfortunately losing Sharon to married life in the near future. By 10 p.m. the bouncers are called into action for the first time, expelling a man in his late twenties, or early thirties.

Later that evening, about 1 a.m., as the kebab shops fill up and the bars empty onto the streets, I see some familiar faces from Reflex. The young lad who was dancing with the woman from the hen party is urinating on a graveyard wall, talking loudly but indistinctly to his friend who is standing a few metres away, eating fried chicken. I wonder how much they have contributed to the local economy tonight, not least supporting the local takeaway businesses and ensuring that the council need to employ a street cleaner to clean up piss and chicken bones before the shoppers, retail employees, museum goers and families reclaim the high street.

The vast number of chain pubs that line the nation's high streets represent a continuation of Ritzer's (1998) notion of rationalisation. Ritzer highlights the rationalised and standardised experience of consumers in relation to a visit to a McDonald's restaurant. His main point is that McDonald's restaurants represent a highly automated system that is both completely rational, in that it is highly efficient and also irrational in that it rails against innate qualities of humanity such as creativity and interaction. The process of McDonaldisation has pervaded high streets and shopping malls across the globe, as O'Brien and Harris (1991) have identified through the increased dominance of multiple retail companies within British urban environments. As the major players within the sector vie for market dominance, individual identities are whittled away as the developments become characterised by a homogeneous array of tenants to the extent that 'high streets are becoming almost indistinguishable from one another' (ibid.: 110). These ideas of 'experienced homogeneity' have been explored by a number of commentators (most notably David Sack (1992) and Alan Bryman (1995)) with respect to the Walt Disney parks. Within the parks of Disney World and Disneyland consumers are provided with narratives that make consumption part of the experience itself, while they go to great lengths in order to ensure that the actual act of consumption is not explicitly acknowledged. Sign value is prioritised over use-value, while much is made of cultural semblance, with historical juxtaposition a common theme (see Bryman, 1995).

The commentary that surrounds the development of retail parks and leisure parks outlined above may, to a greater or lesser extent, be applied to certain developments within the NTE. Consider the high street in the vast majority of towns and cities across the UK. Wetherspoon's, Pitcher & Piano, O'Neill's and Walkabout are just a few of the branded outlets that offer precious little in the way of distinctiveness, and like their retail and leisure equivalents offer unbridled homogeneity in terms of commodities on offer, staff manner and dress, even down to the carpets, fixtures and fittings. Hadfield (2006) invokes a *Which? Pub Guide* criticism levelled at chain operators for their:

> tendency to submerge the individual 'units' in conformity, make them all the same beers, same look (you can bulk buy that nice Irish green paint) and a series of managers who pass through. Such practices make sound business sense (economies of scale, etc.), but it doesn't make for a very interesting product. (Turvil, 2003: 23 cited in Hadfield, 2006: 49)

Ritzer's critique of these homogenised drinking spaces would most likely centre on their importance as a symptom of a larger shift within global capitalism from a social form that is locally conceived, controlled and rich in indigenous and distinctive content, to one that is centrally controlled, conceived and contains little or no distinctive content. However, discussion of the impact of this rationalisation so vilified by Ritzer (1998) underestimates the ability that participants within the

NTE have to interpret the social structures with which they are faced. Consumers appear to be aware of the creative limitations and faceless homogeneity of the chain bar but gain their own sense of enjoyment from, as well as invest their own personal meanings into the framework of that social structure through pursuing the ultimate 'good time' and liminal pleasures promised by continued participation within the NTE. This is exactly Žižek's (2008) point that the oppressive nature of capital isn't 'hidden' from us. To a greater or lesser extent, as exemplified by a number of respondents, we are aware that these pubs and bars are united through homogeneity. They are all the same. Far from preventing us from participating within the consumer economy, far from stopping us going to these pubs and bars, the knowledge that we have allows us to continue to act in the ways that directly propagate capitalism. So, despite knowing that the barrels behind the bar in the Irish pub are fake, purchased from the same outlet as the horse brasses and the pewter tankards that adorn the walls, we drinkers continue to frequent them and to value the experience that awaits us there.

The antithesis of the chain bar is also extant within the NTE, fighting for its market share. If we look more closely we can identify independent pubs, locally brewed beers, cocktail and champagne bars – the list is endless. For some, these venues and associated products are to be valued as superior to the mass-marketed homogeneity of the chain bar or theme pub. However, the pursuit of the profit motive belies these differences in a way perhaps best understood by Theodor Adorno.

Adorno considered the products of the culture industry as intrinsically driven by and linked to economic factors, arguing that the economic rationale that lay behind the production of consumer goods under the capitalist system was equally applied to cultural goods designed for mass consumption through the use of standardisation. He argued that within the culture industry, standard components are combined in order to result in a final product that is capable of attracting mass audiences. The ingredients are reinvigorated or put together in different combinations from time to time in order to prevent audiences losing interest, although each new 'product' is instantly recognisable thanks to the individual features of its component parts. The perception of 'new' is little more than an illusion veiling an essentially standard skeleton beneath:

> The works which are the basis of the fetishisation and become cultural goods experience constitutional changes as a result. They become vulgarised. Irrelevant consumption destroys them. Not

merely do the few things played again and again wear out, like the Sistine Madonna in the bedroom, but reification affects their internal structure. They are transformed into a conglomeration of irruptions which are impressed on the listeners by climax and repetition, while the organisation of the whole makes no impression whatsoever. (Adorno, 2001: 40)

With regard to music, Adorno identified structural differences between types of music that could be used to define similarities and differences and judge music according to how well it measured up to its 'ideal type'. On the surface, the two ideal types that Adorno suggested appear to frame the 'serious' as more valuable and superior to the 'popular'. He highlights a number of features specific to type, such as the statement that there exists a necessity for 'serious' music to maintain a self-conscious relationship between the piece of music as a whole and its constituent parts. Popular music on the other hand does not require this relationship between the whole and its parts, and thematic development is eschewed in favour of repetition. Differences in the structure of composition of these types of music, Adorno argued, are related to differences in listening responses, suggesting that within aesthetic and intellectual terms the serious type held a position of superiority. In order to appreciate the serious type of music, the listener must be willing to put in a certain degree of effort in order to gain a maximum level of engagement and enjoyment of the piece. Popular music, however, contains cues to prompt automatic responses and thus may be consumed with little thought or effort on behalf of the listener. This regression to familiar and standardised formulas, Adorno argues, increases social conformity and domination (see Adorno, 2001). Indeed, regression closes off:

the possibility of a different and oppositional music. Regressive too, is the role which contemporary mass music plays in the psychological household of its victims. They are not merely turned away from more important music, but they are confirmed in their neurotic stupidity, quite irrespective of how their musical capacities are related to the specific musical culture of earlier social phases. The assent to hit songs and debased cultural goods belongs to the same complex of symptoms as do those faces of which one no longer knows whether the film has alienated them from reality or reality has alienated them from the film, as they wrench open a great formless mouth with shining teeth in a voracious smile, while the tired eyes are wretched and lost above. Together with sport and film, mass music and the new listening help to make escape from the whole infantile milieu impossible. The sickness has a preservative function. (Adorno, 2001: 47)

What then, would Adorno make of the relentless production line of 'stars' created by *The X Factor* television format, commodified, marketed and merchandised at the time of their inception, with key changes and harmonies as certain and predictable as the jibes of the judges. Of course pop music is just one element of an entire culture industry that prides itself and even markets itself on its ability to cut straight to sugary gratification without the need for the consumer to expend effort. Reflexive impotence neither asks nor requires the individual to put any effort into decoding cultural forms (see Fisher, 2009), a phenomenon that is reflected within the NTEs of towns and cities across Britain.

So let us consider the NTE with its plethora of 'popular' chain pubs, bars and restaurants juxtaposed with what Adorno might have termed 'serious' or 'authentic' drinking establishments. Within the pages of the *Telegraph* newspaper can be found a review of a public house that appears to rail against all that is 'popular' about the generic high street:

> The Blue Bell ... is, thank heavens, not a historic inn. It is not a generic olde worlde, black-and-white timbered, grockle-trap swanking that it has been in Fossgate since smocks were in vogue. It does not have leaded windows, copper warming-pans or squat faux-tapestry stools surrounding dinky oak tables. Nor does it have a barman in a black waistcoat and open-necked, off-white shirt who does not know pale ale from pilsner, but can play the soft-drinks dispenser with the dexterity of a text-messaging teenager. Furthermore, it does not have a slovenly waitress in a black threadbare skirt offering a laminated menu that has a potted history of the pub and offers a variety of burgers and vegetarian bakes from the microwave. York boasts a pub for every day of the year. Unfortunately, some of them are historic. They tend to celebrate bygone days with Beefeater nostalgia and Brewers Fayre antiquity. (Edwards, 2003)

These 'Real Ale' pubs with their variety of beers, ales and ciders sourced in the main from independent, local breweries exude a degree of smugness over the 'popular' chain bars. The landlord and bar staff are keen to communicate the degree to which they take pride in the intricacies of the keeping, choice and presentation of the beers they sell, and tasting notes take on the level of pretension more usually reserved for bottles of wine in the Sunday supplement of broadsheet newspapers. Getting drunk is, for many of the patrons of these establishments, discounted as merely a 'side effect' of consuming 'decent beers and having decent conversation with friends'. Similarly, cocktail and champagne lounges employ jazz musicians to infuse the atmosphere with sophistication, and the wide variety of spirits, champagnes and wines serves to intimidate the uninitiated. Contrasting sharply with these establishments are the 'popular' chain bars, which require little in the way of 'effort' to drink in. For the vast majority of those spending their evenings in these venues, getting drunk is expected, compulsory, even necessary – an ambition that is realised through rapid consumption of sugary alcopops, generic lager and ubiquitous spirit drinks beneath an umbrella of chart pop and repetitive beats. The bar outlined at the beginning of this chapter at first appears to fall between the two categories – despite being a chain bar, it serves a comprehensive cocktail list served by a raft of well-trained and knowledgeable staff. However, the grand piano in the corner stands silent as the night gets under way, supplanted in favour of relentless bass and instantly recognisable chart-toppers.

The differences between 'popular' and 'serious' drinking establishments are not as polarised as we might first suspect, and it is possible to identify core elements of similarity despite the apparent distinctions between the drinking places. Within the context of 'Real Ale' pubs we might assume conspicuous consumption to be absent – drinkers vocally distance themselves from the 'chavs in The Slug and Lettuce'. However, extolling the virtues of one beer over another imbues the drinker with a crude form of distinction amongst their peers (Bourdieu, 1984), while the conspicuous consumption of champagne and a knowledge of wine are tools with which to demonstrate or perhaps weakly suggest a valued form of cultural capital (ibid.) as surely as the brand loyalties and brand identification that we associate with the high street establishments. The key point here is that there is a level of prefabrication and ubiquity that runs through all of these establishments, from the real ale pub to the cocktail lounge. In Baudrillardian terms, they are representing a layer of simulacrum that prevents the individual from achieving an authentic encounter with the real.

5
Youth, Adulthood and the NTE

Growing up, in the simplest of terms, appears to be about stability. Getting a job, settling down and having children are all seen as key markers that one has successfully made the transition from impetuous, reckless youth to dependable, self-aware adulthood. The term 'transition' here is key, lending its name to a swathe of literature, although over the past couple of decades, its use has become increasingly contested. Recent literature is moving away from the notion of a categorical concept of youth, acknowledging diversity and dependence on specific personal experiences of social division and inequality, rather than a staid, logical, step-by-step progression through to the 'goal' of adulthood. The term 'transition to adulthood' is, in its most basic form, misleading in that it suggests that young people make one transition to adulthood, which serves as a clearly defined destination at which they 'arrive'. If we accept that a number of markers do exist that indicate a change in condition or status, not only is their meaning likely to be inconsistent across different groups, they are not necessarily as significant as researchers may assume, and also are not necessarily permanent (Wyn and White, 1997; Furlong and Cartmel, 2007). Leaving home, marriage and employment are all transitory and reversible, and are unsatisfactory as static milestones from which to measure an individual's movement toward adulthood. Indeed, on closer inspection it appears that age is a less important factor in determining common and shared experiences and characteristics of youth than perhaps we would assume, suggesting that the line between youth and adulthood is increasingly blurred (see Cote, 2000; Barber, 2007; Calcutt, 1998). This chapter adds to the literature around youth and alcohol consumption, perhaps building upon Burnett's assertion that 'being (or even becoming) "youthful" is part of being thirty something' (2010: 85).

These changes are of course linked to a number of broader changes in the economy, as well as reflecting instability and uncertainty within the labour and housing markets. It would seem fair to assume that the expansion and promotion of further and higher education and the increasingly fluid nature of capital naturally lead to a largely positive experience of increased levels of upward mobility and equality of opportunity. In reality, the obverse appears to be true, with social inequalities increasing and the chasm between rich and poor continuously widening, while there is mounting evidence to suggest that large numbers of graduates are failing to achieve the employment opportunities that match their expectations or particular skill-set (Fisher, 2009). With the prospect of unfulfilling, insecure jobs within the service industries beckoning, large numbers may be expected to fall under the influence of the infantilising aspects of consumer capitalism (Lasch, 1979; Barber, 2007), becoming perhaps irreversibly enveloped in the sign-value system of consumerism (Baudrillard, 1984). The uncertainty and anxiety resultant from the widespread incorporation of neoliberal market principles appear to have had the unsettling effect of rendering long-term planning not only undesirable but, for many, impossible (see Southwood, 2010; Lloyd, 2012). The low-paid nature of many service industry jobs in call centres or coffee franchises, regardless of whether they are seen by many graduates as temporary or some kind of 'stepping stone' to something better and grander, has a number of knock-on effects. The lack of financial reward is compounded by high house prices and an exclusionary mortgage market which places access to the property ladder beyond the reach of all but a minority of individuals.[1]

Of course, this was not always the case. During the 1950s and 1960s, domestic and housing transitions tended to occur soon after the completion of the school-to-work transition. However, from the 1970s onwards it is possible to trace a widening of the transitional gaps between school to work and 'flying the nest' of the parental home (Jones, 1995). Recent years have witnessed a number of significant changes in housing and domestic transitions, with a variety of options seemingly commonplace (living alone, with friends, partners, students, work colleagues, sheltered accommodation) with no logical or set movements between. In the period since the 1980s, it is possible to discern a number of changes in the stage at which young people tend to leave the family home largely characterised by an increase in the number of young people that live with their parents. Changes in employment conditions have made it more difficult for individuals (especially those from working class families, but undoubtedly this is an issue that crosses class boundaries) to leave home at an early stage, while the opportunity offered by university and higher education for 'living away' is in many cases a temporary status change. Indeed, it has become common for many to return to the family home upon graduation (Chalabi, 2014). The ability of young people to leave home can be seen as directly affected by a number of factors, perhaps most importantly the supply of jobs and the availability of economic support. A similar temporal extension exists in terms of childbearing, which (especially within the middle classes) is characterised by (within Europe as a whole) an average gap of three to seven years between a female entering her first full-time job and having her first child (see Nicoletti and Tanturri, 2008).

While some may surmise that the changes outlined above are to be celebrated, resulting in young people being gifted a broader range of choices and freedoms, the real beneficiaries are those companies, corporations and businesses that are able to exploit this period of elongation. With vast numbers of young people unable to access the mainstream of what would formerly have been termed 'adult' society, it seems highly probable that they are becoming exposed to the processes of infantilisation that are propagated through global consumerism (see Barber, 2007; Lasch, 1979). Additionally, regular excursions within the leisure industries have the effect of distracting many young people from making the decisions that are necessary for completing the transition to adulthood. This suggests that the concept of 'youth' and 'adulthood' as distinct social categories is being leached of both meaning and relevance, with 'youth lifestyles' becoming commodities to be purchased.

Youth culture for sale

Put simply, youth culture is no longer the preserve of teenagers. Such has been the level of commodification within almost all aspects of society that major elements of youth culture have begun to merge and inform those more usually termed as adults, as part of a process of 'life stage dissolution' (Hayward, 2012). While age and youth are inextricably linked, 'youth' is not necessarily determined by age (Hockey, Robinson, and Hall, 2010). A billion-dollar industry has grown up around the successful construction and framing of 'youthfulness' as an aspect of lifestyle, and perhaps more pertinently, a saleable commodity. This 'youthfulness' is influenced by external factors such as work, education, interpersonal relationships and so on and is partially internalised as an aspect of identity. Meaning is bestowed upon the concept of youth by those who relate to its cultural norms, thus rendering it a fluid lifestyle rather than a static position on a linear life course. Perhaps most importantly, it is clear that 'youthfulness' has been harnessed by the culture industries (Adorno, 2001) as part of a complex strategy that is geared toward ensuring a commitment to consumerism as a marker of identity. This process is captured in the development of the global marketing industry, which in the time since the Second World War has achieved the status of a mass phenomenon (Barber, 2007). This global marketing machine harnesses the young as early as possible through injecting messages around consumer products into the cultural lives of children. By the age of ten, 78% of children list shopping as one of their favourite activities, and will be familiar with 300 to 400 brands (see Barber, 2007; Hall et al., 2008). Children are seen as 'evolving con-sumers' (Bakan, 2005) and represent future generations of compulsive consumption. While many of sociology's left-liberal commentators erroneously discuss the freedom bestowed on consumers by consumer capitalism (see Douglas and Isherwood, 1979), or concentrate on ele-ments of enjoyment and good times that are to be drawn from the consumer marketplace (Heath, 1999), it must be acknowledged that the freedom, such as it is, is critically limited to a degree of choice from an essentially meaningless menu (Adorno, 2001). Also present within the process of global consumerism are a number of somewhat insidi-ous psychosocial processes formulating the compulsive drive of the consumer – narcissism, fetishism and superego injunction that have the ability to push the individual into an arena of enjoyment, and also in some cases beyond into the painful realm of jouissance (see Žižek, 2002). Considered in these terms, it is hard indeed to imagine where 'freedom' might be found, and it is no wonder that conceptualising a transition to adulthood is an increasingly difficult task.

This evident link between consumer capitalism and youth belies the common-sense understanding that youth culture is edgy, rebellious, non-conformist and hedonistic. Even the emergence of rave culture in the 1980s did not challenge the dominant power structures in the way that media reports and some academics believed. While the drug use and illegal parties associated with rave culture can be understood as a challenge to the authority of the police and legal system, Reynolds (1998) points out that rave culture is in fact compatible with a conform-ist lifestyle and describes it as 'controlled hedonism', while the club scenes in resorts such as Ibiza that flourished in the wake of rave culture are little more than sites of 'unadulterated consumerism' (see Briggs, 2012, 2013). Any claim of resistance or subcultural values around dif-ferent music genres and scenes therefore becomes problematic, as we are forced to acknowledge the ability of consumer capitalism to ingest any semblance of rebellion in order to replenish the culture industries and keep capitalism moving forward, as Adorno and Horkheimer (1997) were keenly aware.

The concept of 'pseudo-individualisation' developed by Adorno and Horkheimer (1997) locates music as a vehicle for the standardisation of audience reaction, alongside the maximisation of economic dividends. Within contemporary music 'scenes', we can see an exemplary instance of the ability of the culture industry to mass produce the same product over and over again, with only nuanced changes which appear to be identifiable only by those who seek value and meaning within its cultures. Indeed, society is littered with examples of cultural forms and artefacts that suggest subculturalism or radicalism, with the potential and intent of destabilising capitalism, yet on closer inspection, these turn out to be little more than 'narratives of dissent' (see Hall and Winlow, 2007) that are embedded within capitalism itself. In this way it is naive to suggest that meaningful resistance exists at the point of consumption. Even for those individuals who claim to see the truth, who believe they are impervious to the deceit of capitalism and vociferously decry the homogeneity, the environmental damage and the inequality, who buy organic produce, who wear fair trade clothing, are still fulfilling their role as worker-consumers. However, far from threatening the dominant ideology, these dissenting consumer behaviours are incorporated by capitalism and become part of the energy it requires to perpetually move forward.

While appraising this process we should note that consumer capitalism needs no propaganda in order to thrive. Unlike, for example Stalinism, the interests of capitalism are unaffected, or perhaps more accurately even served, by allowing people to recognise that capitalism is inherently unjust, exploitative and unequal. Once this truth is out in the open we are able to return to the comforting hypnotic state provided by consumerism. We know in our hearts that capitalism is bad and consumerism ultimately banal, yet act in discordance with this (see Badiou, 2002; Fisher, 2009), conceding that capitalism is the 'least worst option' (Badiou, 2002).

In light of this interpretation the dance music around which the rave 'movement' was built is indicted as little more than a cog within the culture industry. Its surface rebelliousness and its supposed distance from the mainstream are precisely what the market needs to keep moving forwards. In this way, all underground scenes help consumer capitalism by suggesting diversity, excitement and resistance to homogeneity. If these scenes did not exist, if our music possessed only an *X Factor* sameness, and if the night-time economy (NTE) was made up only of corporatised branded outlets, then consumers would quite quickly be able to identify the uniformity of products and experiences and so withdraw their custom. Of course, the history of the rave scene suggests quite clearly how cultural forms generated by 'the street' can be appropriated by the market. As one musical trend becomes so popular that it begins to be picked up by the mainstream, a new musical street-generated trend is precisely what the market needs to prevent terminal exhaustion. We can see a similar process in new products that are supposed to possess an anti-consumerist or ecological aspect. We can now buy mass-produced corporate products in order to display our anti-corporate political sensibilities. We can buy locally sourced meat from our polluting, tax-dodging, local-culture-destroying supermarkets if we are worried about the ecological implications of transporting food from the southern hemisphere. Let there be no mistake: there can be no resistance at the point of consumption.

It is not difficult to draw parallels with any of the other youth-oriented trends that are forced to the fore of the national consciousness, not least the excesses connected to the hedonistic playgrounds of the NTE. This is representative of the broader ways in which capitalism ensures that even disobedience is an acceptable way to conform. What today passes for cultural radicalism can be viewed as little more than a vociferous montage of off-the-peg alternative lifestyle signifiers (see Hall and Winlow, 2008) which, far from having the effect of railing against the system and raising hell simply serves to reinforce the image of liberal democratic state capitalism as welcoming dissenting voices and alternative points of view. Fisher uses the example of 2005's Live 8 event to illuminate exactly what this means, indicating that protests tend to share an almost 'carnivalesque background noise to capitalist realism' (2009: 14), organised by the global elite who have much to gain from the continuation of capitalism. As protests against capitalism fail to propose a viable alternative or shape into active, politicised resistance, it is guaranteed that small and mainly insignificant aspects of culture and political life may change, although without the core structure of liberal democracy and free market capitalism ever being threatened.

Binge drinking within commercialised and standardised drinking spaces often harbours a surreal air of simulacra, and a tentative but persistent sense of disjuncture, that something isn't quite right. The stylised venues that serve as arenas for these drinking behaviours are often quite separate from the world around them, and are conspicuously absent of any indicators of locality or history. The fake ought to be easy to spot and decried as such. But such is the embedded nature of consumer capitalism, the glaringly obvious is accepted 'as is', and the endless replication present within the NTE seems of little consequence to the main customer base. Baudrillard's (1983) assertion that reality has been superseded by simulation seems nowhere more starkly exemplified than upon the night-time high street. The excess and hedonism synonymous with a night on the town, and touted as symbolic of youthful exuberance and vitality is so legitimised and neutered by its role within the 'culture industry' that it ceases to be the arena of subversive youth behaviour, instead inviting 'adult' participation.

Indeed, in many respects it is impossible to find any examples of autonomous private leisure, as seemingly all forms are engulfed by commercialised leisure culture informed by the cold reality of the profit motive. The past few decades have witnessed the corralling of 'free time', forcing the gratification of desire through and only by means of consumerism (see Bauman, 2001), a truth that appears at odds with the creative arena of hedonistic abandon that is promised by the night-time leisure industry through myriad marketing devices. The perpetuation of this myth of ultimate gratification through consumption figures predominantly in the business strategies of the culture industries, while eccentricity and diversity have been supplanted in favour of predictability and formulae in order to provide for the mass audience and placate the principle of capital accumulation (Debord, 1983). As Adorno and Horkheimer state:

> The assembly-line character of the culture industry, the synthetic, planned method of turning out its products (factory-like not only in the studio but, more or less, in the compilation of cheap biographies, pseudodocumentary novels, and hit songs) is very suited to advertising: the important individual points, by becoming detachable, interchangeable, and even technically alienated from any connected meaning, lend themselves to ends external to the work. The effect, the trick, the isolated repeatable device, have always been used to exhibit goods for advertising purposes, and today every monster close-up of a star is an advertisement for her name, and every hit song a plug for its tune. Advertising and the culture industry merge technically as well as economically. In both cases the same thing can be seen in innumerable places, and the mechanical repetition of the same cultural product has come to be the same as that of the propaganda slogan. In both cases the insistent demand for effectiveness

makes technology into psycho-technology, into a procedure for manipulating men. In both cases the standards are striking yet familiar, the easy yet catchy, the skilful yet simple; the object is to overpower the customer. (1997: 163)

Horkheimer and Adorno articulate the interwoven nature of the relationship between mass culture, advertising and consumption within the consumer society. Advertising serves to induce the individual to identify with a number of 'imagos' within society, while:

> The defiant reserve or elegant appearance of the individual on show is mass-produced like Yale locks, whose only difference can be measured in fractions of millimetres. (Adorno, 1981: 154)

It now seems impossible to think of leisure as disconnected from spending money. If our desired form of leisure is watching television, then in order to see the latest season of *Breaking Bad* or *Boardwalk Empire*, we must subscribe to a specific satellite TV channel. Films and sports events are available on a pay-per-view basis. We need to have a large flat-screen television to gain the most out of our viewing experience, and a wireless surround-sound system to gain credence as a connoisseur. If we want to go walking in the Yorkshire Dales or the Lake District, we must position ourselves as serious ramblers in the eyes of the Big Other through our Brasher walking boots, Berghaus jackets and titanium walking poles. We must spend money on car parking, memberships to the National Trust and GPS satellite navigation equipment as the leisure industry thinks up innumerable inventive ways to part us from our cash. We can now identify an epoch in which young and maturing consumers are exploited within the world of work while concurrently being manipulated in spheres of leisure through a package marketed in line with neoliberal political orthodoxy as liberating, opportunistic and gratifying. Commercialised leisure represents a creative utopia in which hedonistic pleasure, lifestyles and self-discovery can be effortlessly blended with the help of consumer items that lend themselves to being used as tools to aid in this voyage of self-discovery and the construction of status and identity. The inexorable rise of consumerism ensured the rapid growth in importance of celebrity and ostentatious wealth, as indicative of social hierarchy and aspiration as the forces of marketing combined to parade a succession of imagos, or desirable ideals in front of the consumer, encouraging individuals to purchase and discard akin to the wealthy elite and celebrities that dominate consumer culture.

This cultural mire creates an enduring habitus into which successive generations appear set to be inducted.

While youth lifestyles may be informed and captured by a series of imagos through consumption of music, fashion, drugs, alcohol and violence, it is far from guaranteed that the maturing individual will eschew consumerism and the compulsion to consume in order to attempt to satiate desires created by the global culture industry (Lash and Lury, 2007). Television programming serves to maintain aspirations and desires by constantly reminding viewers that they need to be consuming in order to occupy a valuable position in society. Programmes such as *Cash in the Attic* encourage viewers to discard old, perhaps treasured objects and auction them, enabling them to purchase new consumer goods, often a new TV or a holiday abroad. The message is clear: to constantly be active in the consumer markets – your old stuff is worthless – trade up, trade up. Similarly, a host of programmes inform us that our homes need redecorating, our gardens are boring or we are admonished by Jeremy Clarkson for having a car that is deemed 'uncool'. In this way, the intrinsic worth attributed to the hedonistic playgrounds offered by the night-time leisure industry is transferred onto other leisure pursuits should we tire of hedonistic excess within bars and clubs.

While it may seem that a simple meander through the Freeview channels on our televisions offers enough evidence for the pervasive, seductive and all-encompassing nature of consumer capitalism, the news that British household debt is currently estimated at £1.4 trillion (Credit Action, 2013) leaves us in little doubt as to the pressures applied to individuals to maintain a constant display of cultural knowledge, which more often than not is defined and achieved through the sign-value and exchange value bestowed by the market.

Understanding adulthood

While significant amounts of psychological research and theory have centred upon adult development (see, for example, Erikson, 1978, 1980) sociology seems to have remained mysteriously quiet on the subject. Instead, adulthood is often treated as the yardstick against which the 'other' is measured in terms of 'childhood', 'adolescence' or 'old age'. In other words, adulthood as a construct is often somewhat taken for granted, and remains implicit in much sociological analysis, rather than being the focus.

A number of social markers of adulthood exist, which have traditionally stood as indicators of attainment or non-attainment of adult status, such as stable full-time work, stable relationships, independent living and parenthood. These social markers provide reference points as to what constitutes a 'finished' human being as opposed to an 'unfinished' adolescent 'human becoming' (Blatterer, 2007).

The concept of 'standard adulthood' (Lee, 2001) is borne out of the Fordist economic principles prevalent only a few decades ago, which gradually became synonymous with a way of life that centred on goals of long-term stability and economic growth (Harvey, 1989). Businesses valued employee loyalty, and would reward it with promotion. The consequence of this was simple but important nonetheless – defined career paths, with solid and predetermined milestones on the way, while at the end of it lay a guaranteed government pension providing a secure retirement. The ageing employee too, was valued – seen as experienced rather than expendable – with job security increasing with age and the accumulation of tacit knowledge. These social conditions came hand in hand with a value system that was generally unchallenged until the 1960s (Goldthorpe et al., 1968; Edwards, 2000). Heterosexual, nuclear families were the normative ideal, as were early marriage and family formation (Fox, 1967; Edholm, 1982). Despite the dawning of a new age of liberalism with its emphasis on relativism and diversity, this standard adulthood as a desirable norm remains. Perhaps most distinctly, there is a clear trend for individuals to take longer to reach adulthood than did previous generations (see Cote, 2000). However, this simple certainty is complicated by evidence suggesting that there is a connected ethic for children to grow up quickly and adopt the trappings of a consumerised adulthood as quickly as possible (see Barber, 2007). One thing for sure is that we are in a state of flux. The traditional life course has undoubtedly been challenged by the processes associated with global consumer capitalism, and the old certainties have all but disappeared. What we are left with is a paradoxical situation whereby the transition to adulthood can be said to have at once been lengthened and shortened, characterised by consumer 'kidults' and a period of 'arrested adulthood' (see Calcutt, 1998; Cote, 2000; Barber, 2007). As maturing individuals are encouraged and rewarded for taking on semblances of youth and children are forced to mature, the subject is denied any real chance to inhabit a fixed, stable, socially sanctioned and endorsed identity. Indeed, it becomes increasingly difficult to determine processes of identification from the cultural symbolism of consumer capitalism. Much of the literature highlights a move toward a more problematical transitional period from youth to adulthood than in the past, and it is probably right to do so. However, it is worth thinking about the possibility that the meaning of adulthood itself has changed.

What then, is to be made of the 34-year-old male, living in a shared house, working in a temporary or insecure low-wage job, playing football at the weekends and going out drinking with his friends who are largely in similar situations, rejecting commitment both in work and in love? It is perhaps too simplistic to suggest that these individuals are rejecting or delaying adulthood. However, as Winlow and Hall (2006) have noted, many young people suggest that dealing with the here and now, with the problems and anxieties of unstable labour markets and increasing levels of competitive acquisitive cultural pressure is sufficiently difficult to forestall any serious biographical planning.

Infantilisation

The notion of a prolonged non-adult state has been developed by a number of sociologists. Cote (2000), for example, talks of 'arrested adulthood' and a 'perpetual adolescence' distinguished by a tendency to avoid making commitments due to the demise of adult roles. Tanner and Arnett (2009) suggest a process of 'Emerging Adulthood' that locates centrally hedonistic and narcissistic behaviour as characteristic of the liminal space between youth and adulthood. Calcutt (1998) refers to 'arrested development' and 'erosion of adulthood', suggesting that a new political order has emerged whereby the 'victim' is lauded, and adults are infantilised. Hollands (1995) suggests that young consumers are experiencing blockages in their transition to adulthood, structural obstacles that result in prolonged periods of 'post-adolescence'.

Here, to be 'middle aged' or 'old' is not so much defined by years and months, but by 'staying in' and succumbing to the more traditional concepts of 'adulthood'; to have the vim, vigour and perceived agency of youth curtailed by the process of becoming adult. As a result, musical taste and appreciation alongside clothing and drink choices provide an opportunity for the individual to prove that they are still young, desirable, 'fun' and culturally significant. Of course, the grammar of this discourse is provided through the symbolically loaded items available in the consumer marketplace.

In order to understand and contextualise these claims, it is useful to revisit the Freudian model of infantile narcissism, a concept reinvigorated in recent years by Slavoj Žižek. Here, this phrase is used in the psychoanalytic, rather than the pejorative sense, and the analysis presented in no way implies a simple critique of childish selfishness among the research group. Rather, the body of work associated with infantile narcissism is used to create a more nuanced analysis of subjective psychological responses to the manifold pressures that bear down upon the post-political subject.

Processes of identity creation and maintenance appear to take place against the backdrop of an 'infantilist ethos' (see Barber, 2007) which serves to generate attitudes, desires, habits and preferences that seem to not only legitimise but also encourage childishness among adult consumers. Infantilisation as a social process induces childishness in adults, as well as maintaining those elements of childishness within children who are 'growing up'. The maturing individual is diverted from taking on traditional adult concerns, instead entering a form of biographical stasis, the pause button pressed during a period in which they are most susceptible to consumer symbolism and marketing messages.

This concept is worth dwelling on a little longer. If we are to refute those claims which suggest that committed participation within the NTE is a simple reflection of rational choice and identity creation within a postmodern milieu, then it becomes necessary to look to the individual unconscious, and delve into theoretical psychoanalysis.

Freud walks into a bar ...

Freud's most well-known work focuses on the repression of instinct as the id, ego and superego compete for control of the individual. Harbouring instinctual drives and impulses, being guided by the pleasure principle with no concern for social norms, responsibilities or expectations, the id is kept in check by the ego, which must convince the id to be more reasonable in its demands, defer gratification, and fit in with society. The efforts of the ego are bolstered by the existence of the superego, which introduces the feelings of shame and guilt upon the indulgence of the id. The result of this is that primitive desires are repressed, and the mind learns to control them.

Freud speaks of guilt and shame when giving in to base desires, mechanisms which famously prevent us from sleeping with our mothers and killing our fathers, but perhaps more pertinently may also be integral to preventing us getting into debt, turning up late and hung over for work and relentlessly pursuing the next sexual encounter. This, however, is a situation that Žižek (1991) suggests has reversed to the extent that individuals are made to feel guilty or ashamed of the fact that they are *not* giving in to their desires. Consequently work is viewed as a necessary inconvenience that serves to delay the indulgence of the id, and anything that delays hedonistic gratification is to be avoided at all costs.

The role of the superego in the contemporary quest for enjoyment within consumer society requires unpacking further. Within Freudian thought, the superego is the agency of morality as opposed to enjoyment, restricting the amoral id. However, within *The Ego and the Id* an association is made between the superego and obscene enjoyment, as 'the superego is always close to the id and can act as its representative vis-à-vis the ego. It reaches deep down into the id and for that reason is farther from consciousness than the ego is' (Freud, 1960: 45).

As McGowan (2004: 29) notes;

> The superego receives its energy from the id, the seat of the subject's enjoyment, and this provides the superego with its ability to be excessively cruel ... The obscene dimension of the superego manifests itself in the very form that the superego takes – that is, as a relentless injunction that never leaves the subject alone.

Freud (1930) also develops the concept of narcissism, suggesting that this forms the bedrock of the human psyche, present from the point of birth. Narcissism is ascribed to the fact that we are born too soon, in a state of 'prematuration' (Lacan, 2001). This primary narcissism is reined in during the process of socialisation as the individual becomes acquainted with the social norms and expectations of the dominant culture. If this attenuation does not take place, however, narcissism enters a secondary stage, whereby personal gratification takes priority over social goals and conformity. Indeed, if this secondary narcissism is permitted to take on the position as a primary element within the individual's life course, then narcissism becomes pathogenic. This secondary narcissism should not be viewed simply as innate selfishness winning through; rather, it should be seen as a reflection of the inadequacies of personal socialisation, directly and irrevocably connected to the broader failings of 'culture' as shall be discussed later.

This process of cultural infantilisation ensures that certain features of childhood impact on adult culture, becoming transformed and reintegrated into mature behaviour in such a way that retains childish aspects within a mature adult setting. Hence, childlike qualities and motifs are often seen as desirable by adults, who may be witnessed engrossed in a Harry Potter book on the tube on the way to work, or sit at home in their 'onesie' playing video games and chomping Haribo sweets (Kids and grown-ups love it so!). Furthermore, the adult attachment to gadgets such as the latest iPhone, or plasma screen TV can be viewed as representative of a broader slide into commercialised abstraction with the aim of soothing the anxieties and dissatisfactions that are bound up with real adulthood, both in the formal economy and culture more generally. Similarly, it is possible to view alcopops and drinks such as Corky's Vodka Shots, which revolve around recognisable flavours such as Skittles, Cola Cube or Cream Egg, as appealing to the cult of the child as much as they are accused of being marketed toward underage drinkers. Indeed, drinking cultures appear to be inseparable from a variety of childish motifs, from drinking games to the legitimisation of childish behaviour and separation from the emotional and mental demands of more formal culture.

Consumer society and the unconscious

The frequent misrepresentation of the consumer and the consumerist dynamic as one of freedom, invention and reinvention is simplistic, implying a particular ideological background that appears unwilling to relinquish its attachment to a raw Cartesian subjectivity. From this analytical viewpoint the unconscious roots of desire are largely ignored, which results in a failure to account for intricacies that explain just how individuals become ensconced within the complex folds of consumerist society. Indeed the process of assimilation may be traced back into childhood, and the formation within the unconscious of a very specific mode of identification with external objects and signs, which in turn contributes to a predication for an interminable desire of consumer goods and symbolism. Key to the perpetuation of the processes of capitalism, however, is the continuation of this desire and pursuit of the new throughout the life course.

Earlier versions of capitalism were characterised by functional Symbolic Orders with a system of moral regulation and reality-testing mechanisms, which allowed the maturation process to take place unfettered in the vast majority of individuals. As the maturation process evolved, the unconscious, with its associated infantile narcissistic demands would tend to be displaced onto other, more mature concerns such as art, politics, science and love (Hall et al., 2008). In Lacanian terms, the Symbolic Order is reliant on the individual's acceptance of the Name-of-the-Father, or the laws and restrictions that control both desire and the rules of communication – 'It is in the name of the father that we must recognize the support of the symbolic function which, from the dawn of history, has identified his person with the figure of the law' (Lacan, 2001: 50).

The rapid introduction of consumer capitalism, however, has a distinct impact on 'growing up', effectively derailing what was previously a relatively stable and reliable progression to a traditional form of adulthood. In this way, the maturation process is steered away from objects and signs that appeal to the mature individual or those that are not overtly beating the drum of consumer capitalism. At the same time, we can identify a stark reduction in the emphasis on prohibition within the social order, an identifiable reorientation of the cultural superego (Žižek, 2000). The processes that Baudrillard (1984) identifies as contributing to the commodification of everyday life essentially undermine authority figures and emphasise the importance of enjoyment, a fact drilled home relentlessly via the medium of mass and social media preaching messages unimaginably far removed from the ideology of the 'work ethic' synonymous with an earlier age.

While the selfishness and greed associated with narcissistic personality types have long existed (see Lasch, 1979), we can point toward a more recent emergence of a culture that facilitates and celebrates these traits, indicating that the social conditions involved with late capitalism are responsible for awakening latent narcissism within individuals. We need look no further than the supremely popular television show *The Apprentice*, for a stark exemplar of how hyper-individualism, symbolic violence and greed are praised, rewarded and encouraged.

The impact of these changes on the individual, and the effect of the derailing of the maturation process can be further explained through a deeper exploration of the life-worlds of these committed consumers within the NTE. It is to two of these individuals that our attention will turn in the following chapter.

6
Drinking Biographies

This chapter explores the practical realities and lived experiences of two individuals whose continued involvement in commodified night-time leisure has had a profound impact upon their sense of self. These individuals were of particular importance to this study, as without their role as 'gatekeepers' to the continued pursuit of hedonism, much of the research and insight contained within these pages would simply not have been achievable. They fulfilled the role of gatekeeper not only in the methodological sense (see Whyte, 1959), but also in a more direct, straightforward sense in that they act as cultural gatekeepers within their own extended friendship networks, sending out texts, getting people motivated and ready to go out, determining which bars to go to, whose round it is and so on.

Rob, whom we shall hear more about below, was an old school friend of mine, who, through a chance meeting in a pub was able to 'plug me into' a social network that was heavily ensconced within the arena of commodified pleasure that constitutes the night-time economy (NTE). During the course of my research I bore witness to a number of key events within the life course of Rob and his cohort of thirty-something, white, socially included men. Andrea, who will be discussed later in the chapter is of particular importance, as she was able to introduce me to a range of her female friends, whom I was able to observe on a night out without fear of accusations of stalking or appearing to be simply 'weird'. Andrea was keen for me to see the NTE from the viewpoint of her social group, and consequently was invaluable in facilitating access to otherwise closed social settings. There are right ways and wrong ways to stare at a group of women in a bar, and I am grateful for the tolerance and humour they showed me in the sometimes clumsy or naive methods I used to extract information relating to age, occupation and other personal aspects of their lives for the purposes of social research. While gender differences have been somewhat marginalised throughout the course of this piece of work, I feel that the inclusion of a mixed-gender range of participants has greatly enriched the core arguments presented here, and with Andrea's help I was able to significantly broaden my sample.

Both Rob and Andrea are white and in their mid thirties. They are both socially included individuals of a similar socioeconomic background. Rob has come to realise that the freedoms offered by the consumer economy are hugely offset by the necessity to work in paid employment in order to obtain the means necessary to access the circuits of consumption that will allow him to satisfy his own need for personal possessions. Further pressures and anxieties are revealed around paying rent, saving for a deposit on a house and fulfilling the traditional and properly adult roles of husband and father. At the same time he displays a tangible reluctance to end his continued participation within the NTE. Andrea meanwhile, has bought wholeheartedly into the image of the NTE that many of its key stakeholders are keen to advance. Throughout the course of the research she was keen to impress upon me that the NTE could provide a space to enact friendship, community and camaraderie, and she sees involvement in it as the only viable alternative to the more sedate cultures of traditional adulthood. She clearly sees herself as young, single and unfettered by the restrictions and obligations that come with the traditional markers of adulthood.

Rob

I am sitting with Rob in a city centre pub purporting to be the oldest in the city, although it is not alone in this claim. A narrow alleyway between two buildings opens up into a small courtyard where a number of smokers congregate, then it's through the main door of the pub into an expansive space divided into four separate areas. The bar runs the length of the largest of the rooms, while two of the others are what are usually termed the snug and the smoking room – the latter a moniker that must grate with the assortment of people currently huddling under meagre cover outside, glowing tips of cigarettes visible through the steamed-up windows as the rain begins to fall. Rob and I are in the snug, a room with a fireplace and perimeter bench seats with six round tables and a number of low bar stools clustered here and there. I am drinking a pint of bitter, while Rob is slowly sipping a pint of Guinness, extolling its restorative virtues following a heavy night on the town. It is impossible not to consider the historical features of the pub as we sit and talk – the pub's owners have certainly done little to subdue the heritage of the building, with 'historical' artefacts lodged in every available nook, while a rich tale of the pub's history adorns the back of the laminated menu that lies on our table. The incongruity of the plastic-covered potted history of the establishment is indicative of a transparent attempt to cash in on the historical niche that is occupied by this pub, a mechanism employed by wily landlords and breweries across the land who are eager to sell a dose of experiential history along with their trendy bottled ciders and fizzy continental-style lagers (see Chatterton and Hollands, 2003; Hadfield, 2006, for a more in-depth discussion of this phenomenon). History too is being discussed in our little corner of the pub as Rob reminisces on a number of his earliest drinking experiences. Rob's earliest flirtations with alcohol mirror the experiences recounted by a number of other authors whose research takes place within the arena of juvenile drinking cultures. 'River parties' were as their name suggests parties that took place on the banks of the river, on the outskirts of the city, away from all but the occasional dog walker, and out of sight of parental supervision or other sources of authoritarian gaze. Alcohol would be liberated from the household liquor cupboard – some would bring whole bottles, while others purloined a little from a variety of spirits bottles, creating an unpleasant cocktail that would be unlikely to grace the faux-aged pages of the menus Rob now peruses in the city's up-market cocktail lounges. This baptism of fire seems to have set the tone for Rob's drinking career as these parties, and the occasional teenage shindig at the house of parents trusting enough or perhaps foolhardy enough to leave their home in the hands of their offspring, provided a springboard into the world of excessive alcohol consumption, alcohol-related sickness and vomiting, sexual adventure, violence, and bravado. Furthermore, these episodes served as a portal into thymotic storytelling and creation of cliques of 'cool' inside the school gates. Reputations could be made or ruined, boys qualified as studs, becoming men, while girls were branded as 'slags' or 'slappers'. Rob ruminates on one of his former classmates, wondering if she has escaped a rumour that she administered oral sex to a horse.

Entering the more legitimate world of drinking in pubs was the next step for Rob. He reels off the names of a number of city centre pubs renowned for their lax approach to age verification. Within these establishments barmen would ask for confirmation of date of birth by means of a verbal confirmation of age – a tactic that would not catch out those who had worked out the logistics of birth dates and quickly and confidently gave the 'correct' answer, earning the right to consume beer on the premises. While some of Rob's peers – mainly girls – were able to pass for much older, either through fake ID or simply looking more mature, Rob was cursed (or perhaps blessed, given contemporary society's preoccupation with youth) with looking several years younger than he was. Consequently his night-time leisure opportunities in the realm of the newly burgeoning NTE were limited to frequenting those bars where possession of official identification was not enforced.

Looking back on the formative days of his drinking career, Rob appears on occasion almost whimsical. He recalls his days at university and in the few years that followed while he was working in low-paid, low-stress jobs as a parade of halcyon days where his concerns were limited to accessing enough money to go out, frequenting cheap student nights and happy hours in the town centre. During these years Rob enjoyed the many and varied distractions that are available to a young man unfettered by the practical impediments of work and family, standing as he was at the edge of a seemingly infinite vista of mesmerising possibilities:

> I just pissed away my time at university really, and was pretty lucky to get a Desmond[1] ... but at the time, going out, seeing bands and getting pissed all the time were more important than revising for exams, writing essays and all that sort of thing.

After graduating from university and returning to his home town, Rob was reluctant to move back into the family home, so necessity dictated that he found a job. Unwilling to compromise on the lifestyle of hedonistic excess that he had become accustomed to during his time as a student, the employment he was looking for had to include flexibility, anonymity, a low level of difficulty and little in the way of responsibility. The retail sector appeared to tick most boxes for Rob, so he secured himself a job on the shop floor at the local branch of a chain of bookstores. The work was not demanding, and the team he worked with was young, and appeared to consist largely of people in a similar position to himself, content with low-paid, transient labour in return for earning enough money to pay rent and participate within the lower echelons of the consumer economy:

> We used to get pissed or stoned pretty much every day of the week back then ... we used to either go to the Sam Smith's pubs [a brewery,

known for its cheap, own-brand alcohol] and drink D-Pils, which was about 6% and would get you fucked, or during the week, we would drink in the [student-oriented pub] a lot, which used to be about a pound a pint on weekday nights. A lot of the time we would go on to a club which would have a student night on, and dance to northern soul or Motown. Everyone [in his shared house] had shit jobs back then, and we would all be going in still pissed, not having time to shower or anything. One time [one of our mates] passed out on the sofa, so we drew on him with a marker pen, and he didn't realise 'til he got to work and his boss told him to go and look at himself in the mirror. None of it mattered, because if you got sacked from your job, you could get another one pretty much the same day ... no one was bothered.

Rob soon began to tire of going to the 'same bars, week in week out' and decided to follow a couple of other friends who had made the journey down south to London. He was able to secure a transfer to a branch of the bookshop on the King's Road, and lived in a flat with a school friend who had just qualified as a teacher. Rob was drawn to the social and cultural possibilities of the city, but due to his low-wage job, found himself marginalised, and unable to access many of the circuits of consumer culture that were orbiting just outside of his grasp. His wages from the bookshop were enough to cover his rent and share of the bills, but left him with little extra to go to bars and clubs, watch bands, buy music, clothes and own a mobile phone. Rather than succumb to the spiritual inconsequentiality that was denoted by being unable to maintain a presence within the consumer economy he took out a bank loan to finance his lifestyle, enabling him to join the ranks of ostentatious consumers, if only temporarily and with financial consequences that would remain with him into his thirties.

   Once all available avenues of consumer credit had been exhausted, Rob decided to return north, where he felt able to adopt a more responsible attitude toward his spending. He took up his old job in the bookstore, and resumed the lifestyle that he had previously grown tired of just under two years earlier. He cultivated a large social network consisting of people he met at work, and a number of old school friends who found themselves similarly tethered to their home town.

When I came back to Vikton, everything was fine, a lot of my old friends were here, and there were a really good bunch of people working at the bookshop. After a while though, things began to change ... Craig left to go and live in Manchester, Chris trained as a policeman and Anthony and a couple of others left the bookshop to get proper jobs at the council or [other office work]. As everyone else started earning more money I realised I was getting left behind with no chance of getting a house, going on holiday or anything else like that ... everything I earned was going on rent, credit card bills and paying back my loans.

Rob found it difficult to get past the interview stage for a number of office-based jobs. The years of instrumental living, choosing the direction that offered him maximum flexibility in terms of being able to participate within the NTE had left him with a sparse résumé. Eventually however, he succeeded in getting some agency work at a low-level administration job which later turned into a permanent contract. Armed with relevant experience on his CV, he was able to successfully get a job at a credit card payment processing company as a customer relationship manager. This job was a significant leap in terms of responsibility, workload and intensity, requiring Rob to reappraise a number of aspects of his lifestyle as he neared his 30th birthday:

I did stop going out drinking as often when I got the [agency] job, but the thing was that it was flexi-time, so I didn't have to be in until 10 a.m., which made it quite likely that if people were going out to watch the football or whatever, I could really get stuck in and not worry about being at work at 8 a.m. or anything ... With [the new] job though, they are really strict, and expect you to be in early and leave late, and you have to be noticed to be doing that if you are going to stand any chance of getting a promotion. Because of that I have to go in sometimes on a weekend if we have a big project on ... so basically I don't do anything during the week any more, which while it's good in terms of saving money and not turning into a fat bastard, is really shit if there is something good on and I want to get pissed but can't. Before, I could just take a sick day pretty easily as well, which didn't really matter because it was agency work, but I just can't take a sick day here. It's really frowned upon and the work just mounts up if I am away.

Rob's change in employment status was not the only factor curtailing his halcyon days consisting of the endless pursuit of hedonistic pleasure, for he also became involved in a 'serious relationship'. His only other romantic involvement to last more than a few months since leaving university was during his second stint at the bookshop during his mid twenties, during which time he dated a student who worked in the shop during her holidays. Although he would visit her during term time, and she would be back at weekends, it was a largely instrumental relationship in that they both lived separate lives in the time they were apart, and few plans were made for the long term. His current relationship, however, bears more of the hallmarks of commitment, with shared holidays, friendship groups and culminating in moving into his girlfriend's house. This arrangement has resulted in Rob being kept 'on the leash', as he laments the fact that the 'lads' night out' is more or less a thing of the past, to be revisited only on the rare occasion:

> She was away for a week with her family a few months ago ... I had a brilliant time, different takeaway every night, watched all the football, and had a mad night out round the town Friday and Saturday.

The fact that opportunities to participate within the NTE are severely limited by constraints of both work and home life is clearly an irksome inconvenience for Rob, although he does not appear to be seduced by the NTE to the extent that his relationship with paid employment is reduced to one of pure instrumentalism. He expresses a desire to progress at work, to follow the traditional path of pension contributions, promotions and paydays, despite the fact that they are not compatible with the pursuit of pleasure within the NTE. He is keen to buy a house with his girlfriend and is attentive to the housing market and conversant on the subject of mortgages and repayments, surveys and Home Information Packs (HIPs). He is even beginning to bow to pressure from his girlfriend to start a family, a situation that he admits to being fiercely resistant to only a few months ago.

We might expect the competing factors that are integral to a 'traditional' adulthood to act as a lever, prising embedded individuals out of the consumer playground represented by the NTE, that once 'real world' pressures of mortgage repayments, family commitments and career progression loom large, the pull of the NTE and the associated arenas of conspicuous consumption would dissipate. Instead, what appears to be happening for a significant proportion of adults and certainly a feature of the participants within this study is that the value of participation within the NTE appears to be increased. Individuals such as Rob begin to accept that they are no longer able to maintain such an active presence and must choose which nights they decide to go out to a greater degree than they have found necessary previously in their life course, but because of this fact, not in spite of it, the whole experience is endowed with more significance and importance. As Rob testifies:

> I seem to get a lot more pissed these days than I used to. It's just like, the fact that we don't get to go out as often makes it much more of a big deal ... you are much more up for it. I don't really drink through the week, and only go out one night of the weekend ... [my girlfriend] usually wants to go out for a meal or stay in and watch a film or something on the other night ... so when I'm off the leash I just really go for it and don't know when to stop ... I know that past a certain point I'm going to be in shit with her anyway [for getting drunk], so I think I might as well carry on.

The conflict between the two life-worlds of 'traditional' adulthood and participating within the NTE is referred to frequently by Rob, although it appears that rather than being a genuine sticking point, creating a sense of guilt at the prospect of going out and spending money that should be contributed to the desires associated with more traditional concepts of adulthood – the deposit for a house, a new sofa, weekends away, this instead serves simply to fuel his desire and motivation to purchase experiential pleasure within the arena of bounded hedonism. As traditional adulthood closes in on him from all sides, the NTE provides him with supposed means of experiencing the 'Real' (Žižek, 2002), purchasing a 'time out of time' (Presdee, 2000) in which the rigidity and expectation laid upon him by his 'adult' identity can be temporarily discarded.

Looking to the future, Rob appears focused on a number of areas. He has desires to get on the property ladder, an objective only made remotely attainable due to an inheritance left to him, which has enabled him to greatly reduce the weight of debt that he had accrued in terms of personal loans, student loans and credit cards. He wants a house with three bedrooms; a garden and it must be within walking distance of the centre of town as well as having potential for expansion either through a loft conversion or extending out at the back. He wants to furnish it and decorate it with 'new, cool stuff'. He wants a new job, not merely a lateral move of the type that characterises many of the changes in employment within the aurora of job insecurity and transience to which many people are limited under the influence of global capitalism, but one which offers more in terms of promotion and pay increases. He plans to contribute to a pension, and is aware of the importance of job security in the light of potential commitments to mortgage repayments, and the likelihood of having a child in the next couple of years. While as mentioned above, Rob claims to be 'not in any rush to have kids' he has recently come under increasing pressure from his partner who has 'started to talk about nothing else'. He seems likely to capitulate sooner rather than later, despite claims that he is keen to wait until the new job and house are under his belt. Most of these 'changes' spell little more than an evolvement of consumer desire, despite Rob's belief that he has 'changed' or 'matured'. While he may claim to have outgrown the desires that shaped his involvement within the NTE during his younger years, Rob has simply become drawn toward alternative outlets for his desires that offer fresh incarnations of consumer fetishism. The pressures and anxieties that characterise Rob's existence under global capitalism result in what can be described as a psychosocial tug-of-war, a phenomenon that appears to be peculiar to this generation. Although this notion will be explored in greater depth over the coming chapters, suffice to say that Rob is not alone in being simultaneously drawn toward the narcissistic playground proffered by consumer capitalism, and yet finding himself tethered to the remnants of the more traditional Symbolic Order under which he was socialised.

Andrea

Andrea is 34 years old, and has lived in Vikton since the age of 11, when her parents divorced and she moved north with her sister and mother. Single for the past six years, she epitomises the subject matter of writers such as Barber (2007) and Calcutt (1998) who write of the processes of infantilisation and arrested development.

Her biography of alcohol consumption appears to be unremarkable in that she started drinking with friends in public spaces, 'drinking Mad Dog 20/20 [a low-end fortified wine] around the benches', frequently to the point of vomiting and passing out. This would often lead to the concoction of 'plausible' stories in order to try and convince parents that illness was due to non-alcohol-related causes:

> We used to tell our mum a right load of bullshit to try and hide the fact we had been out getting pissed, blaming a dodgy pizza, or even central heating at a friend's house. I was actually talking to my mum about this a few months ago and she said 'you must have thought we were stupid, some of the rubbish you used to come out with'.

The thread of deceit carried on for Andrea and her cohort once the lure of the burgeoning NTE began to reel them toward its neon glow. In order to pass for 18 years old, enabling them to access bars and clubs on the city high street, they obtained temporary one-year passports from the post office, at a cost of just a few pounds and provision of proof of identity. Made of card, these were relatively easy to alter. Andrea describes how 'the way the 6 was written, it did look a bit like a five ... I was really gentle with it and managed to make it look like it said 1975'.

Andrea lists the pubs on the drinking circuit, stating that the aim was to 'go to as many pubs as possible and get as drunk as possible, as quickly as possible'. She talks of the level of excitement that she felt as she drank up the novelty of joining the droves of other consumers eager to partake in the opportunities for liminal excitement proffered by the NTE:

> Oh yeah, we used to go to Sailors, it was dead exciting with all the lights and the wall of video screens. It was always packed and dead easy to get lads to buy you drinks and that.

The attraction of the NTE was clear; it was a portal into adulthood, a rite of passage and confirmation of maturity as Andrea and her friends were able to shed the vestiges of childhood and immature practices of the surreptitious consumption of alcohol in parks. For Andrea and her friends, this was truly a promise of excitement, standing as they were on the shores of a hedonistic consumer paradise. One cannot help but notice how this viewpoint has been reversed to the point that the NTE is for many consumers representative of youth and vitality, providing them with an arena within which to stretch the boundaries of concepts of 'youth' and 'maturity'.

Having left college after completing A-levels, but declining to continue to higher education, Andrea signed up with several temping agencies and found employment in a number of low-wage and insecure jobs. While living at home, this arrangement suited her as she was able to spend freely within the consumer markets, go on holiday to the Balearics or attend a number of music festivals at short notice, before simply taking up another temporary contract on her return. By her early twenties, however, a desire for an increased level of independence led to her moving out of her mother's house and renting a room in a shared house with a group of friends. However, this was far from a stable living arrangement, and she would often move house at the end of a tenancy agreement, or on several occasions move back to her mother's house in order to save money for another deposit or simply to save money during periods of unemployment or underemployment.

The way that Andrea talks about her formative drinking years is very much indicative of a learning process, whereby she develops a taste for more sophisticated drinks, away from the Ready-to-Drink alcopops and the cheap ciders, to an appreciation of wines and spirits. However, to read this as a cultivation of more sophisticated taste may be too simplistic. The use-value of alcoholic drinks is still, as it was in the parks, sitting on the park bench, its ability to deliver the physiological and mental changes upon the site of the body that are related to drunkenness, while still taking into account the economic cost of the operation. However, while some drinks, such as cider or snakebite and black, a concoction of lager, cider and blackcurrant cordial, may fulfil these criteria, they are considered by Andrea and some of her friends as the preserve of younger drinkers. She is ready to admit that the cost of alcohol is an issue, and speaks of facing financial hardship or 'being skint' toward the end of the month, a condition that involves having to make decisions of whether to get the bus home or spend her bus fare on another drink; budgeting further by eating evening meals at friends' houses or at her mother's house. However, she is eager to maintain the façade of an identity within the NTE that portrays her as able to afford to drink without sacrifices elsewhere in her life.

Throughout her twenties, Andrea maintained a regular presence in the NTE, spending weekday nights and indeed the majority of her time in her local pub, the White Horse. Another 'historic' pub, 'the Horse' consisted then, as now, of three bars positioned around a central courtyard with picnic-style benches and framed by hanging baskets. While two of the bars serve food, the largest room hosts music on one or two evenings a week and contains the ubiquitous fruit machine and quiz machine. This bar tends to be populated by the 'locals', many of whom stop to greet Andrea as they pass the table at which I am conducting the interview, whereupon I am often given an appraising look and an occasional nod of the head.

With the arrival of the weekend, Andrea and her girlfriends would undertake a number of ritualistic procedures that are today replicated throughout the entire country. She describes how she and her friends would meet at one or another of their houses, wine or vodka in hand, and spend a couple of hours drinking, listening to music and 'getting tarted up' before hitting the bars and clubs. Regardless of whether they were in a relationship or not, the weekend was time to go out and immerse themselves in the hyperreality of the NTE. Andrea talks about how an air of excitement surrounded the whole going out experience as she traversed her twenties, and I can almost discern the rose-tinted glow as she gushes enthusiastically about the experiences and memories shared through the medium of alcohol and the NTE. Then, as now, it is the drinking experience that Andrea and her friends value, rather than the drinking itself. However, what emerges as a common thread for a number of respondents is the progression to a point whereby the positive experience of one is impossible without the other, leading to the presumption that getting drunk leads to and is synonymous with good times.

As Andrea heads through her thirties, little has really changed. She can still be found in her local pub most nights of the week, is still working in the same administrative job that she has held for the past four years. She is still living in rented accommodation, although now lives in a flat on her own. Her approach to going out on a Friday and Saturday appears to have mellowed a little; although she and her friends still adhere to the same routine, they are more critical of the places they go and the younger drinkers with whom they share space within the pubs and clubs of the high street.

> When you go out on a Friday, Saturday night and it's loud and it's noisy and there are loads of people, you don't get to catch up with people as much. We haven't really been to a night club for years, but that is a lot to do with late opening. Before late opening, this place would shut and you would have to [move on], and we would be like 'Club Z anyone?' Now you don't need to pay to get into a club, where it's idiots, hot and expensive and you can't hear anything, and if you want to dance and sing along to good music then you can do that too.

The desire that Andrea intimates toward 'catching up with people' certainly differs from her earlier drinking experiences, when listening to her friends droning on about jobs, boyfriends, housing and so on would have actively impinged upon the enjoyment of a night out, rather than becoming integral to it. She continues:

> There are too many hen parties on the other side of the river, anywhere over the bridge, from The Slug and Lettuce onwards. They think that they can charge 6 quid for a glass of wine or whatever, and they aren't anything special, they just have a view of the river, apart from that they are full of chavs and are just shit. It's the dark side. It takes you ages to get served, there is nowhere to sit or even stand, it's too expensive and really annoying, oh and the toilets as well are

dead pretentious with the unisex basin to wash your hands and the fountain and everything.

Andrea is keen to give the impression of having matured as a participant within the NTE. Primarily, her technique for doing this as we have witnessed above is to emphasise the way in which her chosen beverage and preferred location have changed as a result of her advancing years – or (perceived) increased levels of sophistication, to put it in a kinder way. Additionally, she suggests a virtual loathing of her younger self, labelling those in an equivalent position to her younger self as 'other'. She is separate to them, and indeed almost their diametric opposite. She positions herself as a tactful, knowledgeable and civilised consumer (although importantly still a consumer). The creation and depiction of the 'other' within the arena of the NTE suggests the myth of the self-constitutive community built around shared leisure practices (Engineer et al., 2003). Rather than forging a community with shared identities and norms, the NTE is in fact populated by many individuals who display an advanced antagonism towards others with whom they share leisure spaces.

> The older you get you do change your drinking habits. Some pubs are more child-friendly for example, it all depends on what you want from your night out ... When we were 21, we were out on the pull and would just go on a crawl, drink move on, drink move on, whereas we aren't really as interested now in standing in crowded bars bopping to Cascada or something, getting off with random blokes and never seeing them again or any of that ... I think drinking evolves with the person. Like when you are younger you haven't got any inhibitions or hang-ups, you are just full of confidence.

She also seeks to distance herself from the distinctive way that she feels 'lads' drink on a night out:

> Lads can't really do the social drinking thing, they just go out and get absolutely hammered and don't come home until the pubs are shut and it's kicking out time, they can't just sit around and have a glass of wine like us.

Andrea and numerous other respondents go to great lengths to articulate how they are utilising the composite elements of the NTE as tools with which to create identity and indicate themselves as 'cool', savvy and perhaps sophisticated individuals. However, this is to deny the influence of the might of the NTE as a capitalist organism, a basking shark with a vast mouth open wide to filter as much as possible into its cavernous belly. The truth is that consumers are offered such a variety of experiences under the umbrella of the NTE that their quest for the new and novel on the night-time high street is never satiated. By definition, these consumers are 'neophiles' (Campbell, 1989) in as much as they seek out the new, but importantly, the 'new' is just a reconfigured version of the old. Satiation is never achieved, as desire regenerates, with a good night out merely serving as a foundation on which to build towards the next one. This is Lacan's point, in that it is impossible to satisfy desire, because desire itself indicates a state of non-satisfaction. In this sense, desire can only be terminated rather than satiated due to the fact that it is signalling a lack, or an absence of. Desire is a self-sustaining mechanism that doesn't really seek satisfaction (as one might understand it) in terms of an end-goal (see Žižek, 2008). Therefore, as a particular bar or club begins to lose its appeal, another is ready to slot seamlessly in and take its place. This process is usually understood by the consumer to indicate 'progress': away from something that has become staid and banal, and toward something that appears different, possessing new and more positive characteristics. For Andrea and her friends, value is placed upon the familiarity and recognition that they receive from drinking in their local pub, while associating forays outside of this environment as in turn exciting events, and something that they have started to enjoy less. While they may protest that they have matured and reached a higher level of distinction or sophistication through their journey from cheap cider and flavoured wine-coolers to premium lager and white wine by the bottle, premium spirits and cocktails, the effect is merely illusory. Andrea speaks also of how the experience that they wish to glean from their continued participation within the NTE has also metamorphosed; from the desire to get as drunk as quickly and as cheaply as possible (Andrea mentions one anecdote referring to how they used to take non-prescription painkillers prior to drinking, in the belief that the alcohol would affect them more quickly, while others refer to drinking lager or cider through a straw to achieve the same goal) to a desire to spend more time 'catching up with friends' and drinking wine because it is 'more sociable to share a bottle of wine', with less emphasis on the goal of getting drunk.

Between 17 and 23 was pub crawls, getting dressed up doing all that and getting into clubs, then since then it's been progressively getting more the social aspects of it where you just go out with your mates and sit down round a table, talk, discuss things and put the world to rights and all that. Definitely prefer it now because it is about spending quality time with your friends, it's not about going out and pulling, meeting people ... which is probably where I am going wrong seeing as I am 33 and still single. And that gives you a bit of a problem, because I don't see myself meeting someone in The Horse and I wouldn't want the kind of person you see on a night out on a pub crawl, younger chav-people banging into you.

However, the choice and variety that is on offer within the NTE is utilised by Andrea and her friends, as the desire for the new and exciting is impossible to stifle completely:

> We need to go to places that are different, with just the girls, because no blokes are going to approach you or whatever if you are out with a group of mates, most of which are lads. But on the other hand I would rather meet someone through a friend of a friend or something like that rather than just some random in a bar. But in somewhere like Vikton, it is difficult to meet someone that you don't know through however many degrees of separation or whatever.

Drunkenness is in fact often referred to by Andrea as little more than a coincidental side effect of drinking socially. In fact, she bemoans the lack of an 'off switch' that allows her to drink from 'when we finish work at 4 p.m. to still being out drinking at 4 in the morning'.

Andrea identifies a number of other changes that have taken place relating to her and her friends' continued participation within the NTE. There is a level of concern vocalised surrounding the physiological effects of drinking alcohol, as she complains about looking 'rough' the morning after a 'session'. She also alludes to a heightened level of concern about memory loss after a particularly big night out, usually on a Friday or Saturday night:

> I've started to suffer terribly with 'booze blues' where I wake up in the morning and if I can't remember the whole night, and I just have a fear that I've done something terrible. When I was younger I didn't give a toss, and I think I used to remember more. The older I've got, the memory loss thing has started to creep in and now I can wake up in the morning, be fine and then think 'Christ, I've got no idea how I got home' and that's more in the last two or three years. Not the memory loss thing as much as the worrying about it.

For Andrea, there appears to be a clear delineation between two different types of drinking. There is the going to the pub after work, which
is couched in terms of just going for 'a glass of wine' in order to help
'de-stress' or 'chill out'. However, far from being a staid or sophisticated evening of restrained alcohol consumption along the lines of the
European café culture famously envisioned by the Blair government,
there is the underlying excitement of the possibility or perhaps likelihood that the evening is going to turn into what Andrea terms 'a bit
of a session':

> There's that thing of 'ooh' is anyone going to say they're going to go
> home, then if they do it's like 'nooo'. Everyone starts off just saying
> or thinking that they are going to just have one glass of wine, then
> the second bottle comes, and we end up having at least a bottle each.

Weekend nights out, however, are seen as a little different, with part of
the enjoyment appearing to be the ritualistic aspect of getting ready,
and the opportunity to dance, 'meet people you haven't seen for a while
or don't usually see' tempered only by the assertion that it can 'be a bit
mad'. Andrea expresses concern at the fact that going too 'mad' on a
weekend night out has the effect of ruining the precious commodity
of weekend leisure time, and states that she feels worse about 'wasting'
her weekend with a hangover than she does in going to work in paid
employment with a hangover:

> I'm not really career minded. I'm quite happy in the job I'm in,
> but I'm not interested in career development, promotion or what-
> ever. I'm not going to change my lifestyle for my job, because it isn't
> that important. I don't have a mortgage, I don't have kids or any
> other financial commitments so I'm just not that bothered about it.
> I certainly didn't have my heart set on being a civil servant when
> I was a kid. I wouldn't have minded going to university, but life
> doesn't turn out like you want it to, my mum didn't have any money
> and I had to go and get a job straight from school.

It is not hard to draw some comparisons between the instrumental
nature of attitudes to work and the importance placed upon leisure
time, discussed in preceding chapters. Indeed this is representative of a
key theme that we will see drawn through the following pages.

When I ask Andrea about the future, she finds it necessary to clarify
what I mean, as if it hasn't really occurred to her. She seems aware that

the aspirational lifestyles sold through global media and the consumer economy are largely unobtainable, and is realistic enough to concede that the transient nature of employment, relationships and even health preclude the certainty that may have been characterised within an earlier epoch. Her consciousness seems for the time being to be firmly rooted in the immediacy of the present, and although eventually she paints me a picture of what she perceives the future to hold, it is to some extent framed in ambivalent terms, and tells of a desire for the status quo to remain for the foreseeable future.

I hate the thought of me in ten years' time being like this, but I remember saying that ten years ago. I feel like I am still 22 or 23 in my mental age. I don't feel like I'm ignoring life, it's more of a sideline while things sort themselves out. If we didn't go out all the time then what would we do? Just sit in and watch telly programmes, *EastEnders* and have that as a life? A lot of people I know at work do that, and I just don't think that's the way to live. It's more acceptable to do things this way now.

In five years' time I hope by then I have met someone and have a family. I always thought I would be married and have kids before I was 30. I was with Lloyd for six years, got engaged and so on, but there was no real level of commitment there. You can live with people and share bills or whatever, but it can end at any time and you are back to square one. I've never been bothered about getting married, but I would like to think that I would have a more settled kind of lifestyle. I would still like to go out and drink, but maybe, you know, not every night. If you have someone you want to spend time with and want to go home and see them, spend time with them, then going out would get bypassed a lot of the time.

A lot of my friends are starting to get married and have kids, and Sara for example was still coming out, even though she was not drinking while she was pregnant. When you have a toddler or slightly older kid, you are OK to leave it with family. Other friends though are having their lives completely altered by getting married, kids, whatever, and that makes me think that maybe it is better to fit it in as much as possible now while you still have time. I know they wouldn't want to swap their children for the world, but I know they would like to still have the freedom that I have ... We have so many choices and there is so much going on, getting married and losing independence and so on ... I don't see it as a good thing. Having the kind of networks of friends and the girls and that, it's the way to go ... My mum and dad nag at me about the fact I haven't got a husband, brood of kids and all that. Family parties and all that, and my auntie will whisper in my ear – don't leave it too late, and I'm like fuck off, I'm only in my thirties. All my cousins are married and have kids, so it's a bit of an issue.

Although clearly aware of the societal factors existing to draw her back into a more traditional life course, such as familial pressure exuding the expectation that she settle down with a man and set up home, Andrea is seduced by the promises of the NTE. Her explanatory mechanism positions her as the discerning consumer who makes a calculated and fully rational decision to 'leave behind' the mediocrity of career building and prime-time television viewing, applying value to more rewarding and pleasurable pastimes. This is actually a viewpoint that is clearly in harmony with many liberal academic accounts (see, for example, Skelton and Valentine, 1998; Malbon, 1999). However, while failing to give her any real sense of satisfaction, this explanation also fails to adequately explain her current approach to consumerised leisure. In many ways her account is similar to some of the street criminals interviewed by Hall et al. (2008), who appear to construct these positive narratives as an ideological fall-back position, a means of momentarily convincing the self and others that the future is bright and the subject remains in control of its own destiny. Andrea actually appears to show little commitment to this narrative, and beneath it is possible to discern an undercurrent of bleak nihilism, a depressive hedonia (see Fisher, 2009) that seems increasingly to characterise a culture at the end of history.

This illusory nature of youth and vitality within the sphere of the NTE is hit upon by Andrea herself as she recalls thinking that drinkers of around her own age, when she was younger, were 'sad' or 'embarrassing', although she deflects any uncomfortable feeling that this might evoke through a thin veil of selective feminism:

I'm happy doing this until I settle down and have a family, but then again when I was younger I would be sitting in a bar and see people not a lot older than we are now, mid to late thirties or something and I would think to myself 'There is no way I'm going to be doing that when I get to your age because it's just like embarrassing,' and I'm still doing it now and can't see that it is embarrassing. I guess I'm not married or have kids, so my lifestyle fully allows it. The more acceptable it becomes for women to be single and not married off with children I think the more normal that this becomes.

Andrea (despite her protestations to the contrary) is still committed to indulgence and captured by the spectacle of consumer excess. The bottles of wine after work are not the epitome of the socially constructive café culture ostensibly sought after by Blair's New Labour government, and while Andrea may believe that she has full creative control over her social engagement, it is clear that she is in fact bound by a number of complex psychosocial factors that are shaping her identity and perpetually propelling her back to the market in search of something more, processes which will be explored in much greater detail over the coming pages.

Last orders?

The above case studies give a clear snapshot of the pressures that the subjects of this piece of work find bearing down upon them as they attempt to reach an uneasy compromise between the socialisation processes that form a key part of what may be termed traditional adulthood, and their desire to maintain a presence within the NTE. While following chapters will explore how meaning and identity are extracted from various aspects and processes of the night-time leisure scene for these individuals, from the above case studies we can glean an insight into the importance and the consistency of the role that alcohol has played in their lives from their teen years to the present day. Both Andrea and Rob are embedded within the value system that lies at the heart of social engagement within liberal capitalism, and while financial and cultural success is a goal for them, they resent the necessity to join the 'rat race' of paid employment that dictates to what extent they can succeed within consumer markets. While they acknowledge that flash cars, grand houses and exotic holidays lie out of their reach, they are eager to grasp the cultural markers that identify them as 'cool', 'hip' or discerning whenever their orbits come into touching distance.

7
Desire, Motivation and the NTE

Previous pages have illuminated the global processes that have given rise to a dominant culture of consumerism and infantilisation. This chapter will explore in more detail a number of drives that appear to be affecting the lives of these committed consumers. For many of the people who form the basis of this research, participation within the night-time economy (NTE) has been a constant throughout their adult lives, which are characterised by the use of alcohol as a commodity around which to frame friendships. In the previous chapter, we saw how Rob and Andrea only see their friends on occasions that are mediated by alcohol, creating something akin to dependence on marketised excess as they return time and time again to consume amounts of alcohol that far transgress the government guidelines for responsible use.[1] The purpose of this chapter is not only to investigate *why* these individuals retain such an attachment to the (NTE) as they progress through their thirties and continue to nurture an identity that is firmly ensconced within the machinations of global consumer capitalism, so much as it is to delve further into a consideration of the derivation of enjoyment that they extract from the NTE. Respondents often reported that a bad night out was not uncommon, and complained of the repetitious nature of their excursions. However, despite the financial implications of wasting money on a bad night out, and despite the option of seeking alternatives of neighbouring bars or even neighbouring cities, these individuals return interminably in search of the elusive great night out.

Commitment to the NTE comes with a price tag, wherein alcohol is merely one part of the consideration. Transportation, drugs, clothing, entry to clubs, pizzas and kebabs all contribute to the cost. Aside from these expenses, felt keenly in the wage packet and wallet, there are a number of negative externalities concomitant to commitment to this lifestyle. Respondents spoke of the impact of hangovers and weight gain, indicative of a paradox. While consumers are encouraged to enjoy, to never let an opportunity to experience all life has to offer pass by, they are also under increasing pressure to look good, to be fit, sleek and alert. Failure to adhere to these cultural norms can result in a form of anxiety and *cultural inconsequentiality*.

Media coverage revolving around the NTE has shaped the public perception of how those frequenting bars, pubs and clubs tend to behave, and while the pub-crawl has been rebranded to some extent, with local heritage and small-brewery beers providing the focus to an array of 'ale-trails' across the UK (see Spracklen et al., 2013), popular perception is likely to involve marauding groups of young males and females indulging in weekend circuit drinking. It therefore becomes important to explore the extent to which older adults who are still regularly participating within the NTE experience the night out in a different way to their younger counterparts and in terms of their own biography.

Motivations within the NTE

The attraction of alcohol as an intoxicant is an area that has been well covered by a number of commentators (see MacAndrew and Edgerton, 1969; Plant et al., 1997; Babor, 2010) with a general consensus being that it provides a legally and socially acceptable means of altering one's perception of the world as well as an individual's place within it. The evolution of night-time leisure as pubs and more traditional city centre buildings are converted into Vertical Drinking Establishments (see Chatterton and Hollands, 2003; Hobbs et al., 2000; Hadfield, 2006) resulted in a wealth of drinking establishments and experiences targeted at a range of consumers. This provides an opportunity for drinkers to cast off the shackles of daytime comportment, be released from 'normal' identity, responsibility and associated behaviours where the boundaries of social control are relaxed (see Presdee, 2000). The perception of relaxation outside the bounds of the workaday mentality may be heightened in vast numbers of individuals by lives otherwise characterised by monotony and drudgery, or lack of contact with peers of similar interests. For this reason it is likely that those consumers who are at work during the day, or at home caring for children, invest very specific meaning into participation in the NTE.

Entrance into the full-time labour market, home ownership and the other factors associated with 'growing up' and 'settling down' reduce opportunities to participate within the NTE quite as frequently. However, it is clear that the majority of respondents made clear distinction between work life and leisure life, an observation that will be explored more thoroughly in due course. A more complex picture emerges for those respondents who are mediating the role of parent with that of dedicated consumer. Michelle is a 35-year-old single mother to a four-year-old girl. She studied away at university, and worked in low-level management jobs in London and various other locations. She doesn't get to go out drinking as often as other respondents in this study, and the occasions she does go out are dictated by fitting around her child's routine and the availability of her parents to be able to help out with childcare. She likes being surrounded by her friends, and appears to fear that if she fails to maintain an appearance within the NTE then they – or she – will simply evaporate into nothingness.

> I don't see going out as needing a break from responsibilities, unwinding or any of that – in fact the opposite, because I feel guilty for going out. But people drop off the radar if they don't go out. There's the fear that if you keep saying no to people then they stop asking. If you keep turning people down, they will assume you are going to say no every time and you drop out of the loop. I think I have got the balance just about right.

Michelle displays a level of concern at being left 'out of the loop' if she doesn't go out every weekend but also has a very clear set of ideas about what her role as a mother should constitute, which results in a more traditional arousal of guilt surrounding the conflict of going out, and the awareness that she is perhaps contravening a social norm by leaving her daughter in pursuit of her own hedonism. However, it is likely that this period of abstinence serves to make the attraction of the eventual and inevitable hedonistic excess that will accompany her re-entrance into the NTE all the more potent. Michelle's particular position of being a single mother to a young child makes her acutely aware of a number of elements surrounding socially sanctioned responsibility, while her embryonic relationship with a man who is very much embedded within the NTE forces her to confront the power and importance of youthful consumerism. She thereby occupies a particularly narrow cultural peninsula from where she both consciously and subconsciously attempts to deny a number of social processes that may drag her further from the 'ideal' of youthful and hedonistic independence and toward middle-age mediocrity and anonymity.

When I started going out again [after the birth of her child and break-down of her relationship] it was odd. I was living over at my mam's and used to go out with a [male] friend in a similar situation and we would just go into town together. I used to go out once a fortnight, just because I didn't want to go out more often, just didn't want to be away from her. I wouldn't go out unless there was a reason, like a birthday or celebration you know, but I was having more and more of a laugh and now usually the weekend is reason enough. It's such a social thing, Belle [daughter] wasn't at school, all my friends were at work, so I could be in all day and not see another adult all day, and not even be able to go to the shop if Belle was asleep or whatever.

Michelle is not alone in framing the experience of participating within the NTE as something other than the normal routine. The pubs and bars of the high street are the spaces in which relationships and friend-ships are sought, developed and maintained as well as offering refracted images of the Real. For Michelle and other respondents who had family responsibilities, the NTE offers an opportunity to regress to forms of behaviours that would have been far more commonplace in the years before having children:

Yeah, on Thursday night I was really drunk – I tried to open the taxi driver's door on the way home – he went mental. We were in the taxi and saw Milly [a friend of Michelle's] and all that lot com-ing out of [the club], so rather than faffing, well I didn't think of opening the window, I just opened the door and shouted ... don't even know what I shouted, and the taxi driver wasn't happy, [my boyfriend] was going mad. I was just really drunk. I don't remember a right lot. I remember bits, you know when you cringe and think 'Did I say that?' Got home around 2 a.m. I think, don't know how I got so drunk, I met all the girls in The Slug and Lettuce, and was drinking wine. I don't usually drink wine, I've been drinking halves recently because I've always been doing things the next day and haven't wanted to get too drunk. But I just couldn't get enough of it on Thursday.

Earlier chapters have addressed the new forms of labour that emerged under the shadow of post-industrialism and discussed the decline of dis-tinct and more traditional forms of biographical development. We have explored the relationships that are widely held as responsible for increased levels of anxiety within youth cultures surrounding the construction of identity in a cultural milieu devoid of historical reference points and pre-dictable pathways, while social hierarchies have been steadily eroded by the instability of contemporary labour markets and top down implementation of neoliberal ideology. Consumer culture has not only destroyed the traditional social hierarchies but has replaced them with interminably transient, rolling cultural hierarchies with tumultuous impact upon the very nature of young people's lives (Hall et al., 2008; Winlow and Hall 2006). The people at the very core of this book are among the first to feel the impact of this in their teenage years and represent the first cohort to be carrying its legacy deep into what may traditionally be termed adulthood.

The majority of my respondents are employed within the field of 'service sector employment' and many have spent years moving only laterally along the rungs of an essentially dissatisfying career ladder. For these individuals, there exists a real sense that work is little more than an inconvenience which is to be tolerated or endured as merely a means through which to fund a presence within the consumer market; clothes, music, furnishings and of course nights out – indeed, all the trappings of global consumer capitalism. The accumulation of such riches has the effect of imbuing the individual with the communal symbolism that in years gone by would have been found within traditional communities through religion, geographic location and class, a phenomenon exten-sively explored by Bauman (2007: 75):

> More often than not, the 'totality' to which individuals are to stay loyal and obedient no longer enters their life and confronts them in the shape of a denial of their individual autonomy, or as an obliga-tory sacrifice like universal conscription and the duty to give their life for the country and the national cause. Instead, it presents itself in the form of highly entertaining and invariably pleasurable and relished festivals of communal togetherness and belonging.

For the individuals here, the sources of identification adopted for the purposes of leisure are weighted with more significance than other dimensions of life. On a weekend, or in the evening, distanced from the perceived pressures, responsibilities and boredom of work they were able to be their 'true selves' and spend time with their 'real mates' rather than work colleagues, other mothers at mother and baby groups and so on. In this way, respondents were referring to the 'second life' described by Bakhtin (1984). The rest of the time, it is necessary to foreground facets of their core identity in a pragmatic and instrumental manner in order to manage the situation and their actions within it (see Simmel, 1921). Nowhere is this better exemplified than in the case of Evan, a 33-year-old firefighter. Having graduated with a degree in languages and studied an abortive year at law college, Evan experienced the general uncertainty tinged with ennui that has become a hallmark of youth transitions before applying to join the Fire Service. This career has lasted more than seven years, but is due to end upon his recent successful application to return to university to undertake a course in natural science. He talks at length about the necessity to suppress elements of what he might think of as his core identity in order to align himself with his work colleagues:

> I'm not really looking forward to my leaving do. It's incredible how little I have in common with [my work colleagues]. I mean I get on all right with them, but there's absolutely no chance of me having a decent conversation about music or anything that I'm interested in. And they don't really know anything about me. I mean, they know I'm getting married, and they know I support Newcastle, but they don't know I used to be in a band or any of that stuff. I mean, they'll all be talking about the latest episode of *Top Gear* or *Britain's Got Talent* or whatever moronic reality TV show is on at the moment, and I just sit there and it all goes over my head. And most of the stuff they say, you know, about anything that is on the news at the moment is just them regurgitating the *[Daily] Mail* or the *News of the World* and just holding the most basic views about everything like immigration or whatever, and I've given up trying to argue against them because it's just impossible. I get on all right with them, and have a laugh and stuff at work, well you have to really, but I just don't have anything in common with them. They are the type of people, I'm serious, who have become firefighters just to impress women when they are in [a nightclub], so a night out with them is just awful. Last Christmas do, for example, I just left after a while and went and met some mates in a different pub, so I imagine that's what I'll do [when it's time for my leaving do]. All they do is wind each other up about having shagged each other's wives, girlfriends, daughters, whatever, and talk racist or sexist bollocks, and that just isn't me. Obviously I laugh along and sometimes it is actually quite funny, but it just isn't really me.

Evan's working persona appears to be somewhat compartmentalised, isolated even. While his chosen occupation has been noted for its adherence to hypermasculine norms, and has been documented as generating group cohesion and worker solidarity (Thurnell-Read and Parker, 2008), Evan's work identity seems to be characterised by a daily determination to complete each shift as a relatively isolated individual. His planned return to university is perhaps a contributory factor, allowing him to position himself as on the way to something better, and the acquisition of status and qualifications that will allow him to put further distance between himself and his colleagues at the fire station. To this extent his work biography is seen to be a product of constant adaptation, with the hope that the next move will provide some form of reward. However, the reality of this quasi-romantic viewpoint may turn out to be ultimately unfulfilling as the life course takes on the character of an incessant journey towards a non-existent destination.

For some of the respondents there is evidence of a realisation that the good times can't last. They have already experienced some degree of loss of previous freedoms, and are aware of the obligations that lie just ahead. The here and now is therefore to be celebrated as frequently as possible.

Steve is 36 years old and upon leaving school worked in the retail sector, before securing some better-paid work through employment agencies. He is currently employed through an agency that contracts out to large offices, but like many employees in his situation, his job is far from secure. Meeting him at his shared house near the city centre, the furnishings are typical of many rented houses in a marketplace dominated by buy-to-let landlords, although he is surrounded by a number of expensive items that cement his loyalty to consumerism – an Apple MacBook, Sony TV, iPod, hundreds of CDs, the list goes on. Although he is dressed casually in jeans, T-shirt and Converse trainers, he is proud of the fact that his clothes are purchased from 'boutique' stores rather than common or garden high street shops.

> I like to wear stuff that other people won't be wearing. You don't want to be in a bar in town or whatever and look up and see some other cunt in the same top as you, do you? I'll go through to Leeds or Manchester every now and again rather than just get stuff from Topman or Next or whatever, that all the mongies in town wear. This T-shirt and these jeans are ... well I'm not sure of the label to be honest, but I got them from [a designer clothing store] and haven't seen anyone else in the same.

Steve appears to be acutely aware of his age and the possibility that his commitment to consumerism and a sustained attachment to maintaining a presence within the NTE have had the effect of essentially derailing his progress through the more traditional life course:

> I really need to get two things sorted out this year – a pension and buying a flat. I mean, for fuck's sake I'm 36 years old. I can't live in rented accommodation for the rest of my life, and I don't want to be working in B&Q to pay off my mortgage when I'm 70. I've never got round to getting a pension either so I really need to start thinking about that.

Pensions, owning property, progressing up the career ladder are all factors that contribute to the process of 'being' adult, reliant on the conveyance of symbolic efficiency. It is never enough for the individual to know they are an adult, the Big Other must know it too, through monthly deductions from the pay cheque. It is the Big Other that confers an identity upon the fragmented, decentred individual, bestowing upon it symbolic efficiency, recognised by everyone else and acting as a determiner of socioeconomic positioning. Žižek outlines how this works by referring to a joke in which a man with no small amount of psychiatric problems went to the doctor believing that he was a grain of corn. After being cured and sent home, he rushes back into the doctor's office concerned that there is a chicken outside who might eat him. The doctor duly explains that he is not a grain of corn and is in fact a human being, to which the man replies 'well *I* know that, but does the chicken?' (see Žižek, 2009). Put simply, the man is still a grain of corn until his status as a human being is confirmed by the Big Other.

Following this line of reasoning, it is possible to argue that for many of my respondents their status as adult fails to be confirmed by the Big Other due to the fact that they lack the symbolic accoutrements associated with being 'grown up'. This lack or void can be filled by engaging with consumerism, which allows the purchasable symbolism of youth, vigour, and perpetual adolescence while at the same time, the markers of traditional adulthood remain unachievable and for some untenable. Status as young and cool is confirmed through possession of certain clothes, or possessions that may be considered superfluous or indulgent to the traditional social order. As Žižek (1999: 330) explains, this symbolic efficiency takes place not at the level of:

> 'reality' as opposed to the play of my imagination – Lacan's point is not that, behind the multiplicity of phantasmic identities, there is a

hard core of some 'real Self'; we are dealing with a symbolic fiction, but a fiction which, for contingent reasons that have nothing to do with its inherent structure, possesses performative power – is socially operative, structures the sociosymbolic reality in which I participate. The status of the same person, inclusive of his/her very 'real' features, can appear in an entirely different light the moment the modality of his/her relationship to the Big Other changes.

So when looking at the motivation of individuals to return time and time again to the night-time high street, we can postulate that there exists a relationship between a desire to present attributes that, while in themselves are not necessarily youthful, are certainly other than synonymous with adulthood as traditionally perceived. Similarly, importance appears to be placed upon the maintenance of friendship bonds created and perpetuated within the bounded liminality offered by global consumer capitalism through the guise of drinking places and spaces within the NTE.

The problems for the individuals I encountered during this piece of research are that the contemporary world issues two interrelated but also seemingly mutually exclusive injunctions. I conceive of this in terms of a psychosocial tug-of-war, for individuals are at once commanded to be normative, responsible citizens, and are simultaneously expected to fulfil the role of dedicated hedonist committed to pleasuring the self in socially prescribed ways. This exemplifies the problem of contemporary subjectivity. Even if we choose to be a respectable 'adult', the fundamental and irreducible lack that lies at the core of subjectivity (see Lacan, 2001) is experienced through the haunting shadow of what might have been – continually subjecting the individual to the injunction to abandon respectability and commit to indulgence. And of course the opposite is true. Consequently, as appealing as the idea of a coherent, fixed and stable identity free from regrets might be, it is impossible in the Western world. It is this realisation that has prompted a spawn of literature that relates growing mental health problems to the onward march of twenty-first century global capitalism (James, 2007; Fisher 2009; Dorling 2010).

A characteristic that may yet prove to be distinct to this generation is the challenge found in the necessity to balance these two opposing yet insistent forces – they are more than aware of what makes up a 'responsible' adult lifestyle, yet are unable to ignore the siren song of consumerised hedonism. This results in a complex plate-spinning exercise that is managed with varying degrees of success.

Among some respondents, there appeared to be a generalised resistance to the more traditional nodes of socialisation, and a preference for a level of individual autonomy over social interconnectedness. For Steve, from whom we have heard earlier in this chapter, the potential for loss of personal freedom that he equates with embarking on a romantic relationship is a source of terror. Throughout our meetings he recounts tales of friends and acquaintances whom he perceives as having their personal autonomy curtailed through their involvement in what he interprets as an outmoded and undesirable form of relationship. He recounts with derision anecdotes that portray his contemporaries as 'under the thumb' or otherwise failing to follow the hedonistic lifestyle they once enjoyed alongside him:

> The problem is that if you get a bird now, they are going to want to have kids straight away. Our mate Dave, for example, I was out with him last night and he was saying to me – don't get married now ... it's all trips to IKEA and never seeing your mates. That's why if I got a bird – I was explaining this to a mate's girlfriend the other day and she looked horrified – I would want her to want to go on holidays on her own with her own group of friends. I'm not against having a girlfriend, I just don't want my life to change, be told what to do and all that.

Variations of this theme were a commonality throughout the research, with individuals happy to measure the quality of their relationships compared to those of their peers in terms of personal freedom and the permissiveness of partners to their continued participation within the NTE – as a unit, but also on an individual level. Again, we hear from Evan:

> You've got to feel for Benno [one of his friends]. He is just so under the thumb it's ridiculous, which is going to cause him problems down the line. His Granddad just died last year, and he inherited about twenty grand, which he always used to talk about using to go back to university. Well that's all out of the window. [His girlfriend, whom he currently lives with in her house] has got it spent already as a deposit for a place to buy together, and she wants to have kids as soon as they have bought a house, and she just doesn't understand that it would be beneficial for both of them for him to go and do a master's like an MBA or something. I'm lucky I suppose, because Debbie [fiancée] is younger, so isn't desperate to have kids yet, and

understands that it's important to do what you want to do. She is totally supportive of me going back to university, and doesn't give me any shit about going out with the lads or whatever. It's just about not taking the piss really – I don't want to go out every night of the week, so I suppose it just doesn't cause a problem. Benno though, struggles to get a pass out[2] to watch both Champions League matches in a week, and has no chance of going out on a Friday if he is out on a Saturday.

Evan's lack of empathy, along with his obvious disgust that his friend is having to compromise on his personal goals indicates a point of view that mirrors that of Steve. He elevates his own relationship to that of the ideal – and positions the other as borderline oppressive. By placing the other relationship in a negative light, he is able to justify his own insistence on autonomy – a break away from more traditional relationship organisation.

A number of the respondents studied throughout the course of this work appear to be caught in something of an ideological impasse. On the one hand, they are aware that marriage, property, family holidays and so on, are, broadly speaking, an inevitable feature of their life course, but they are also so deeply ensconced within a dominant ideology that demands their continued participation in the NTE. There is a sense that they are staving off the inevitable through continued participation within the NTE, or perhaps their rejection of it, no matter how temporary, is viewed as a rejection of traditional elements of life course, the rat race, the mill and so on. While this may be conceived of as a motivation for perpetual presence in the pubs, bars and clubs, there exists an unresolved problem, in that their involvement and consumption within the NTE serves to power many of the instruments of capitalism against which they believe they are rebelling in their commitment to their own leisure and freedom. They believe that they are the 'winners' in the game, working to live, making their job serve their own enjoyment while their place within the Symbolic Order is cemented through the completion of their roles within it. For example, Steve knows that he has to go to work in order to be able to go out at the weekend and buy the clothes that speak volumes about his tastes, interests and style. While he would rather not work in his administrative role, to give up work would relegate him to a much lower socioeconomic stratum, not through the loss of status conferred as a member of the labour force, but through his inability to display the ownership of material goods.

They do not know it ...

It seems plausible to explain the motivations of the target population of this piece of work with Marx's maxim that he invokes to define false consciousness; 'they do not know it, but they are doing it'. We could interpret this to mean that these participants do not know what they are doing with regard to drinking within the NTE. That is to say that they misperceive the reality of their situation. While they believe that their continued pursuit of hedonistic pleasure within the arena of the night-time high street is an expression of their own freedom, they fail to grasp that this freedom and commitment to hedonistic excess is precisely what the market needs to rejuvenate itself. A parallel to this interpretation may be drawn with the Marxist analysis of commodity fetishism, as paraphrased by Žižek (1991: 31):

> Money is in reality just an embodiment, a condensation, a materialisation of a network of social relations – the fact that it functions as a universal equivalent of all commodities is conditioned by its position in the texture of social relations. But to the individuals themselves, this function of money – to be the embodiment of wealth – appears as an immediate, natural property of a thing called 'money', as if money is already within itself, in its immediate material reality, the embodiment of wealth.

The Marxist interpretation of wealth, of course, is essentially an expression of inequality, representing the deficit between the value of the labour required to make a commodity, and the value of the commodity itself. As the value of the commodity tends to be more than the cost of making it in monetary terms, it means that the labourers are essentially exploited for the work, rendering wealth as little more than unpaid-for labour. However, the social make-up of labour is masked by the circulation of commodities and the money used to pay for them, essentially creating a shroud of mystery around the true value of money, as individuals treat it as if it were inherently valuable. The true value is of course located within the relations of the people that make the commodities, and those that profit from the labour. Nevertheless, they remain unaware that when they treat money as valuable in itself, they are wrong.

Within the NTE, we see individuals on a very basic level trading a significant proportion of their labour for what they perceive to be unlimited freedom of choice, and an authentic experience that stands in contrast to the dull grind and predictable monotony of the working week. However, freedom of choice within any consumer market is impossible on any meaningful level. Consequently, when individuals who are so invested within the NTE use the drinking spaces and alcoholic beverages in line with fashion and style to gain these experiences, we could argue that they are misperceiving their activities and situation. However, this reading of events fails to take into account an important factor that has become apparent through the course of interviews with some participants. There is in fact a level of awareness that all is not as it seems. For example, Evan feels he has discovered an inherent cynicism at work within the NTE:

> Of course [a city centre bar] is a business, and they will do everything they can to screw you out of as much money as they can. That's why Irene and Paul [owners of the bar] buy you a drink now and then – they know that you are going to come back every time you go into town, and bring your friends and tell your friends what a great bar it is and all that. So they give you a free shot, which costs them next to nothing, and you pay for their holiday in New York.

Evan, like a number of other consumers within the NTE is showing an awareness that bounded hedonism offers little in terms of authentic experience. Many consumers appear to be aware that the alcohol products on sale are vastly overpriced and that the 'experience' of drinking in town is little more than a marketised device to part a fool and his money, and yet time and time again these individuals *act* as if there is so much more concealed within. The fact that this act continues despite people being aware of its falsity confirms to us that the ideology of liberal capitalism is hard at work, and is located within the actions of people themselves, rather than, as one might suspect, the knowledge of people. So while their knowledge or belief may locate them as savvy consumers, their actions contradict this to an almost baffling degree. The fact that people continue to participate within the NTE, despite their knowledge that an authentic experience is not on offer is a rather neat example of what Žižek (1989) refers to as *fetishistic disavowal*. Here, Žižek is moving beyond the description of ideology as false consciousness – 'they do not know it, but they are doing it', toward the assertion that 'they know very well what they are doing, but still, they are doing it' (ibid: 24–25). As such, Evan's cynical conformity reaffirms, rather than threatens the prevailing social order and the supremacy of the NTE.

Desire and fantasy on the night-time high street

> I've had a few crap nights out recently actually. Nothing specific –
> like I haven't gone out and had the shit kicked out of me or anything
> like that – just kind of nights where you wish you hadn't bothered ...
> just bumping into people you would rather avoid, spending loads of
> money, that sort of thing. (Kevin, 32)

A common response among respondents was that a bad night out was
no rare occurrence. A bad night out could consist of any number of
factors, such as falling out with partners or friends, the loss of personal property or other tangible effects. However, much of the time,
the quality of the night out could be boiled down to a base economic
formula – the amount of pleasure gained as relating to the economic
expenditure. Although on the surface simplistic, respondents found it
hard to verbalise just what it is that accounts for a 'good night out'.
When talking about positive past experiences they often found it hard
to focus on one definitive evening, rather selecting amusing anecdotes
and snapshots from an experiential smorgasbord of different nights
out, creating a fantasmic 'selective composite' night out. However,
the key element in the individual return to participate in the NTE is
the belief and hope that *this* weekend will provide everything that it
promises, a belief that is enabled by this process of *hedonic amnesia*.
Indeed, the 'fantasy' of a great night out provides the route to and
object of desire. Fantasy in this context is not concerned with fantasy
to replace the lack of an object, but rather a blueprint or formula
for the ultimate in (bounded) hedonistic pleasure. As far as desire is
concerned, it is too simplistic to conceive of desire as simply a question of 'What do I want?' Instead, the question can be rephrased as it
relates to the *others'* desire – 'What do *others* want from me? What am
I to them?' This element of intersubjectivity is described by Freud in
his report of his young daughter fantasising about eating a strawberry
cake – rather than the simple hallucinatory satisfaction of a desire
(that she wanted a cake, was unable to get one and so fantasised about
eating a cake as a substitute), the girl noticed while she was eating a
cake that her parents gained a great level of satisfaction from seeing
her seemingly enjoy it. Consequently, the fantasy of eating a cake is
really an element of identity formation, of playing the part that satis-
fies her parents and subsequently ensures her position as the object of
their desire (see Žižek, 1997). It is not hard to conceive of a continual
presence within the NTE as a strawberry cake fantasy designed to

bolster an identity that will satisfy the perceived desire of the friendship group.

So what makes a good night out? The answer to this question lies in the attraction of the NTE that we have discussed earlier in this piece of work – namely the partial removal of the traditional guardians of social and moral order as well as the removal of issues of responsibility and 'normal' comportment which contribute to the attraction of the NTE discussed above. The very element of drunkenness too has become synonymous with the NTE, and a commodity within its own right. The relaxing of social and legal sanctions within the realm of the NTE provide a potential for excitement, danger, hedonism through behaviour that is acceptable and normalised within this sphere, but subject to control and sanction at all other times. It is these factors that maintain the allure for consumers within the NTE, so we must assume that they are elements that form the basis for a good night out. The culture of drunkenness that pervades the UK is the key to enjoyment for a number of these respondents. Within this culture, alcohol is perceived to lower psychological inhibitions, conferring upon its users the quality of gregariousness, giving them confidence and access to a mind-set of visceral humour that is denied to the temperate. From out of this culture emerge exploits and tales that become mythologised and recounted to willing audiences time and time again.

Tales of extreme drunkenness and determined drinking are common within the literature on the NTE (see Winlow and Hall, 2006; Briggs, 2013), and committed older participants do not prove an exception. Nights out tend to consist of rapid, frequent consumption – perhaps seated in the early part of the evening, but soon evolving into standing room only, moving to bars with little in the way of seating and much in the way of loud music. These conditions prohibit conversations with more than one person at a time, while even that conversation has to be carried out in close proximity, hand cupped to try and steal an advantage over the music. Rounds of drinks are bought within fairly small groups of four or five, but a number of side-rounds appear to spring up as shots – sometimes tequila, but often, in line with the neophilic proclivity of the consumer – of whatever drink is most heavily marketed and pushed by the bar staff. At the time of writing, Jägermeister appeared to be a popular choice. This is a bitter-sweet dark shot, syrupy in consistency and consumed either neat or as part of a Jägerbomb. Here, the shot glass containing the Jägermeister is dropped into a half-pint glass containing Red Bull, a sweet, lurid, caffeinated soft drink, prompting a ritualistic raising of the glass, and swift consumption of the mixture. Mike, a 37-year-old office worker has amassed a collection of glassware around the area of bar against which he is leaning:

> Ah yes, Jägerbomb. Well I don't really like drinking pints anyway, I drink Jack and Coke, but a Jäger is just something a bit different isn't it? I mean, I suppose it must give you a bit of a buzz with the Red Bull in it, but it's more of a gimmick, just a bit of a laugh. Also, if someone buys me a drink I tend to just get a Jäger, because it's only £2.50, whereas a Jack and Coke is more like taking the piss as it's nearly a fiver, but pints [which most people seem to be drinking] are only £2.75.

The consumption of vast quantities of alcohol was a fundamental part of the night out for the drinkers that form the core of this study, a fact that brought with it a number of problems from the point of view of the researcher, but more pertinently indicating that the arena of alcohol-related hedonism becomes an awkward place to negotiate while sober. This has ramifications for individuals within friend groups who do not want to drink alcohol on a particular evening, and also for pregnant women who may find themselves slipping out of participation within the NTE if they choose to not drink alcohol throughout their pregnancy. Individuals who are expressing a desire to avoid excessive consumption of alcohol on a particular evening may find themselves subject to a number of different strategies designed to goad them into alcohol consumption, from having drinks forcibly pushed into their hands therefore obliging them to join a round, to general abuse with regard to their sexual orientation. As far as excuses went, having to work in the morning was not seen as sufficient, while pleas of financial issues would be greeted with offers of short-term loans. Having to drive a car that evening was often met with a suggestion to pick the car up in the morning, but was a more successful excuse, and one that I, in my role as researcher, used on a number of occasions through the course of my research to deal with those times when I felt one more night of serious research might in fact do me some serious lasting physical damage. Others, such as Rob in the example below, invoke medical 'sick-notes' in order to extricate themselves from a perceived duty to go out:

> I'm just going to have a quiet one this weekend. I've been to the dentist and my wisdom teeth are playing up. Last time this happened my cheeks puffed up like this, so I'll probably be on antibiotics, so

I won't be able to drink so I think I'll just stay in and save myself for [an upcoming trip to London] (Rob, 33).

Even in this response, Rob finds it necessary to qualify his decision to stay in, backing it up with medical evidence and the reassurance that he will be out in force in due course.

For female respondents that were or had recently been pregnant, a kind of self-imposed quarantine seemed to be in force. Charlotte is 36 years old and has come into her local pub on a Sunday afternoon with some friends and her three-week-old baby girl:

This is actually the first time I have been out since Maddie [the baby] was born. I mean, the last few months you just don't want to, like you are just so massive and fat and knackered all the time. You just don't want people seeing you like that anyway. But before that I just couldn't be bothered. I'd come out for a glass of wine every now and again, but it just isn't as much fun when everyone else is getting pissed and you are just sitting there sober.

Hannah is 38 and currently pregnant with her third child. Her partner and father of her unborn child is employed at a bar in the city centre:

Well this is my third time [of being pregnant] so I'm pretty used to it all now actually, I come into the pub once a week to see Bobby, and I'll have a couple of halves of lager and just laugh at everyone as they all get pissed. I go out if there is something different going on like a birthday or [a friend's] band is playing or something.

There are a number of social conventions that get built up within a cohort over the course of creating a drinking biography. Topics of conversation appear to largely avoid the subject of paid employment, again relating to the fact that this is very much viewed as time outside of the normative monotony of the workplace, although of course, the belief that these 'fun' times represent time external to capital is little more than fetishistic disavowal, as described above. There are, however, exceptions to this unwritten rule. During the course of my ethnographic research, I found myself in the company of groups of people who while working in different locations, would meet up for a 'quick drink' after work in the city centre. Within this setting, it appeared much more acceptable to discuss matters pertaining to the working week, as well as more mundane matters around housing, money and other tales of woe.

Within these surroundings the pub appeared to be performing a much more traditional role of providing a buffer point for these workers to unwind, and air issues that may be troubling them in a vernacular and perhaps cynical way that may be unsuitable somewhere else.

The role of the carnival has been touched upon in previous chapters, but its role here, in terms of providing desire with an outlet, a symbolic space in which it can be released without the usual prohibitions, indicates that it is a concept worthy of revisitation and expansion. The carnival, as Bakhtin describes, serves as an interruption to the daily routine and offers brief, exhilarating intervals between interminable instalments of dull monotony. Within this 'time out of time' (Presdee, 2000), the oppressive hierarchy of values is temporarily reversed, the most arduous elements of reality are frozen, while the kind of conduct that is prohibited and sanctioned as shameful within the 'normal' scheme of things is practised with flourish and abandon. The importance of periodic carnival lies in its pivotal function within social renewal. The toil and mundanity of the everyday is tempered by the fact that the subject continually keeps one eye looking forward to the carnival and the hedonistic prospects contained therein. For some of my respondents, it appears that the longer they have to wait for carnival to come round again – that is to say the longer the gaps between bouts of (albeit commodified) excess, the higher the level of enthusiasm with which they submerge themselves within the hedonism proffered by the NTE. Evan alluded to this within one of our interviews. The fact that his profession as a firefighter was organised around a shift system of four days on followed by four days off meant that a conventional weekend off would occur only once a month:

> It's just not the same when your 'weekend' is on a Monday and Tuesday – it's really hard to get anyone to come out for more than one or two pints, and I'm there wanting to really get stuck in. All it means though is that when my days off are actually properly over the weekend is that I'll get ringing round everyone, making sure they are going out, no excuses!

For Evan, the injunction to enjoy is denied for three weekends out of four due to external limitations put into place by the nature of shift work. This, when viewed in conjunction with his earlier indications of choosing not to socialise with his work colleagues whenever possible appears to contribute heavily to the realisation of his desire to partake in hedonistic excess when the opportunity arises. Like Charlie in the

Roald Dahl book *Charlie and the Chocolate Factory*, whose access to pleasure through the medium of chocolate is severely limited, Evan confines himself to only nibbling the corner, making the rare occasion of gorging himself all the more pleasurable in comparison. But why is it that Evan (and a number of other respondents within this study) fails to be satisfied with deferring gratification? It is simply not enough to take at face value the stock answers that respondents gave when asked why they continue to participate so wholeheartedly in the NTE of 'enjoyment', 'to have a laugh' and so on. Perhaps part of the answer may be contained within the work of René Girard, whose work on 'mimetic desire' suggests that the individual's desire (remaining active within the NTE) does not originate from within themselves, but is rather derived from other people's possessions, desires and actions. Girard argues that people learn to want what they want from other people, and make judgements about an object or activity's value through assessing to what degree other people want it – the process of mimesis. Whereas in Girardian thought, the process of mimetic desire as it pertains to commodities results in unrest, violence and the creation of a scapegoat mechanism (see Girard, 1986; Vaughan, 2002), the outcome for the denizens of the NTE with its aggressive culture of global consumerism is likely to be an exacerbated struggle with the traditional roles of adulthood in which individualist, hedonistic values are likely to win out.

The glimpses into the life-worlds of maturing participants within the NTE outlined above confirm suspicions that it is too simplistic to distil the motivations and desires involved in the practice of hedonistic consumption on the night-time high street into the pursuit of mere enjoyment. Similarly, to suggest that committed and sustained participation in the NTE is indicative of these individuals 'kicking against the system' (Cohen, 1955) in protest at their entrapment by global capitalism, caught within a string of unsatisfying and unstable employment is to imbue them with a greater degree of reflexivity than was evident through both ethnographic observation and interview data collection. Rather, they appear swept into the NTE by the current of global capitalism that they have been subject to throughout their lives. The NTE provides a stage upon which they can earn social capital, ostentatiously and conspicuously consume goods, through the adoption and appreciation of styles of dress, music and chosen location for alcohol consumption. Indeed, Veblen (1994: 47) describes this process, noting that:

> In order to avoid stultification, he must also cultivate his tastes for it now becomes incumbent on him to discriminate with some nicety

between the noble and ignoble in consumable goods. He becomes a connoisseur in creditable viands of various degrees and merit, in manly beverages and trinkets, in seemly apparel. Closely related to the requirement that the gentleman must consume freely and of the right kind of goods, there is the requirement that he must know how to consume them in a seemly manner.

Bringing this chapter to a close, it appears that the desire expressed by these consumers to 'be themselves' within the NTE is perhaps a little misleading. We are not witnessing individuals in possession of a series of alternate personalities, although it is fair to assume that the facets of their selves that are unleashed throughout the course of hedonistic excess are more intrinsically satisfying, offering as they do fleeting glimpses of the Real. The relaxing of social sanctions throughout the evening and the suggestion of carnival are strong pull factors against the ties of a more traditional sense of adulthood. While we have touched upon elements of identity within the NTE in the above discussion, it is a complex area and needs to be discussed in greater detail over the coming pages.

8
Identity

Alcohol has been identified by a number of authors as an important factor in the marking of social identity (Hollands, 1995; McCreanor et al., 2005). This is a revelation which has not escaped the producers of alcoholic beverages and their associate marketing departments – consider, for example, the recent advertising campaign from Carling, who suggest that 'you know who your mates are', or the sparkling wine that is advertised through the assertion that 'Lambrini girls wanna have fun'. This appears to be a global strategy, with consumers in the US being told that 'Great times are brewing', while Canadians are urged to proclaim 'I Am Canadian' (see also McCreanor et al., 2005).

This chapter examines a number of processes related to creating and maintaining identities within and by means of participation within the night-time economy (NTE). Under global capitalism, it is no longer possible to maintain one single identity; one constantly has to re-evaluate and adjust in line with circumstances and the features of Liquid Society (see Bauman, 2005). Indeed:

> [This] trend is self-sustained and self-invigorating. The focusing on self-reform self-perpetuates; so does the lack of interest in, and the inattention to, the aspects of common life that resist a complete and immediate translation into the current targets of self-reform. (Bauman, 2005: 11)

A recurrent theme for the respondents within this piece of work appears to be a necessity to wear identities like masks, presenting alternative facets of identity for in the workplace, among family and while participating in the NTE. This process was identified as early as the beginning of the twentieth century by Simmel (1903) who postulated that the effect of the urban metropolitan existence was to require individuals to bend their subjective personality at the whim of objective and impersonal social factors, producing conditions in which new excesses and excessive actions are required in order to define individuality. This presentation of a range of identities appears to result in an almost regimented compartmentalisation of the various aspects of their lives and consequently identities. This was a phenomenon that Winlow and Hall (2006: 29) duly noted in their study of younger consumers of night-time leisure, where they identified a commonality among respondents:

> Indicating that ... life can be clearly compartmentalised and judged according to the instrumental utility and potential benefits and pleasures of each sphere. Work is unimportant aside from the fact that it provides the funds for other, more pleasurable spheres of personal activity ... work identity is a product of [a] daily determination to get through each shift as an isolated individual as quickly and with as little difficulty as possible, without forming close personal ties.

Similarly, a common thread appears to be a creation of identity that is based on a complex dynamic of 'otherness'. Certain bars and clubs are denigrated as 'being full of kids' or playing 'shite music', creating a distinction based on a sense of 'coolness' that is associated with their particular cohorts and venues they frequent. The complexity surrounding the issue of 'coolness' has been addressed in earlier chapters, where I leaned toward a definition that portrays 'coolness' as somewhat of a faux sense of community based upon an abstract symbolism, with distinct links in terms of its origin to the interests of capital (see Heath and Potter, 2006). This is linked closely to further identification with certain bars, drinks and behaviours, with a high level of criticism levelled at revellers who are unable to hold their drink, like different music or drink certain brands of alcoholic beverage.

Identity and lifestyle are two closely related terms used throughout this chapter. Although they have been used and discussed elsewhere in this piece of work, it is worth reiterating to some extent the way in which the terms will be used over the following pages. The purpose of this chapter is to analyse the ways in which respondents discuss the venues they choose to drink in, the drinks they consume and the company they keep. The focus will remain on to what extent the continued participation within the NTE of these older drinkers can be said to be integral to their construction and maintenance of identity, and in what way they can be seen to be 'choosing' distinctive lifestyles. The concept of lifestyle here is closely aligned with the work of Pierre Bourdieu (1984). Within his description, Bourdieu (1984: 73) posits lifestyle as 'a system of classified and classifying practices' and a 'unitary set of distinctive preferences which express the same expressive intention in the logic of each of the symbolic sub-spaces, furniture, clothing, language or body hexis'. The concept of lifestyle is also indelibly bound up with the concept of distinction – lifestyles are relational, connected to other lifestyles through complex and intertwined processes of distinction, whereby certain combinations of attributes and activities are imbued with value, quality or correctness, while others are discarded to the gutter of the cultural highway. Here, it is beneficial to view the work of Baudrillard (1993) alongside Bourdieu (1984) in order to fully understand the processes that form the experiences of individuals within the NTE. Respondents talked of being 'left out of the loop' if they failed to persistently partake in 'nights on the town', although it would be too simplistic to reduce an explanation of this to the effects of peer pressure. At the heart of the anxiety surrounding failure to indulge in the commodified hedonism of the night-time high street lies the principle of symbolic exchange (Bourdieu, 1984; Baudrillard, 1993), and it is the failure to competently exchange action within the NTE which can result in a crisis of the self, as they are rendered inconsequential in the eyes of the Big Other (see Žižek, 2002).

It is through these processes, and the palpable fear surrounding the looming possibility of cultural obsolescence that we gain a sense of how the ways and means with which we forge an understanding of our biographies and self-identity are bound up with the faux creativity and acquisitive characteristics of consumer culture. The battle for symbolic and cultural capital is hard fought, and the reoriented superego engenders a sense of shame upon encountering any missed opportunity to garner this imaginary capital, against a background of the insecurity and anxiety that is characteristic of consumer culture (Hall et al., 2008).

Where have you been tonight?

Throughout the course of the research, it became clear that particular bars bear significance to regular consumers in terms of bestowing them with, or providing a platform from which to display or earn social capital. Steve, whom we met in the last chapter, frequents a bar in the centre of town that is owned by a husband-and-wife entrepreneurial partnership. Steve has established a relationship with the owners, enjoyed a brief romantic interlude with the bar manageress, and has developed a vast network of friends and acquaintances through the time he has invested into maintaining an active presence on the premises.

> I was in the Spotted Pig the other night and bumped into Jacquie and Vince [the owners of the bar that he regularly drinks in]. We stayed there pretty late and just got pissed ... it was a good laugh. I've been going to [their bar] quite a lot recently actually, the downstairs bit has really got too townie and chavvy, but upstairs is better, and they usually play decent music unless there is a party on or something and they bring their own DJ. Plus I hardly ever have to spend any money there, [the owners] are always buying me drinks.

I suggest that the benevolence that he receives is far removed from what could reasonably be considered friendship, a comment that appears to rile Steve, who responds somewhat indignantly. This indignation appears rooted in distaste associated with the fact that elements of symbolic exchange that are interpreted and reproduced as indicative of friendship and affection may in fact be more ideologically related to the profit motive:

> No, I think they actually like me, I mean they know that I don't really like a lot of the people that have been drinking in there recently and I think it is full of cranks, and they have been asking my advice on how to stop that sort of crowd coming in. I'm pretty sure the staff [like me] as well, I'm actually pretty good friends with a few of them, who also give me loads of free drinks when I go in. You can't say that's all part of some kind of business model can you? They don't give a fuck about the business, and they don't gain anything from giving me free drinks, do they?

The relationship that Steve outlines in the above excerpt is strongly indicative of the departure from the strong friendship and community bonds that were extant in the modern era, and the move toward the 'pure' relationship outlined by Giddens (1991) and Bauman (2005). Bauman suggests:

> Relationships are fast turning into the major and an apparently inexhaustible source of ambivalence and anxiety. In a liquid, fast-flowing and unpredictable setting, we need firm and reliable ties of

friendship and mutual trust more than ever before. Friends, after all, are people we can count on for understanding and a helping hand in case we stumble and fall ... On the other hand, though, those self-same liquid and fast-flowing settings privilege those who can travel light; if changed circumstances require a fast move and starting anew from scratch, long-term commitments and any ties difficult to untie may prove to be a cumbersome burden – ballast that needs to be thrown overboard. (2005: 108)

Steve's relationship with the owners of the bar he frequents would appear to be a friendship that represents the definitions provided by both Giddens and Bauman exemplified above. The primary indicator of friendship seems to be based on his receiving of free drinks, although the more cynical may suggest that this also acts as some sort of loyalty incentive to ensure that Steve returns to the bar week in, week out and brings his extensive group of friends and acquaintances. As far as I know, they have little contact outside of the context of the NTE, and the occasions they meet are rarely organised, as they are based on a loosely coincidental grounding. Consequently, the owners of the bar benefit from their friendship through the custom that he brings through the door, while Steve receives social capital that is invaluable to him in regard to maintenance of his identity within the NTE.

As the above shows, within the heart of the NTE, friendships tend to be largely instrumental, selective and fragile, due to the fact that they are based in little more than the utilisation and style of cultural objects and a mutual knowledge of comportment within the circuits of consumer signification (see Winlow and Hall, 2006, 2009). Indeed, instrumentalism within contemporary friendship groups may be the result of the fact that:

Bonds are no longer rooted in anything more profound than the instrumental display of lifestyle symbolism and cultural competence in the circuits of consumer signification, and at the moment this seems to be having a corrosive effect on the more enduring friendships upon which the communal, social and political solidarities of the past were built. (Winlow and Hall, 2006: 53)

Further to the concept of instrumentalism that appears to be established within the social and working lives of many of the individuals recorded here, the majority of individuals participating within this piece of work are seen to be actively treating identity creation as a vocation, facilitated by the seemingly vast array of tools at their disposal. Commercialised leisure, not least in the guise of the pubs and bars of the night-time high street is ground into everyday life and laden with meaning, becoming central to their sense of self and belonging. As the bodies they inhabit begin to age, and a realisation dawns that other aspects of their life are underdeveloped, we can discern a complex array of anxiety, tension and pressure that hold a mirror up to the fragmented, individualised and increasingly isolated aspects of society. These identities that come to the fore within the context of the NTE have been years in the making, and for some are too valuable to be simply discarded as the pressures and expectations of the culture in which they were primarily socialised attempt to drag them away from the pull of commodified hedonistic excess.

An exemplar of commitment to participation within the NTE in the face of more traditional commitments is Billy, a 40-year-old joiner. He has a reputation for being on the drinking 'scene' for as long as anyone can remember, and I had been told a number of anecdotes relating to his hedonistic exploits before our meeting, stories that abounded with sexual conquest, superhuman absorption of hard drugs and sometimes violent interludes. I recognise him as a character I have seen at last orders in a number of pubs in town, still dressed in his work attire, from his high-visibility vest down to his dusty and dirty steel toecapped boots, holding court at the bar in the booming tones of the drunk and self-important. I am sitting at the bar with him on this occasion, at around 7 p.m. on a Saturday night, and he sits opposite me, grey-haired, overweight and in a checked shirt with jeans and smart-casual trainers, smelling strongly of freshly applied aftershave. Our conversation revolves largely around the 'good old days' before marriage, kids and a weighty mortgage that he procured at the height of the housing market. He is married with two children under eight years old, and explains to me that having a 'massive night out' and 'getting fucked up' stops him getting depressed about financial pressures that are facing him as a consequence of the current financial crisis, particularly as it relates to the construction industry. He finds himself torn between supplementing his income through selling illegal drugs, and adhering to the remnants of the traditional Symbolic Order that continues to demand that he adopt the role of father and family man:

> Just as an example right, take hanging doors. In a big block of flats, offices or whatever, a few months ago I would have been looking at

40 quid a door, I'd turn up and the door would be right there, someone would have put it right there for you and all I had to do was hang it and move on to the next one. I was making serious money, and that's just hanging doors, you know. These days, the guys that would set up the doors for you, just go and get them and lean them up against the wall or whatever, their jobs are gone, and I get paid 10 quid for hanging a door. I have to go and get the door myself, lug it up a load of stairs or whatever then hang it, before moving on to the next one. Seriously, some weeks, I am making about 175 quid. It's hardly fucking worth it. I could be making fucking loads more than that selling gear [cocaine]. I could make a phone call now, and go and get some really good shit, cut it and shift it all tonight, make about 300 quid, but I really don't want to do that. I've got the girls, and I just want to graft and do things right by them. It's fucking tempting though I'm telling you. Especially when you think about the fact that I am coming out and dropping 30 or 40 quid tonight on getting pissed.

The problems experienced by Billy are mirrored by Wilson, a 32-year-old scaffolder. Although habitually participating in the Vertical Drinking Establishments of the city high street on a Friday and Saturday night, his recent redundancy has resulted in a challenge to a number of aspects of his life, having to move back into his family home, and scraping together enough money to get down the pub and see his friends:

I got made redundant a few months ago by [the scaffolding company], so me and the bird have actually had to move back into my parents' house for a while, just until things sort themselves out a bit. I'm actually just getting a bit of money together by doing odd jobs around the estate, handyman sort of stuff, gardening, whatever really, just enough coin so I can get out on a weekend, keep me in beer and that. I'm thinking of setting up as self-employed and doing it properly, get a van or something.

These identities that have been so long in the making are bound up within the specificities of the NTE. The processes of identity formation that were synonymous with the prevalence of Fordism are all but inaccessible to the vast majority of individuals, and so consequently they must look to the commodified hedonism of the NTE to source alternative or supplementary means of creating identities. As Malbon states with regard to the 'clubbing' scene of the 1990s, the appeal of the NTE lies in its ability to offer experiential consuming, defined as:

> A form of consuming in which nothing material is 'taken home', but which can nevertheless produce important memories, emotional experiences and imaginaries (remembered imaginations) that can be sources of identification and thus of vitality. (1999: 183)

All in all, Malbon is suggesting that stories and experiences gleaned from participation in the NTE are integral to forging a sense of identity. Little wonder then, that for these individuals, there is little incentive to adopt a more staid, traditional version of adulthood when we consider the importance placed upon (never mind the financial and temporal investments that have been sunk into) identity creation within the NTE.

Youth and vitality

Key components of global consumer capitalism are (as explored in more detail earlier) the marketification of youth and vitality. Legislation put in place to deter underage drinking, stating that models used in alcoholic drink advertisements should not look under the age of 25 perhaps have the effect of normalising participation within the NTE for older drinkers, while these adverts portray drinkers as having fun, laughing and pursuing youthful activities. Whether or not alcohol marketing has any effect, intended or otherwise is an oft-debated point, but it is certainly symptomatic of the wider issue of the elongation of the period of youth within the life course, as explored earlier within this piece of work.

Consequently, the role of alcohol consumption within the NTE is as an activity imbued with symbolism in terms of youth. Standing around in bars drinking and laughing has become a symbol of youthful vigour. Contact with members of the opposite sex, the underlying potential for conflict, ribaldry and liminal pleasure has become more than just a habit for these individuals; it is a portal to the vestiges of youth, a time before mortgages, rent, unfulfilling employment, and uncertain futures. Charlotte, Katherine and Andrea are all in their mid thirties, and work in an administrative capacity for one of the larger employers in the city. We meet in a bar, and perch on tall wooden stools that are grouped around taller tables, the design of which is to compel drinkers to stand around when the bar is busy, rather than waste space through allowing seating in the more traditional pub-environment style. Today is a

Monday evening, however, and the bar is quiet, with many of the after-work crowd thinning out and we shift uncomfortably on the unforgiving furniture, our drinks at chest height in front of us. The furniture is clearly designed for the crowd, with little in the way of comfort to offer the solitary drinker. Charlotte exemplifies the link between youthful connotations of participation within the NTE and their importance to identity creation as she recounts an anecdote that refers to her partner, Kevin who is 32 and works in the same office complex as Charlotte and her friends:

> Yeah, well we've started calling him the Peter Pan of getting pissed, because he just isn't going to grow up [laughs]. He just drinks and gets fucked up like he is still 18, and I don't know if he could handle it better then – actually I don't think he could – but these days he just gets so arseholed he's just all over the place. Friday night he comes in, he's been out drinking straight from work and I can hear him dropping his keys, missing the keyhole, scratching all round the door and all that. I was going to go and open the door, but I thought I would just see how he got on on his own, I was just sitting on the sofa pissing meself at him. Well anyway he gets in eventually, and he is just falling all over the place, banging into the table. And I'm all like this [adopting a stance like a goalkeeper faced with a penalty-kick] just trying to protect [their three-month old daughter] in case he falls on her. He wants to wake her up and pick her up and that, but I'm like 'that's not really a good idea Kev'. Eventually, he just stumbled up the stairs to bed and passed out with all his clothes on [laughs], it's like I don't know which is the kid sometimes.

Charlotte's description of the events and the light-hearted delivery of the tale is indicative of a number of important factors. It is indicative of a process of individualisation, as Charlotte expresses no dissatisfaction with her partner's decision to go out and get drunk without her on a regular basis. Indeed we learn that this grace is returned on the remaining night of the weekend, when Kevin will compliantly stay at home with the baby and the dog, in an epitome of domesticity, while his partner is 'out with the girls' embracing the noise and excitement of the NTE. Kevin's desire to remain an active consumer within the NTE is no surprise to Charlotte. They met through mutual friends within the drinking arena, and would regularly be drunk either together or individually throughout the week as well as at weekends.

The above account has the potential to be viewed (or told) in a completely different light. With mortgage repayments, and expenses commensurate with the birth of a new baby, Charlotte could understandably be concerned at the fact that Kevin is spending upwards of £60 on getting drunk, splashing money around on rounds of drinks and Sambuca. There are also the moral implications with regard to health. Some sectors of society may insist that Kevin has a moral responsibility to look after his own health now he is a father, a lifestyle choice that would perhaps preclude him from drinking pints of lager and downing several shots of Jägermeister within minutes of clocking off work, a conundrum indicative of the paradox of the injunction to enjoy (see Žižek, 2006) discussed earlier. Additionally, the fact that Charlotte has to steer her partner away from their child as he returns home in a condition that could potentially prove hazardous to the infant could be viewed as a cause for concern, especially in the light of high profile cases of child neglect in the media. However, this incident, and indeed the wider behaviour of which it is symptomatic is positively rather than negatively sanctioned. While Charlotte may have some private concerns, it would not be suitable to air them within the habitus of commodified hedonism within which these individuals reside. Instead, the story is used to convey the youth and vitality that still exists within them, the momentary escape from the remnants of the traditional Symbolic Order, in spite of the constraints put upon them by post-Fordist employment and traditional markers of adulthood such as property ownership and parenthood. Indeed it is true to say that Kevin has integrated alcohol consumption and getting pissed into the very core of his identity – certainly within the habitus of the NTE, but with results that have on occasion bled through into his working life as well. Charlotte takes up the story:

> I think the worst time was when he was coming back from [a music festival]. He had booked the Friday off work so could get down on the bus, but they didn't let him have the Monday off, so Kevin thought 'Fuck it, I'm going anyway'. Well, the bus was getting back into Vikton on Monday morning about 8, so Kevin just got it to drop him off in town and he went straight to work. Bearing in mind he had been [drinking] all weekend and doing pills and God knows what else, he was in a right state for going to work. Well he turned up, then his boss took one look at him and drove him home. I mean actually drove him home. How bad do you have to be for that to happen? Getting sent home from work is one thing, but your boss

actually driving you to your door because you are in no fit state to work is just ridiculous [laughs]. I think he ended up getting a proper bollocking for that.

The above anecdote is interesting as it creates a picture of how commitment to hedonism and liminal or carnivalesque behaviour is condoned or perhaps even celebrated within the cohort of dedicated participants within the NTE. Charlotte's story provides an example of the transference of an event – being sent home from work due to being unable to fulfil his role as an employee adequately due to excess drug and alcohol use following a weekend of hedonistic excess – that in a number of ways could be viewed as irresponsible or damaging to future job prospects into a form of social capital that is used to bolster his standing within the cohort of participants within the NTE. His clear prioritisation of leisure over workplace commitments highlights the pull being exerted on individuals to remain active and visible within the arena of commodified leisure within the NTE. The culture of narcissism (see Lasch, 1979) is alive and well in Kevin and a number of his contemporaries that feature throughout this work as the injunction to enjoy is followed to the letter. Were Kevin to cancel his entire weekend plans due to the minor inconvenience of having to be present at work on the Monday, he would be denying the injunction to enjoy.

Alcohol as an identity marker

We have touched upon the fact that the concept of alcohol and spaces in which alcohol is consumed have the potential to play an important part in the signalling of identity and place in the world (see McCreanor et al., 2005). For drinkers of a generation ago, frequenting the local pub under the umbrella of Fordism, the market-share dominance of beer was threatened only by the steady growth in consumption of wine (see Burnett, 1999), and consumers would likely stick to one brand. Alcoholic beverages were largely anonymous once they crossed over the bar due to the choice of glassware being limited to straight or dimple glass for pints or half pints of beer, lager or mild. Wine choice would be by colour only, while the range of spirits and mixers was rudimentary and uncomplicated, with cocktails unheard of in many parts, while in others designated the stuff of Del Boy, the aspiring yuppie character from the British sitcom *Only Fools and Horses*.

Alcohol advertising on screen and in print has necessarily moved away from portraying such themes as sexual success and 'avoiding appeal to the young, links with youth culture or sex, tough or daring behaviour and irresponsible serving or drinking of alcohol' (Advertising Standards Authority, n.d.) toward portrayal of older drinkers, and in the case of the majority of advertisements, an encouragement of male viewers to make cognitive links with mischief, friendship and camaraderie. As much of the literature discussed earlier in this piece of work suggests that marketing and branding can be important factors in the identity creation of younger consumers, the observations that I have made with regard to the elongation of youth within the life course and the entrapment of older consumers within the cultural maelstrom of consumer capitalism suggests that alcohol advertising and branding is likely to assume some significance for the individuals studied here. To deny that advertising and branding has any effect on older consumers, to confer upon them the ability or desire to turn away from the experiential and commodified forms of leisure and the meanings that can be attributed to it is to totally underestimate the pull being exerted on these consumers by the powerful injunction to enjoy. Indeed, these individuals are in a position of some precarity, as they negotiate the utilisation of culturally significant objects in order to try and assuage desire and the quest for the real that is perpetuated by the fluid nature of the market. Having said that, there is little evidence to suggest that participants within this study were influenced to any great degree in the choice of alcohol they consumed in terms of brand as a direct result of assimilation through exposure to advertising – certainly not to the same degree that Hastings et al. (2005) suggest that younger drinkers are influenced by marketing processes surrounding the sale of alcohol. Older drinkers tend to offer different explanations of drink choice for different occasions, providing an opportunity to bestow an element of distinction on their choice, while economic factors also played a part in the choice of beverage for some:

> We'll often share a bottle of wine between the three of us after work. It's just sociable isn't it? Plus it's a lot cheaper than buying three double vodka and Cokes or whatever ... a bottle of wine is only nine quid here, whereas for doubles, you are looking at about a fiver ... there's just something quite relaxing about chilling out with a bottle of wine after work. (Andrea, 33)

I join Andrea and her friends; they are indeed sharing a bottle of white wine, ordered from the specials board, and advertised by means of glossy signs in the window and on folded card on the bar. It is a Blossom

Hill Chardonnay, and would be unlikely be eulogised on the hand-drawn chalkboards found in an up-market wine bar. Two of the girls mask its astringency with lemonade, poured from a half-pint glass that the two of them appear to be sharing. The choice of wine, and indeed the variety of wine is made from a largely economical standpoint, and also from a perspective that allows them to drink a considerable amount of alcohol. They are buying in a round system, so the shared bottle eliminates price disparity between drink types, while they are guaranteed to drink a bottle of wine each if they all buy a round. This has the effect of legitimating the decision to pursue hedonistic pleasure on a work night, as for the sake of equality, they have to each purchase a bottle. By this time their commitment to pleasure is complete, and the night is likely to continue further afield.

For Paul, a 37-year-old IT systems consultant, his choice of drink is linked strongly with the maintenance of his identity within the NTE. He is sitting at the table outside the bar at which we have conducted a number of meetings, drinking Jack Daniel's and Coke in a glass branded with the JD logo. He explains to me that he sometimes thinks he is in the bar more often than in his own house:

> All the staff know that this is my drink. And this is my glass, there are only one or two of these glasses behind the bar, the rest are just those normal spirit glasses ... they know to serve it in this glass with a couple of ice cubes and up to the top with Coke ... Jane [the landlady] was saying to Ian at the bar, she said 'This is like [Paul's] second home here,' and I said 'No Jane, it's more like my first'. I mean, I come here most nights, even if I just stop for a drink, and I sometimes come here on lunch break as well for me lunch or a coffee or whatever. I see people here more often than I do my own family.

Under the societal conditions of late modernity that have been discussed earlier within this piece of work, individuals need to look toward personal resources in order to cement their identity and functional place (see Morch, 1997). Within the realm of contemporary youth studies, the transition from youth to adulthood is seen as both normative and desirable, consisting of a number of 'identity gains' such as:

> securing memberships in adult communities, and being recognised as a fully responsible adult who is accorded certain forms of respect and privilege. A partial list of identity capital acquisitions thus includes: consolidating advanced forms of personal development,

making progress in one's life project, resolving adult-identity issues, securing community memberships that provide identity validation and social capital, and attaining an occupation that is personally and financially gratifying. (Cote, 2002: 120)

There appears to be little evidence in support of the normative view outlined above in terms of the individuals studied throughout the course of this piece of work. For the majority of respondents, a clear and complete transition into adulthood was not a desirable goal; instead the aim was to bring to the fore of their selves those facets of identity that held strong connotations with youth, in many cases shying away from the more traditional concept and reality of adulthood.

Cultural competence

Maintaining and creating an identity within the NTE is not a case of simply going out and getting drunk; through the course of the research undertaken within these pages, it became clear that there exists a complex litany of cultural and social processes that provide the individual with the means to display cultural competence within the arena of night-time leisure. The meanings of specific forms of consumer items are in a state of perpetual fluidity, just as the young adults that form the basis of a number of other studies are under a consistent pressure to display competency and a firm grip on cultural signifiers enabling them to 'stick out' at the same time as 'fitting in'. This process involves distancing themselves from certain cultural items, while being seen to overtly embrace others. Paul:

> I get told what to wear all week at work, so they can fuck off if they think they are going to tell me what I can wear at the weekend too. To be honest if a bar is not going to let me in if I'm not wearing a shirt or the right shoes or any of that shit, then it's not the kind of place that I want to go anyway. Those bars are always full of wankers anyway ... the music is shit, the atmosphere is shit and you just wouldn't get me in there.

Julian, however, disagrees:

> You've got to make an effort when you go out haven't you, wear an expensive shirt, nice shoes and all that, otherwise what's the point? Birds aren't going to look twice at you if you haven't got all that

stuff, especially the younger ones (laughs) ... you've got to go to the right bars as well. Like, the birds in Yates's on a Sunday night [when a cheap drinks promotion takes place] are going to be pretty rough, but they are dirty slags which is a right laugh, and most of the other blokes in there are right gyppos so you are always going to be in with a chance ... I don't really care about the music, it's all about having a laugh, as long as we can get up on the dance floor and dance with some dirty women (laughs) ... We avoid the 'old men's' pubs and the scuzzy dives where all the emo chicks go, and stay this side of town.

While the two opinions seem to emanate from polar opposite sides of some sort of cultural divide, there is in fact little significant difference between them. Both prioritise elements of the NTE that are vital to securing their identity within the night-time arena. While Paul is dismissive of bars that play 'chart' music that is not imbued with the cultural significance of other forms of music in his eyes, Julian is more concerned with engaging women and displaying an opulent lifestyle. Both men have a widely similar aim in utilising aspects of the NTE to bolster and maintain their projected identity in an instrumental fashion. While they may believe that they are moulding and creating unique cultural forms and identities in order to distance and differentiate themselves from the crowd, the mechanism and tools with which they can present their identity are limited to those offered to them by consumerism and the assorted culture industries. The respondents whose opinions are documented throughout the pages of this piece of work were rendered indignant at the suggestion that they were victims of manipulation by the culture industry and more specifically the NTE, believing that the power to create identity lay within the utilisation and reworking of cultural signs. However, the reality is that no matter how strong the desire, to create independent identity through participation within the NTE results not in the creation of a free, self-malleable persona, and not in the capture of a significant degree of control in terms of the identity they present, but only in fleeting glimpses of these as if through a zoetrope, giving no more than an illusion of individuality in identity and utilisation of consumer items.

9
Work, Friendship and the NTE

Working to live

For some of the respondents within this study, participation within the night-time economy (NTE) appears to be kept rigorously separate from their working lives. For some, like Evan whom we met previously, this is due to a process of distinction (see Bourdieu, 1984) whereby he did not possess the same patterns of attributes and activities as did the majority of his work colleagues, while his habitus was afforded little value. Other respondents are wary when it comes to mixing their out-of-the-workplace identity with their workplace identity. Sally, a 32-year-old health professional is one such example:

> I have to be pretty careful about being seen out and about in town. It didn't matter so much when I was working in [a neighbouring city] but now there is a chance that I might see someone out in town when I'm drunk who I have been treating earlier or, say, the son or daughter of a patient. It looks totally unprofessional, but they could also put in a complaint to my supervisor, and I could probably get struck off.

The desire to maintain a professional façade within working hours was repeated by a number of respondents, the majority of whom tended to be in jobs that had a much more designated 'career path' or were in positions of more responsibility. Again, we hear from Paul:

> I'm completely different at work than I am in here [indicates the environs of the bar in which the interview is being conducted]. I have to be really. I'm in charge of a lot of the IT infrastructure for

payroll, employment and stuff for the council, with access to a lot of important shit. Statistics, data management, all that. When I started, the whole lot was in a right mess, so my job expanded into sorting it all out rather than just maintaining it. I'm now going into meetings with guys earning 60 to a hundred thousand and telling them how it is, giving them a bollocking because I haven't got the software I need to be able to do my job properly and so on. That's why I have to wear this suit and tie, and why I'm not out getting pissed all week. I mean, I'll be out for a few after work, but I'm not staying out 'til all hours of the night, mainly because of my job. I can't go into meetings and all that hung over and reeking of Jack [Daniel's]. They [colleagues and bosses] haven't got a clue that I'll be spending all weekend in here off my tits. Having said that, this week I have had to shift a couple of meetings around to the back end of the week because this weekend turned out being quite heavy. I had a massive argument on the Saturday, after having been out all night, in which I apparently called my girlfriend a cunt down the phone, and we weren't speaking at all on Sunday, so I just carried on drinking. 2 for 1 cocktails got really messy and I ended up staying out 'til about 1 a.m., and having to go into work on Monday.

Paul's general approach to his work and his participation within the NTE may be viewed as relatively responsible, as most of the time he succeeds in pursuing what may be termed a more rationalised hedonism. Even the example he gives of having to shift meetings around in order to disguise his hangover indicates a desire to separate the more responsible aspects of his job from the rigours of the weekend's hedonism. However, the lure of the NTE is still strong, and Paul finds it hard to be the first to leave on a night out, regardless of the fact that more traditional pressures of work and responsibility lurk just around the corner – the fear of cultural inconsequentiality as a result of not being there until the bitter end is strong enough to take precedence over other aspects of his life.

Other respondents tended to display a much more casual attitude toward comportment at work and while socialising with work colleagues. Ellie has worked in administrative positions since leaving school at 18. A large core of lower-level employees in her current place of work are sourced from recruiting agencies, before being offered more permanent contracts after a period of around a year, a fairly common practice among large corporations who may have a fast turnover among positions of this nature.

At work, in the office it is kind of divided up into groups of people who like to go out for a drink after work or whatever, and those who don't. It's mostly an age thing I would say, but there are a couple of guys who are in their 50s who love to come out for a couple. They tend to go home in time for their tea, whereas the rest of us might stay out later. Sometimes it turns into a proper session, staying out 'til last orders, which means going into work the next day with a hangover [laughs]. The pissheads in the office are the ones who are sitting with their sunglasses on like this [uses her hand to prop up and shield one side of her head] and trying not to be noticed, just drinking Lucozade.

There is no vocational quality to Ellie's employment. In David Graeber's uncompromising terminology it might be referred to as a 'bullshit job', a job with no immediately apparent *purpose*, and one in which the worker's absence could quite easily go unnoticed. Up until the last few months it has been transitory and unstable, arranged through agencies or on temporary contracts. Membership of a union, or contributing to a pension are not priorities, due to the fact that they divert money from the circuits of consumption. Her present contract allows for flexitime, a valuable tool in terms of late starts that go hand in hand with weekday drinking sessions. Her accommodation too is in a state of fluidity; she appears to move house on average every 18 months, returning to her family home for months at a time while she saves for a deposit and pays down debt. However, as soon as she can she moves back into rented accommodation in the city centre. The desire to be close to the action is tangible, and the fear that failure to partake in the continual flow of cultural symbolism orbiting the NTE will result in cultural anonymity and render her inconsequential maintains her in a perpetual state of anxiety.

For Ellie, work is clearly there to be 'endured, not enjoyed' (Winlow and Hall, 2006). All her employment to date has been concerned with garnering enough money to pay rent, buy clothes and maintain an active presence within the NTE. Shortfalls in any of these areas are temporarily shored up by payday loans, which can provide the financial backing for another night out, addressing the need for immediate gratification:

Towards the end of the month I tend to be pretty skint, and if there's something going on, if people are going out or whatever, I do get a payday loan. It's no problem, because I know that I'm going to pay it back in a few days, so I don't let it get out of control, and a hundred quid loan only ends up costing me the price of a couple of rounds.

In Ellie's eyes, she is being responsible, although the thought of deferring her enjoyment appears to be out of the question. However, later conversation indicates that her debt has mounted up in the past, to the extent that she has had to move back into her parents' home in order to try to pay it off.

A continual theme with regard to paid employment tended to be that its importance was greatly diminished in favour of participating within the consumer market, and the activities and cultural signifiers that this entails. A sense of ambivalence toward work was a key theme, while some were acutely aware of the fragility of their employment status, especially in the light of the fears surrounding recession that were ubiquitous at the time of writing. Sam provides a concise example of this:

I'm waiting to see what happens with my job at the moment. The contractors that I work for are looking like they are going to lose the contract, which means that my job will go, and I will be made redundant. There is a chance that [the main company] will take me on either in the same job I am doing now, or somewhere else – I've spoken to my boss about that and he's a decent bloke so we will see ... I'm not bothered though really, if I get made redundant, I might just go travelling for a while or something, blow all my redundancy, sublet and just fuck off to America and travel around for a few months.

To what extent Sam's nonchalance is affected is hard to discern, but his words accentuate the acknowledgement among individuals within this age bracket of the isolating and transitory nature of employment. Under these conditions, the friendships, group identity and shared biographies that made no little contribution to the culture of the working class fail to materialise, and rather than the camaraderie of the shop floor or production line that we would have witnessed within the traditional working environments (see Willis, 1977; Roberts, 1981), the working lives of many respondents reflect isolation, and a feeling of disjointedness or alienation. As such, work is viewed in purely instrumental terms, lacking a larger symbolic meaning or significance.

Gavin, a divorced father to 5-year-old Stephanie, is aged 33, and works in an office-based job with a largely administrative job description. Although he has risen up to the position of team leader within his job, his real passion is music – Gavin plays the drums in a couple of local covers bands and dreams of an alternative form of income, neatly summing up the instrumentality that looms within so many modes of employment:

> If it wasn't for the fact that I have Stephanie, I wouldn't be working [here] ... I would have jacked it in ages ago ... I dunno, I'd do something to do with drumming, be in a band, teach drums at the college or something. I certainly wouldn't be devoting my life to those fuckers.

Friendship and the NTE

Within Andrea's group of friends there appears to be a level of mistrust of romantic diversions, and she seems quick to label partners of friends as 'controlling', which masks an underlying fear that regular participation within the bounded liminality of the night-time drinking circuits is limited by time and the end of freedom looms on the horizon.

> I know it sounds harsh, but I was actually well pleased when Verity [a friend] broke up with her boyfriend; he was just so fucking controlling, telling her when she could go out, and always coming out with us ... since [breaking up with her boyfriend] we have all seen her loads more often, and she seems a lot happier, just seems to be more herself, you know? You can't beat being single to be honest. I haven't been in a proper relationship for about six years now. Obviously I've had a couple of *things*, you know, but I look around at my friends, who are always having some sort of issue or another to do with relationships, and I think 'What's the point?'

Andrea's assertion that her friend is happier out of the relationship and has returned to being 'herself' does not appear to be based on a concern for her wellbeing, but rather acts as an example of the instrumental nature of friendship as discussed earlier in this chapter. Andrea's friendship with Verity is based upon her value as someone to go out with, and her perspective is heavily skewed by the value that is placed by Andrea upon Verity's continued presence within the NTE. In the case of a number of respondents, the construction and maintenance of friendship serves to act as a springboard from which the individual is able to make an impact through the achievement of distinction and significance within the culture of night-time leisure. As the act of 'going out' remains high on the list of important activities within the life-worlds of these individuals, friends are seen as tools to facilitate the entry into the circuits of consumption, and as such are often 'activated' through the means of communications technology as the weekend draws near. The following quote from Dan illustrates this:

> I still text and call people about going out, but I tend to use Facebook quite a bit now actually, just to let people know you are thinking of going to a particular night or something. You can set up events on the page itself and invite people to it if you want, but that's really only worth doing if you are actually having a party or something. You can just let people know through the status thing [a feature on Facebook] if you are going out, which is easier than phoning round everybody.

While Katherine describes her contact with her friends:

> There are loads of people who I don't really speak to during the week at all, they aren't the kind of friends that I would call up just for a chat or expect to call me or whatever, but we are still part of the same group [of friends] and will see them at the weekend. I mean, I think that's how you know your proper mates isn't it? You want to just call them up or email them during the week for no real reason, invite them over to your house, that sort of thing.

There appears at first glance to be a distinction between friendships that operate solely within the arena of the NTE, and more substantial friendships that are bolstered by phone calls, texts and meetings outside of the cultural melee of the pubs and bars. However, it is hard to escape the nagging feeling that the vast majority of these relationships exist purely on the basis of their use-value. While the phone calls, text messages and emails through the week appear to imbue the friendship with added-value in the eyes of the individual concerned, the driver appears to be ultimately the ability to cash in on the opportunity to mould and maintain functional identity. In real terms, a brief text or email hurriedly composed during working hours equates with little more than a wave from across the street or a brief exchange of pleasantries. Giddens encapsulates the 'floating' nature of these relationships:

> In contrast to close personal ties in traditional contexts, the pure relationship is not anchored in external conditions of social or economic life – it is, as it were, free floating ... Modern friendship

exposes this characteristic even more clearly. A friend is defined specifically as someone with whom one has a relationship unprompted by anything other than the rewards that that relationship provides. One might become friendly with a colleague, and the proximity at work or shared interest generated by work might help instigate the friendship, but it *is* a friendship only in so far as the connection with the other person is valued for its own sake ... Friendship attachments may have their own inertial elements, but in practice as well as in principle, one only stays a friend for another in so far as sentiments of closeness are reciprocated for their own sake. (1991: 89–90)

It is clear that the issue of identity creation and maintenance is more complicated than the straightforward view of increased and unfettered agentic control thanks to the elements of consumerism that allow us to mould and remould our identities at will (see Giddens, 1991; Elliot and Lemert, 2006). A number of commentators firmly believe that the loss of centralised structures such as local communities and traditional, stable families has led to instability being celebrated. Here, there is an assertion of the plural self, 'free to shift, redefine and to re-emerge' into new spaces, in a glorious revolution that represents resistance against the fixed, orthodox practices (Mort, 1989). In fact the picture that is emerging is one of a complex implementation of structure through which only a severely truncated and essentially impotent form of agency is able to manoeuvre. The limitations and boundaries imposed on agentic control are based in the reorientation of the superego and the compulsion to enjoy through consumption. The market within the NTE and the myriad cultural objects that orbit it are undoubtedly offering a wide choice to the consumer, but the choice is limited to a toolbox, the contents of which enable individuals to display their cultural competence within a limited number of outlets.

The NTE provides the perfect arena within which to create and maintain identity within the postmodern milieu of hyperreality (Baudrillard, 1983) whereby identity becomes indelibly linked to concepts of excess and glittering, commodified images which become more important than reality. Simulations abound, and almost everything appears to be a copy or a parody of something else, whether music, fashion or the perception of 'different' drinking spaces that abound within the NTE. At the centre of Baudrillard's concept of the hyperreal lies seduction, and indeed many of the drinking spaces that occupy the high street circuits can be viewed as fantasyscapes along the same lines as Disneyland or McDonald's, with their levels of vividity, intensity and reality that far exceed what might be otherwise typically thought of as being 'real'. For Baudrillard, images and simulations have the power to intoxicate, compel and seduce to such an extent that the self is crushed, as branded experiences hold more power and seductiveness over the consumer than its reality or constituent parts. Indeed, the following passage could be taken to describe the faux liminality and hedonism expounded by the clubs and bars of any town or city in the UK, as much as it is used to describe Disneyland:

> All of Los Angeles and the America surrounding it are no longer real, but of the order of the hyperreal and of simulation ... it is meant to be an infantile world, in order to make us believe that the adults are elsewhere, in the 'real' world and to conceal the fact that real childishness is everywhere, particularly amongst those adults who go here to act the child in order to foster illusions as to their real childishness. (Baudrillard, 1983: 204–205)

The respondents whose life-worlds have been explored within the pages of this piece of work have invested heavily, obeying the siren call of commodified hedonism. Many have spent beyond their means, relying on the glut of consumer credit at their disposal (see Stiglitz, 2010), squandering financial resources on alcohol, drugs and the trappings of night-time leisure, eschewing the early morning starts and overtime at work which may have propelled them up the traditionalist career ladder, putting their health at risk through excessive alcohol consumption over a prolonged number of years, taking recreational drugs, engaging in potentially risky sexual encounters; purchasing experiences and a licence to access situations of liminality and carnival, on which stories perpetuate and 'legends' are born. They spend time and money on making sure they are wearing the right clothes, listening to the right music, purchasing the latest iPhone to create and maintain identities that clearly hold much more importance and relevance to themselves than their 'other' identities that are ensconced within the remnants of a more traditional symbolic order and workaday monotony. It seems unlikely that these individuals are going to relinquish these identities easily; that they are going to resist the tide of consumer culture and abandon the predominant stage of the NTE. It is unlikely that they will suddenly 'grow out of it' and unproblematically adopt a traditional version of adulthood consisting of the accumulation of material wealth and property. Friendships and relationships have been born and nurtured within the hothouse NTE. Are they really going to survive out in the cold? The following chapter will explore these issues and attempt to envisage what the future holds for these individuals.

10
Conclusions and Futures

The purpose of this piece of work has been to describe and illuminate the lived experiences of committed adult consumers within the alcohol-based night-time economy (NTE) under global capitalism. The participants within these pages are in the unique position of having experienced first hand the inexorable rise of conspicuous consumption in a number of guises, not least the meteoric rise of what has become known as the NTE. Set against the backdrop of epochal changes in the economic and social fabric of society, the experiences and anxieties of these individuals are symptomatic if not representative of the challenges facing a generation. The atomisation and insecurity that is fast becoming synonymous with contemporary adulthood brings to bear a question mark over economic and social development in a future that is made all the more uncertain by the pressures born out of economic recession as we head into the second decade of the new millennium.

It would be naive to claim that the data reported over these pages is representative in terms that would satisfy any but the most sympathetic social statistician, but neither do I believe that it is unrepresentative of the experiences of an increasing proportion of adults who are regular consumers within the NTE within the UK. Indeed the respondents whose stories and experiences are captured within the pages of this book may be described as the very picture of middle England, and I can state with some confidence that others who occupy similar positions within these subsections of society are undergoing very similar experiences across the country and beyond. In addition, this work serves to build upon the findings and concerns outlined by a number of authors writing in the field of youth transitions. The challenges identified as facing young people at this time, such as 'social division, atomisation, instrumentalism, hostile interpersonal competition and anxiety'

(Winlow and Hall, 2006: 181) appear not to be somehow jettisoned from the life-worlds of individuals as they progress through their life course, but instead are exacerbated and ground in, to an extent where they represent the normal order of things rather than a transitional stage. The majority of respondents that feature within this piece of work are socially included and educated, yet are clearly suffering serious and perhaps terminal forms of insecurity and indeterminacy, which may be felt in exacerbated forms throughout the postmodern milieu. Many of these individuals have experienced disjointed childhoods and adolescence and are now experiencing similar levels of fragmentation in adulthood, and it is important to recognise that the absence of social stability, concrete and parallel identities, and shared biographies is in itself a 'structural' element of life under global capitalism.

For the vast majority of the participants within this study, all of whom are aged between 32 and 40, there exists a dichotomy between where they hoped they might end up and where they are headed. Growing up, they shared the same fantasies of children today – the desire for wealth and fame, garnering envy from the 'ordinary person' and entering the cultural and economic elite. These life goals were never really likely, but their existence and allure was unavoidable due to the ways in which fantasies are inextricably bound to the interests of capital. Growing up in the 1980s, they were subjected (if only by proxy) to many of the socioeconomic changes that were buffeting the country at this time. Under New Labour, they were sold the myth of freedom and mobility through education and the dissolving of class boundaries. The promise of education was unbounded achievement and limitless access to the circuits of consumer culture and conspicuous consumption – the emerging benchmark against which success or lack thereof was measured. This neoliberal ideology promised that the removal of state politics and the development of a free market economy would deliver new levels of prosperity and liberation to all who bought into it (see Harvey, 1989). A subsequent programme of privatisation and decentralisation replaced the manufacturing industries and much of the cohesive societal framework that was intrinsically bound up with them.

The promise of education under a New Labour government was that in return for three years of deferred gratification and studying, long-term rewards would be reached through the existence of graduate training schemes and fast-track employment routes. Many of my respondents, however, found themselves ill-equipped for the world of work, as they found themselves slipping into underpaid, unsatisfying and unstable service sector employment. Severed from the communitas and deep bonds experienced by past generations (see Willis, 1977), solace was to be found in the consumer markets that offered tangible and experiential goods on the one hand, but threatened cultural insignificance with the other. Under these conditions, work soon becomes something to be suffered or endured, a necessary evil whose sole purpose is to gain means of access to the consumer markets. A burgeoning leisure industry has of course realised that individuals require arenas in which to show their cultural worth, knowledge and competency – and what better place than the NTE? In the face of this, pension plans fall by the wayside, becoming a member of a union appears archaic and irrelevant within a workplace that is at once both isolating and transitory. Consequently the majority of respondents within this piece of work tended to view work identities as 'other' to their 'real' personalities, and imbued them with little significance.

I have stressed in earlier pages that the magnitude of socioeconomic changes that have swept the nation over the past three decades cannot be underestimated. The relatively clearly defined class system, despite its flaws and shortcomings around the areas of inequality, tension and injustice (Cohen, 1972) was overall imbued with a profound stability that enabled those within it to navigate their own biographies within the context of relatively comprehensible and stable cultural processes and meanings that served to strengthen a sense of identity within a clearly defined social group. It is important to avoid a 'rose tinted' view of this bygone era, for the simple fact that it offers a profoundly unworldly interpretation of human history that can be at best misleading. It is a mistake to presume that all human history is progressive, moving on a path toward ever-greater levels of civilisation and 'freedom'. Nor should we treat history as a simple, linear progression, rather than an infinitely complex process.

While it is impossible to deny that we have witnessed increased gender equality, increased levels of tolerance and many other indicators of the 'progress' lauded by the liberal left, this can in no way be treated as evidence that everything has improved for the majority of people. Increased levels of insecurity and social competition are clearly exhibited in everyday culture, a process that if it cannot be altered could surely be made all the more bearable by a return to the meaningful collective that characterised community values under modernity (see Willis, 1977). This bygone age consisted of mechanics of social stability that resulted in bounded forms of social engagement and a variety of ascetic practices bore within it a series of figurations – social interdependencies that Elias (1994) saw as vital to modernity's 'civilising process', setting the context for the 'sociogenesis and psychogenesis of the sorts of sensibilities and *habitus* that are required for reasonably convivial ways of life' (Winlow and Hall, 2006). A combination of internalised and perpetual cultural forces were responsible for ushering the vast majority of individuals toward a very defined and definite end-goal of adulthood, that was delineated by a number of cultural markers. The disintegration of stabilised industrial economy heralded the rise of service and leisure sector employment, and under neoliberalist ideology, traditional working life trajectories began to fragment as unstable, insecure modes of employment became the norm. This process of fragmentation of traditional communities and the associated diversion of biographies that has accompanied it is seen by a number of commentators (Currie, 1997; Taylor, 1999) as responsible for the dissolution of community values, local obligation, shared resistances and mutual interests. In its place has evolved a culture of individualism that has both created and maintained a society largely based on self-interest, a development that has contributed to the atomisation of the individual, with work becoming alienating and self-identity becoming indelibly bound up with status attainment and consumerism (Winlow and Hall, 2013).

Identity: instrumentality, consumption and individualism

Identity has formed a key theme of the preceding pages of this book. The rise of global consumer capitalism has allowed individuals to mould and switch identities in a way far more complicated than intimated by Simmel (1921) at the turn of the last century, albeit through the purchase of available identities that are made available through consumer circuits. While affirmative postmodernists have certainly overemphasised the degree to which identity is limitlessly malleable, I have attempted to tread a more cautious path, claiming that identities themselves are constrained by the structures of global capitalism and the post-Fordist ideology so prevalent in Western society. However, individuals are able to 'foreground' different facets of their identity in order to achieve a degree of tessellation with their social surroundings. While some respondents may report differently, the truth is that while different behaviours are observable in different social settings, this is not to say that they are 'themselves' in some social settings and acting in others. This was very much evident for individuals who consider themselves to be two different people within their work and leisure lives, but also within incidents where the psychotropic properties of alcohol are used as a trigger to bring to the fore fun-loving, youthful and vibrant aspects of individual identity.

It is clear that individual identity can no longer be so firmly grounded in class position or through involvement within a particular mode of production, and as such identity as a form of social differentiation is bound up with the signs and symbols that constitute the 'identity value' imbued in the consumption of goods and services (see Warde, 1992). Indeed Veblen (1994: 85) indicated that the consumption of goods could act as a primary indicator of social status, commenting that 'no class of society, not even the most abject poor, forgoes all customary conspicuous consumption. The last items of this category of consumption are not given up except under the stress of direct necessity'.

Veblen is of course stating that no matter how poor, the consumption practices of all social groupings are imbued with identity value as well as simply use-value. Nowhere is this more ably demonstrated than within the NTE. As the data showed, the drinking spaces that form the high street circuits are utilised by individuals as ways in which to project their identity and social competence. The global media helps provide a string of imagos, while the 'designer outlet' villages and the designer labels without the 'designer' element of exclusivity make them appear all the more achievable, while the jouissance encountered while striving so hard and falling so short of the illusive 'great night out' ensures the desire to maintain identity within the NTE remains and endures. The cocktail lounges and champagne bars of the city centre provide an arena in which to play out fantasmic identity work wherein the traditional dimensions of life that include political, social, emotional and ethical elements fade into the background to become as indecipherable as the chatter from across the bar. Identity work in this context of course does not relate to behaviour and self as presentation only – it consists of a deeply symbolic internalised form of representation, whereby the individual is 'acting' for themselves as much as for an audience. The evidence presented throughout the course of this piece of work indicates that the individual who maintains a presence within the NTE and who appears unfettered by the inconveniences of paid employment or familial responsibility is perhaps best described as an infantile narcissist, compelled to perpetually consume, not merely in terms of imbibing alcohol, but ensuring that they are wearing the right clothes, listening to the right music and displaying competence within the consumer society. It is this level of narcissism that allows them to so effectively judge other participants within the NTE, using pejorative terminology to describe those who choose to drink in (what are deemed to be) more commercial, soulless venues than the ones that those who are blessed with such distinction and good taste tend to frequent.

The night-time high street achieves its meaning through what Bourdieu (1984) would term an anti-Kantian aesthetic (or popular culture), whereby the preference is clearly for immediate gratification, hedonistic pleasure and overindulgence. For all the differences in meaning that are extrapolated by the consumer in the different drinking spaces, the various forms of alcohol consumption and musical preference, homogeneity looms large over the whole experience, and it is only in the subtle and choreographed nuances that some form of albeit meaningless distinction may be found. Evidence contained within earlier pages highlights the ways in which the processes of 'othering' and differentiation are carried out, as respondents essentially constitute self and group through mechanisms such as defining that which the other is, and therefore that which the self is not. The old means of recognition and distinction that functioned under modernity were taken apart by the onslaught of consumer capitalism, and permanently destabilised. Hall et al. (2008) correctly state that consumption is not simply about freedom, but a defence against humiliation and a response to the need to both fit in and stand out. When respondents were eager to show how their identity was linked to participation within the NTE, there was often a strong sense of desire to avoid the levels of humiliation that befall those who use symbols provided by consumer culture in an alternative or variant way.

The role of employment within the lives of these adult consumers of the NTE was a recurrent theme. Although for some it represented little more than an endurance test in order to be able to acquire the means through which to access circuits of consumption, there was a realisation among others that they were leaving behind them a status of unfettered youthfulness, and there existed an awareness of the traditional markers by which a successful transition into adulthood is recognised. An instrumental relationship with paid employment certainly appears to be the norm for the majority of respondents. From my limited sample I would tentatively suggest that there may be evidence that there does exist a gender differential with regard to attitudes toward work. The women interviewed show a level of concern relating to 'adulthood' that centred around more traditionally feminine roles of becoming a mother and 'settling down' or getting married, perhaps as a result of the heightened level of societal pressure on women to get married and raise a family, a hangover from the modernist era that shows only the slightest degree of abatement. The males that showed concern, however, tended to cite issues such as a lack of a pension as a potential concern as well as a failure to be on the housing ladder, again issues that can be traced back to patriarchal gender roles, whereby the male is perceived as the breadwinner and social status is derived from such issues as owning property. On the whole though, work identities were often framed as less important than leisure identities, and the facets of themselves that were presented when out drinking in the pubs and clubs of the city centre certainly seemed to be those that were viewed with a greater degree of veracity.

The NTE provides us with a lens through which to view the state of friendship and relationships within the context of contemporary adulthood. Again, the data reveals a high degree of instrumentality in the ways in which these individuals approach the majority of their friendships and indeed intimate relationships. Friendship bonds appear often fairly tenuous or to use Bauman's terminology 'liquid' compared to more traditional friendships that would be bound in a sense of communitas. The shared experiences under modernist conditions, however, would have consisted of a much higher degree of gravitas; key moments in each other's closely parallel lives; births, deaths, the perils of capitalist exploitation, all of which would have served to forge tight bonds (see Willis, 1977). The data presented in preceding pages illuminates a much weaker valency among friendship groups, as we witness bonds that exist only within the context of the NTE. Friendship is to some extent distilled down to its use-value, as respondents talk of 'dropping off the radar' in instances when they fail to maintain a presence in the bars and pubs of the city centre. Geographic mobility as well as events such as childbirth, illness or enthusiasm for a new relationship can all sever the bonds of friendship, if only temporarily, as for many individuals a case of 'out of sight, out of mind' ensues. And just as one might speak of the dead, an individual may easily be cast into the realms of sentiment, where conversations begin with 'Do you remember when so and so ...'

Such is the way of the infantile narcissist, who pervades the NTE, and who invests much more meaning in the bacchanalian culture than they have bestowed upon themselves by others. Which brings us to perhaps the most dour aspect of reflections on the findings from this piece of research. Perhaps we are witnessing first hand the birth of the Nietzschean 'last man' (1994), an individual to whom culture, politics, art, love, and altruism hold neither appeal nor interest, and competence in the use of consumer signs and symbols has become the primary way in which a person is judged. For those identified within this piece of work, there is evidence of the last vestiges of a culture within which they have been socialised, the remnants of traditional values and conceptions of adulthood that were ingrained through parental means, a faint ghost of which remains within those participants who speak of desiring a good job, family, a house, who express intention or have already got a pension payment scheme in place. These traces are likely to fade further with ensuing generations, as thymotic spirit, Plato's term for the part of the soul that encompasses pride, becomes more entrenched within the pursuit of identities that form the core of consumerism's system of signs, and the existential terror of being left behind, unnoticed and insignificant further drives the desire to own, display and experience consumerism. Consumer capital will find fewer and fewer obstacles in the way of its hijacking of the maturation process in the individual, reorienting the superego with consummate ease. With children currently bombarded from dawn until dusk with imagos that personify the commodification of everyday life (see Barber, 2007), the Symbolic Order cannot help but be destabilised, with as yet untold consequences recognised by increased levels of interminably unsatiated desire.

Intimate relationships have, for a number of these respondents, been formed within the bounded liminal spaces of the NTE, and just as contemporary friendship bonds are increasingly anchored in little more than tenuous shared experiences within the NTE, allegiance to various football clubs or a shared interest in music, fashion or style, it is likely that many intimate relationships formed in the NTE will not have the core similarities that exist below the surface of a false sense of communitas provided by the existence of the NTE. These couples are likely to return to the pubs and bars either separately as an exemplar of instrumentality toward intimate relationships, or together, in an attempt to capture the 'Real' ostensibly and tantalisingly offered by the NTE, but experiencing increasing levels of frustration and dissatisfaction as their desire fails to be realised.

Many of the respondents whose experiences form the basis of this piece of work find themselves embroiled in an existential and psychosocial tug-of-war that history will reveal as peculiar to this particular generational cohort, as future generations find that the maturation process is hijacked by consumer capitalism at an increasingly earlier stage, and with increasingly less resistance. While of course their individual circumstances vary greatly with some respondents being brought up in a traditional nuclear family, and others raised by single parent families, or even grandparents, the social milieu in which the majority of socialisation took place was one over which the shadow of asceticism loomed. This process has allowed the maturation process to include a partial integration with the Symbolic Order, and while as has been argued above there has been a reorientation of the superego, associating feelings of guilt with denial of the injunction to enjoy (Žižek, 2002), remnants of an epoch in which they were primarily socialised remain. The imprints left by the imposition of generational values have tethered them to some extent in a unique pre-postmodern era although simultaneously exposed to the temptation and hedonistic insistence of global capitalism, afraid of the cultural inconsequence that beckons should they refuse or fail to enter the circuits of consumption. This conflict exists and is manifested as the source of much anxiety for the adult individual who forms the basis for this piece of work. While getting a job is viewed as a necessary route into the hedonistic playgrounds and stages of identity provided by global developments in the nature of liberal capitalism, more traditional markers of adulthood such as marriage and property ownership are held as desirable goals – a hangover from a less consumer-driven economy base. However, failure to achieve these more traditional goals is for many individuals inevitable, as by falling short they are offered the opportunity to couch their failings as 'individuality', 'maintenance of independence' and other language more suited to the 'liquid life' identified by Bauman (2005). We can perhaps borrow from the psychological approach to explaining sociopathy (see, for example, Millon, 2004) and describe socialisation as parasitic, with an emphasis on individualisation, benefiting at the expense of others and characterised by low levels of motivation and deferment of gratification. The birth of the infantile narcissist that has been permitted through the intervention of consumer capitalism within the individual's maturation process allows the individual to view their version of adulthood, be it childless, single, married and so on, as the right way of being adult, a version of rationality that can be viewed as being almost entirely driven by the consumer economy.

Epilogue

Leaving the field

At the conclusion of almost three years of research in the field, participant observation, recorded and unrecorded interviews, I found myself in somewhat of a curious position. No longer having to immerse myself in the hyperreal of the night-time economy (NTE), my need to maintain contact with the disparate groups of individuals who have provided the data on which this piece of work is based evaporated. Although through the previous months and years I had in effect spread my time between several social groups in order to gain a level of insight into their lives and relationship with the NTE that would simply not have been possible through any other means of data collection, I now found myself choosing my own forays into the NTE with opportunities for data collection featuring much further down my list of priorities. I no longer had the need to follow Julian and his friends into 80s theme bars and a string of Vertical Drinking Establishments that had on a number of occasions I am sure, contributed to a severe headache the following morning. I no longer had to trail Kevin into rough pubs to make illicit drug deals in the dingiest corner of a dingier pub. In short, there came a point when I had no need to see any of these individuals any more. I had collected sufficient data as far as I was concerned to furnish the reader with insight into the lives of contemporary adults and their relationship with the NTE. However, I live and work in a relatively small city, and as a consequence I have met several respondents on occasion since. It is testament to the instrumentalism behind their concept of friendship that no ill feeling resulted from the fact that I had seemingly 'dropped off the radar' and our chance meetings seemed genuinely affable, while the fact that we had not seen each other for a few months was put down to being 'one of those things' and had been given little consideration. While my own narcissistic self may have taken a little offence at my absence in their social circles going all but unnoticed, it served to confirm my suspicion that as a friendship on the periphery, their focus was always going to be in the immediate present and on continued instantaneous gratification proffered by the circuits of consumer culture and the NTE. One such meeting occurred with Kevin in a crowded pub, where we both happened to meet at the bar during half time of a football match being screened on a multitude of flat-screened TVs. After a brief discussion revolving around the woeful defensive display being offered by Manchester City, I learned that he was undergoing some relationship problems, and his girlfriend had been staying at her mother's house for a few days with their young baby. He admitted that he expected she would 'calm down after few days' and things would be back to normal. Although he was unspecific about the cause of the argument, simply explaining that she was 'fucking mental', it does not seem unreasonable to suspect that this is in fact (in part) a realisation of an issue raised in earlier chapters, that of individualisation and atomisation within relationships. Kevin's relationship with his partner is one that was created within the hyperreality of the NTE, with the consequence that the comparatively monotonous and staid elements of contemporary adulthood bring to the fore points of contention and conflict. From my brief conversation with Kevin, it appears that the birth of their child has impacted more heavily upon the relationship and his ability to maintain a presence within the NTE than he had anticipated. His frequent trips to watch Manchester City, an event that is likely to involve copious amounts of alcohol throughout the course of a long day, compounded by his desire to be out on the town every weekend appears to represent an incongruity with the role of devoted househusband that he feels that he is unfairly being asked to perform. His partner (according to Kevin) appears to have adopted a much more traditional view with regard to gender roles and appears to have made it clear that his money, time and attention could be better spent at home than 'getting pissed with his mates and wasting money'. This situation is likely to be one replicated the length of the country as partnerships and relationships that seemed to work so efficiently and to mutual benefit under the neon glow of the seductive NTE become strained. Put simply, the realities of having to perform adult roles encompasses a shift in consumption patterns and associated desire from the arena of the NTE to that of the home, garden and driveway, a shift bolstered by the plethora of home improvement magazines, television programmes and advertisements that choke the media channels.

Other respondents that have featured in this piece of work still maintain a strong presence within my social group. A shared interest in football, music and a shared biography that may be viewed as more parallel than most within our 'liquid' society (Bauman, 2005) has led to me maintaining a social relationship with Rob. He tells me that he is coming under increasing pressure to start a family with his girlfriend, and appears to have shelved any plans to return to university to do a master's degree. Despite maintaining that he is not ready to have kids yet, he appears resigned to the fact that it is likely to happen sooner rather than later, and admits to having 'spunked in her' on a couple of occasions, just 'to stop her going on at him about it'. In both language and demeanour, Rob is anxious to display disinterest and nonchalance, resistance to coercion and reluctance in his choices to move toward a more traditional stage of adulthood. Neither has he moved any closer to getting on the housing ladder. The trade-off he made at university in terms of pursuing hedonistic pleasure rather than academic prowess has left him with a qualification that is poorly suited to his current job, and the likelihood of a promotion that would enable him to access a radically better mortgage deal in order to actually realise his newly located focus of consumer acquisition appears slight. The NTE still retains its allure for Rob, and the route to having a good time through the excessive consumption of alcohol appears to be as well-trodden as it ever was. He appears eager to have a good time as often as possible, and continues to link 'a good time' to the consumption of alcohol and recreational drugs, despondent at the belief that these heady days are numbered. He does not appear optimistic about the future, and bemoans the fact that he is never going to have the money or the personal freedom to travel or study further. And indeed the future for Rob, as it does for countless others under the shadow of global capitalism appears to hold little more than a journey consisting of material acquisition interspersed with sporadic episodes of hedonistic excess. While their nature may alter over the years, it is hard to envisage a point at which Rob's life will not be dominated by a parade of imagos that promise advancement toward the cultural and economic elite, a string of fantasies that are inextricably linked to the interests of capital.

Paul too is an individual whom I have met on a number of occasions since the conclusion of my research, although I do not seek him out as I did while requiring his direct input and the access he provided to a number of bars and the people who frequented them. When we met him in an earlier chapter, he was employed within the IT department of council offices. I happened to come across him sitting at the bar of his favourite establishment, idly reading a newspaper and with the space in front of him bereft of any alcoholic beverage. I am killing time on a weekday afternoon, so decide to have a pint, and offer to buy him one. I am surprised to hear him ask for a cup of coffee rather than his staple of 'Jack' (Daniel's) and Coke. He explains that he has an interview with a temp agency coming up later in the afternoon. Further questioning reveals that he has been unemployed for eight weeks, having been made redundant from his job. He has moved back into his parents' home and concedes that he is coming to the end of his meagre savings account, describing himself as close to being 'on his arse', and having started collecting the dole. 'There's just fuck all out there', he explains to me. His predicament exemplifies the fragility and instability of employment under post-Fordism, and it is unlikely that he is going to secure another job on comparable terms to his previous employment. He admits that he is getting to the stage where if he doesn't take the first job he gets offered, it will catastrophically impinge on his ability to maintain a presence within the NTE. He has a tab at his local bar that is spiralling rapidly out of control, and would surely be starting to face more serious problems were it not for the fact that he is able to live at home with his retired parents.

Final word

I hope that this book draws attention to the complexities and fragility of becoming adult in a world that is demarcated by watchwords such as deindustrialisation and postmodernity (see Jameson, 1991). The NTE, characterised by reflections of carnival (Bakhtin, 1984), seductions of liminality (Turner, 1975), simulacra, hyperreality (Baudrillard, 1983) and illusions of the Real (Žižek, 2001, 2002; Badiou, 2007), has provided us with a lens through which to view contemporary adulthood beneath the shadow of global capitalism. As I have reiterated throughout these pages, the meanings attributed to maintaining a presence within the NTE, the motivations involved in 'going out' and the partial or in some cases wholesale rejection of many of the markers of traditional adulthood cannot be understood through applying the affirmative postmodernist rhetoric of increased choice, increased potential and increased freedom. As such I believe that I have provided a theoretical framework that provides us with a much more robust and comprehensive explanation of the role of the NTE within the greater sphere of consumerism. Within this theoretical framework, we can identify huge levels of anxiety resulting in the fear of not being counted as a distinct individual. Forms of 'acting out', ornamental consumption through dress or consumption of alcohol and utilisation of spaces are not rebellion or expressions of freedom, but rather adherence to neoliberal imperatives to be both different and the same, individual but part of a (perceived) collective: in short, to at once 'fit in and stand out' (Miles, 1998, Winlow and Hall, 2006).

As this final chapter nears its end, I feel compelled to defend to the reader what may have been construed as an overly negative or pessimistic interpretation of contemporary adulthood beneath the shadow of global capitalism. Indeed, the purpose of this piece of work has been to draw attention towards and add to the literature that supports the contention (Winlow and Hall, 2013) that consumer capitalism perpetuates inequality and is responsible for a host of problems through its ethic of compulsory individualism and the reorientation of the superego culminating in the injunction to enjoy (Žižek, 1991). The suggestion that the anxieties, isolation and challenges that have been widely identified as facing young people today somehow dissolve as the individual progresses through the life course is to misinterpret and underestimate the all-enveloping nature of consumer capitalism. Indeed the evidence contained within these pages would suggest that many of these problems are exacerbated by the myth of individual freedom attributed to the perpetuation of consumption. The injunction to enjoy, coupled with the passion for the Real that has been explored over previous pages serve to negate much of the freedom attributed to consumer capitalism and the transition to adulthood. Processes of infantilism and the coming of age of the infantile narcissist have removed or masked many of the markers associated with becoming 'adult' in the traditional sense, an issue compounded by the inaccessibility to many of these markers, such as access to the housing market imposed by the inequalities of contemporary capitalism. Where success in the consumer circuits of adulthood is either unobtainable, or unappealing, success within the consumer circuits of the NTE and wider cultural frame provides a viable and attractive alternative. It is insufficient to claim that the NTE serves as a safety valve for the pressures of life under global capitalism, although this is true to the extent that the role of carnival is evident in the liminal excess purchased within the night-time leisure scene. For many, the NTE provides a more appealing focus than the sphere of alienating employment and serves to reward the faithful disciple with access to the Real that is so markedly absent from the alternative. While the majority of individuals are likely to successfully negotiate a path to a more traditional incarnation of adulthood, there is much to suggest that others will not. Andrea, for example, is unlikely to be able to make the transition from living in rented accommodation to becoming a homeowner, for the simple reason that her single status and economic situation make it a far from viable proposition. The financial difficulty that she experiences when having to scrape together the money for the deposit on her rented flat, and the complexities of budgeting her money and balancing her books from one pay cheque to the next does not bode well for her ability to make this transition any time in the near future. For Billy, the allure of easy money (Smith, 2012) through entry into the illegal markets of the drug dealer may yet prove too tempting as the financial noose tightens around his neck due to contraction within the building industry. Although presenting at times a rather dour interpretation of life under late capitalism, it is not my intention to be overly pessimistic. Rather, it is my intention to provide an alternative explanation than that offered by those who believe that as the logic of capitalist markets leaches into and pervades almost every aspect of life, individuals are faced with ever-increasing levels of freedom, choice and wellbeing. The reality, I would suggest, is a future not only of weak community bonds, precarity and atomisation, but also increasing levels of social alienation, political apathy and emotional fragility that are likely to intensify with age, rather than be ameliorated by contemporary adulthood.

Notes

1 Introduction

1. The Bullingdon Club is an exclusive University of Oxford dining club, renowned for drunken behaviour, including the destruction of restaurants, vandalism of college property and fighting. Within the conservative press, however, such 'antics' are referred to as 'playful joshing' while the violence is recontextualised as taking on a 'polite, skittish guise' (see Atkinson, 2006).
2. I have referred to the city as 'Vikton' in this book rather than using its real name, partly to protect the identity of the people profiled in the case studies, and to emphasise that it stands for life and leisure in any number of cities across Britain.
3. A particular kind of bar, sometimes located in a former commercial or retail building, where customers are encouraged through its design to stand rather than sit which in turn facilitates rapid consumption of alcohol.
4. Exceptions to this do of course exist (see Gofton, 1990; Tomsen, 1997; Hobbs et al., 2003; Winlow and Hall, 2006).
5. Happily, on this occasion I was right, and a later chance meeting with Louise revealed that she was in a new relationship and had moved back out of her parents' home, news of which served to somewhat assuage my feelings of guilt.

3 Binge Britain and the NTE

1. The issue of celebrity is an interesting one, which unfortunately must remain unexplored here. Suffice to say we can position the objects of contemporary fetishisation of celebrity as having transcended traditional morality. They are able to fornicate, drink, take drugs in ways that are completely inaccessible to much of society. And while we may believe that celebrity lives reflect some element of the Real, in fact it is more accurate to say that they do not exist – trapped between the 'real' them and their mediatised image, an existential gulf in which they are unable to recognise themselves.
2. Although the direct translation of 'jouissance' is 'pleasure', it is more useful to utilise this term in the psychoanalytic sense, pertaining to an excess of pleasure, that takes on a traumatic, painful element. Therefore, a good meal is pleasurable, but to keep eating beyond the point at which our hunger is satiated becomes uncomfortable to the point of traumatic intrusion, perhaps most aptly illustrated by the Monty Python character Mr Creosote, whose consumption graphically pushes beyond the pleasure principle.
3. The term given to the highly acquisitive pub estate companies who sought large profits by buying up premises and installing tenant landlords who, while ostensibly 'business partners', are tied to buying stock from the pubco itself, and are vulnerable to substantial rent increases.

4 Consuming the City

1. The hyperreality surrounding nostalgia for decades past that is so neatly characterised within the Reflex brand is taken to its logical conclusion by TV chef Heston Blumenthal in his recent show Feasts, in which he creates a 1980s themed meal for a group of minor celebrities. Introducing the viewer to the decade in question from the dance floor of a Reflex bar, pointing out hyperreal fixtures and fittings as genuine representations of the period, he proceeds to cook versions of 1980s food that has lost all semblance of its original form – for example, Blumenthal makes a cheese and ham toasted sandwich, using meat that goes beyond ham, sourced from acorn-fed pigs in the south of Spain, utilising fine black truffles, and cheese that he has subjected to a number of pseudo-scientific processes in his kitchen in order to make it stringy enough to be stretched to incredible lengths.

5 Youth, Adulthood and the NTE

1. Even government attempts to control this market, such as 2013's 'Help to Buy' scheme, are likely to help those who are already relatively wealthy, rather than those struggling to afford a deposit (Collinson, 2013).

6 Drinking Biographies

1. Slang for a lower second class honours degree – Desmond Tutu = 2:2.

7 Desire, Motivation and the NTE

1. Interestingly, many participants within the night-time leisure economy will find themselves at once transgressing government health guidelines while abiding faithfully to the ethic of compulsory indulgence discussed elsewhere.
2. 'Pass out', 'green card' and 'beer licence' are all terms that relate in simple terms to 'permission', usually from their partner, to go out drinking.

References

Ab-inbev.co.uk (2013), Available at www.ab-invev.co.uk/about/about-abinbev/ [accessed December 12, 2013].

Adorno, T. W. (1978), *Minima Moralia: reflections on a damaged life*, London: Verso Books.

Adorno, T. (1981), *Negative dialectics*, London: Continuum.

Adorno, T. W. (1990), *Negative dialectics*, London: Routledge.

Adorno, T. W. (2001), *The culture industry: selected essays on mass culture*, London. Routledge.

Adorno, T. and Horkheimer, M. (1997), *Dialectics of enlightenment*, London: Verso Books.

Advertising Standards Authority (n.d.), Available online at http://www.asa.org.uk/News-resources/Hot-Topics/~/media/Files/CAP/Codes%20BCAP%20pdf/BCAP%20Section%2019.ashx [accessed 12/03/2013].

Amin, A. (1994), *Post-Fordism: a reader*, Oxford; Cambridge, MA: Blackwell.

Atkinson, R. (2006), 'Spaces of discipline and control: the compounded citizenship of social renting', in Flint, J. (ed.) *Housing, urban governance and anti-social behaviour: perspectives, policy and practice*, Bristol: Policy Press, pp. 99–117.

Auge, M. (2009), *Non-Places: an introduction to supermodernity*, London: Verso Books.

Babor, T. (ed.), (2010), *Alcohol: no ordinary commodity: research and public policy*, Oxford: Oxford University Press.

Badiou, A. (2002), *Ethics: an essay on the understanding of evil*, London: Verso Books.

Badiou, A. (2007), *The century*, Cambridge: Polity Press.

Bakan, J. (2005), *The corporation: the pathological pursuit of profit and power*, New York: Free Press.

Bakhtin, M. M. (1984), *Rabelais and his world* (First Midland book Edition), Bloomington: Indiana University Press.

Barber, B. R. (2007), *Consumption: how markets corrupt children, infantilize adults, and swallow citizens whole*, New York: Norton.

Barton, A. and Husk, K. (2012), 'Controlling pre-loaders: alcohol related violence in an English night time economy', *Drugs and Alcohol Today*, 12(2), 89–97.

Barth-Haas Group (2012), Available online at http://www.ibdasiapac.com.au/technical-papers/hops-update---hpa.pdf [accessed 04/01/2014].

Baudrillard, J. (1970), *The consumer society*. London: Sage.

Baudrillard, J. (1983), *Simulations*, New York City: Semiotext(e) Inc.

Baudrillard, J. (1984), *In the shadow of the silent majorities, or, the end of the social, and other essays*, New York: Semiotext(e) Inc.

Baudrillard J. (1988), *Selected writings*, Stanford: Stanford University Press.

Baudrillard, J. (1993), *Symbolic Exchange and Death*, London: Sage.

Baudrillard, J. (1994), *Simulacra and simulation*. University of Michigan Press.

Bauman, Z. (1992), *Intimations of postmodernity*, London, New York: Routledge.

Bauman, Z. (1998a), *Life in fragments: essays in postmodern morality*, Oxford: Blackwell.

Bauman, Z. (1998b), *Work, consumerism and the new poor*, Buckingham: Open University Press.

Bauman, Z. (1999), *In search of politics*, Cambridge: Polity Press.

Bauman, Z. (2000), *Liquid modernity*, Cambridge: Polity Press.

Bauman, Z. (2001), *The individualized society*, Cambridge: Polity Press.

Bauman, Z. (2005), *Liquid life*, Cambridge: Polity Press.

Bauman, Z. (2007), *Consuming life*, Cambridge: Polity Press.

BBC, (2008) Brewer S&N agrees 7.8bn takeover. available online: http://news.bbc. co.uk/1/hi/business/7208341.stm [accessed 13/03/2013]

Beauchamp, T. L. and Childress, J. (2001), *Principles of biomedical ethics*, Oxford: Oxford University Press.

Beck, U. (1992), *Risk society: towards a new modernity*, London: Sage Publications.

Beck, U. (2000), *The brave new world of work*, Cambridge: Polity Press.

Beck, U. and Beck-Gernsheim, E. (1995), *The normal chaos of love*, Cambridge: Polity Press.

Bell, C. and Newby, H. (1977), *Doing sociological research*, Michigan: Free Press.

Bell, D. (1973), *The coming of the post-industrial society*, New York: Penguin.

Bendix, R. and Lipset, S. (1967), *Class Status and Power*, London: Routledge & Kegan Paul.

Berardi, F. (2009), *Soul at work*, Los Angeles: Semiotext(e).

Blatterer, H. (2007), 'Contemporary adulthood: reconceptualizing an uncontested category', *Current Sociology*, 55(6), 771.

Boltanski, L. and Chiapello, E. (2007), *The new spirit of capitalism*, London: Verso Books.

Bourdieu, P. (2000), *Acts of resistance: against the new myths of our time*, Oxford: Blackwell.

Bourdieu, P. (1984), *Distinction: a social critique of the judgement of taste*, London: Routledge & Kegan Paul.

Bourdieu, P. and Passeron, J. C. (1990), *Reproduction in education, society and culture*, Sage, London.

Bourke, J. (1994), *Working class cultures in Britain, 1890–1960: gender, class, and ethnicity*, London: Routledge.

Briggs, D. (2012), 'Deviance and risk on holiday: an ethnography with British youth abroad', in Winlow, S. and Atkinson, R. (eds) *New directions in crime and deviance*, London: Routledge.

Briggs, D. (2013), *Deviance and risk on holiday*, London: Palgrave.

British Beer and Pub Association (2013), Available at www.beerandpub.com/ statistics Online/ [accessed December 12, 2013].

Brown, S. (1993), 'Postmodern Marketing?' *European Journal of Marketing*, 27(4), 19–34.

Brown, P. and Hesketh, A. (2004), *The mismanagement of talent: Employability and jobs in the knowledge economy*, Oxford: Oxford University Press.

Bryman, A. (1995), *Disney and his worlds*, London: Routledge.

Bryman, A. (2004), *Social research methods* (second edition), Oxford: Oxford University Press.

Bulmer, M. (1982), 'When is disguise justified? Alternatives to covert participant-observations', *Qualitative Sociology*, 5, 251–264.

Burnett, J. (1999), *Liquid pleasures: a social history of drinks in modern Britain*, London: Routledge.

Burnett, J. (2010), *Contemporary adulthood: calendars, cartographies and constructions*, Basingstoke: Palgrave Macmillan.

Byrne, D. (1995), 'Deindustrialisation and dispossession: an examination of social division in the industrial city', *Sociology*, 29(1), 95.

Byrne, D. (2005), *Social exclusion*, Maidenhead: Open University Press.

Calcutt, A. (1998), *Arrested development: pop culture and the erosion of adulthood*, London: Cassell.

Campbell, C. (1989), *The romantic ethic and the spirit of modern consumerism*, Oxford: Blackwell.

CAMRA (2014), Available online at http://www.camra.org.uk/aboutcamra [accessed 04/01/2014].

Cassell, J. (1988), 'The relationship of observer to observed when studying up', *Studies in Qualitative Methodology*, 1, 89–108.

Castells, M. (2000), *The rise of the network society*, Oxford: Blackwell.

Cederstrom, C. and Fleming, P. (2012), *Dead Man Working*, Winchester: Zero Books.

Chalabi (2014), Available online at http://www.theguardian.com/news/datablog/2014/jan/21/record-numbers-young-adults-living-with-parents [accessed 12/12/2013].

Chatterton, P. and Hollands, R. G. (2001), *Changing our 'Toon': youth, nightlife and urban change in Newcastle*, Newcastle upon Tyne: University of Newcastle upon Tyne.

Chatterton, P. and Hollands, R. (2003), *Urban nightscapes: youth cultures, pleasure spaces and corporate power*, London: Routledge.

Cheek, N. H. and Burch, W. R. (1976), *The social organization of leisure in modern society*, New York: Harper and Row.

Cloward, R. A. and Ohlin, L. E. (1960), *Delinquency and opportunity: a theory of delinquent gangs*, New York: Free Press.

Cohen, A. (1955), *Delinquent boys*, New York: Free Press.

Cohen, S. (1972), *Folk devils and moral panics: the creation of the mods and rockers*, Oxford: Martin Robertson.

Coleman, C. and Moynihan, J. (1996), *Understanding crime data: haunted by the dark figure*. Buckingham: Open University Press.

Collin, M. and Godfrey, J. (1998), *Altered state: the story of ecstasy culture and acid house*, London: Serpents Tail.

Collinson, D. L. (1988), '"Engineering humour": masculinity, joking and conflict in shop-floor relations', *Organization Studies*, 9(2), 181.

Collinson (2013), www.theguardian.com/money/blog/2013/oct/08/help-to-buy-house-prices.

Coomber, R. (2002), 'Siging your life away?' *Sociological Research Online*, 7(1).

Coomber, R. and Moyle, L. (2013), 'Beyond drug dealing: developing and extending the concept of "social supply" of illicit drugs to "minimally commercial supply"', *Drugs: Education, prevention and policy* 21(2) 157–164.

Corrigan, P. (1979), *Schooling the smash street kids*, London: Palgrave.

Cote, J. (2000), *Arrested Adulthood*, New York: New York University Press.

Cote, J. (2002), 'The role of identity capital in the transition to adulthood: the individualization thesis examined', *Journal of Youth Studies*, 5(2), 117–134, DOI:10.1080/13676260220134403.

Cote, J. E. and Allahar, A. (1995), *Generation on hold: coming of age in the late twentieth century*, New York: New York University Press.

Credit Action (2013), Available online at http://www.creditaction.org.uk/debt-statistics.html [accessed 09/09/2013].

Crouch, C. (2011), *The strange non-death of neo-liberalism*. Polity, Cambridge.

Crow, G., Wiles. R. and Heath, S. (2006), 'Research ethics and data quality: the implications of informed consent', *International Journal of Social Research Methodology*, 9(2), 83–92.

Cross, G. S. (2002), *An all-consuming century: why commercialism won in modern America*, New York: Columbia University Press.

Crouch, C. (2011), *The strange non-death of neoliberalism*, Cambridge: Polity Press.

Currie, E. (1997), 'Market, crime and community toward a mid-range theory of post-industrial violence. *Theoretical criminology*, 1(2), 147–172.

Currie, E. (2004), *The road to whatever*, New York: Metropolitan Books.

Dahl, R. A. and Lindblom, C. E. (1953), *Politics, economics and welfare: planning and politico-economic systems resolved into basic social processes*, Chicago: University of Chicago Press.

de Certeau, M. (1984), *The practice of everyday life*, translated by Steven Rendall, Berkeley: University of California Press.

Debord, G. (1983), *Society of the Spectacle*, Michigan: Rebel Press.

Department of Environment (1994), *Planning out crime*, Circular 5/94, London: DoE.

Dienst, R. (2011), *The bonds of debt*, London: Verso Books.

Ditton, J. (1977), *Part-time crime: an ethnography of fiddling and pilferage*, Basingstoke: Macmillan.

Dorling, D. (2010), *Injustice: why social inequality persists*, Bristol: Policy Press.

Douglas, M. and Isherwood, B. (1979), *The world of goods: towards an anthropology of consumption*, London: Routledge.

Dumazedier, J. (1967), *Toward a society of leisure*, New York: Free Press.

Dumeil, G. and Levy, D. (2013), *The crisis of neoliberalism*, Massachusetts: Harvard University Press.

Edholm, F. (1982), 'The unnatural family', in Whitelegg, E. (ed.) *The Changing Experience of Women*, Oxford: Martin Robinson.

Edwards, A. (2003), 'Pint to Pint: Blue Bell', *The Telegraph*, 11 October. Available online at http://www.telegraph.co.uk/foodanddrink/pubs/3308353/Pint-to-pint-Blue-Bell.html [accessed October 21, 2009].

Edwards, P. (2000), 'Late twentieth century workplace relation: class struggle without classes', in Rosemary. Crompton et al. (eds) *Renewing Class Analysis*. Oxford: Blackwell, pp. 141–164.

Ehrenreich, B. (2010), *Nickel and dimed: undercover in low-wage USA*, London: Granta Books.

Elias, N. (1994), *The civilizing process*, Oxford England; Cambridge, MA: Blackwell.

Elliott, A. and Lemert, C. (2006), *The new individualism*, London: Routledge.

Engineer, R., Phillips, A., Thompson, J. and Nicholls, J. (2003), *Drunk and disorderly: a qualitative study of binge drinking among 18- to 24-year olds*, London: Home Office.

Erikson, E. (1978), *Adulthood*, New York: Norton.

Erikson, E. (1980), 'Themes of adulthood in the Freud-Jung correspondence', in Smelsner, N. and Erikson, E. (eds) *Themes of work and love in adulthood*, New York: Norton.

Ewen, S. (2001), *Captains of consciousness: advertising and the social roots of the consumer culture*, New York: Basic Books.

Featherstone, M. (1987), 'Lifestyle and consumer culture', *Theory Culture & Society*, 4(1), 55–70.

Featherstone, M. (1990), 'Global culture: an introduction', *Theory, Culture & Society*, 7(2), 1.

Featherstone, M. (2007), *Consumer culture and postmodernism*, London: Sage.

Feldman, M. S., Bell, J. and Berger, M. T. (2003), *Gaining access: a practical and theoretical guide for qualitative researchers*, Oxford: Altamira Press.

Ferree, M. M. and Hall, E. J. (1996), 'Rethinking stratification from a feminist perspective: gender, race, and class in mainstream textbooks', *American Sociological Review*, 61(6), 929–950.

Fink, B. (1995), *The Lacanian subject: between language and jouissance*, Princeton: Princeton University Press.

Fisher, M. (2009), *Capitalist realism: is there no alternative?* London: Zero Books.

Fiske, J. (1989), *Television culture*, London: Routledge.

Fiske, J. (1991), *Understanding popular culture*, London: Routledge.

Fox, R. (1967), *Kinship and marriage: an anthropological perspective*, London: Penguin.

Frank, T. (1998), *The conquest of cool: business culture, counterculture & the rise of hip consumerism*, Chicago: University of Chicago Press.

Freud, S. (1930), *Civilisation and its discontents*, New York: Norton.

Furlong, A. and Cartmel, F. (2007), *Young people and social change: new perspectives* (second edition), Maidenhead: McGraw-Hill/Open University Press.

Furlong, A. and Kelly, P. (2005), The Brazilianisation of youth transitions in Australia and the UK? *Australian Journal of Social Issues (Australian Council of Social Service)*, 40(2): 207–225.

Gardner, C. and Sheppard, J. (1989), *Consuming passion: the rise of retail culture*, London: Routledge.

Giddens, A. (1991), *Modernity and self-identity: self and society in the late modern age*, Oxford: Polity Press; Basil Blackwell.

Girard, R. (1986), *The scapegoat*, Baltimore: Johns Hopkins University Press.

globalbrands.co.uk (2014), Available online at http://www.globalbrands.co.uk/component/k2/item/53-corkys-innovates-as-leader-of-liqueur-pack.html [accessed 13/03/2014].

Gofton, L. (1990), 'On the town: drink and the new lawlessness', *Youth and policy*, 29, 33–39.

Goldthorpe, J., Lockwood, D., Bechhofer, F. and Platt, J. (1968), *The affluent worker: political attitudes and behavior*, London: Cambridge University Press.

Graeber (2010), *Debt: the first 5000 years*. New York: Melville House.

Griffin, C., Bengry-Howell, A., Hackley, C., Mistral, W. and Szmigin, I. (2009), '"Every time I do it I absolutely annihilate myself": loss of (self)consciousness and loss of memory in young people's drinking narratives', *Sociology*, 43(3), 457–476, DOI:10.1177/00380385 09103201.

Hadfield, P. (2006), *Bar wars: contesting the night in contemporary British cities*, Oxford: Oxford University Press.

Hall, S. (1988), *The hard road to renewal: Thatcherism and the crisis of the left*, London: Verso Books.

Hall, S. and Winlow, S. (2005), 'Anti-nirvana: crime, culture and instrumentalism in the age of insecurity', *Crime, Media, Culture*, 1(1), 31–48.

Hall, S. and Winlow, S. (2007), 'Cultural criminology and primitive accumulation: a formal introduction for two strangers who should really become more intimate', *Crime, Media, Culture*, 3(1), 82.

Hall, S., Winlow, S. and Ancrum, A. (2008), *Criminal identities and consumer culture: rime, exclusion and the new culture of Narcissism*, Cullompton: Willan.

Hall, T. and Hubbard, P. (1998), *The entrepreneurial city: geographies of politics, regime and representation*, London: Wiley.

Hammersley, M. (1992), 'What's wrong with ethnography', *Methodological Explanations*, 24(4), 597–615.

Hammersley, M. and Atkinson, P. (2007), *Ethnography: Principles in practice*, New York: Taylor & Francis.

Harrison, B. (1994), *Drink and the Victorians: the temperance question in England 1815–1872*, Keele: Keele University Press.

Harvey, D. (1989), *The conditions of late modernity*. Oxford: Blackwell.

Harvey, D. (2006), 'Neo-liberalism as creative destruction', *Geografiska Annaler: Series B, Human Geography*, 88(2), 145–158.

Harvey, D. (2007), *A brief history of neoliberalism*, USA: Oxford University Press.

Hastings, G., Anderson, S., Cooke, E. and Gordon, R. (2005), 'Alcohol marketing and young people's drinking: a review of the research', *Journal of Public Health Policy*, 26(3), 296–311.

Hayward, K. (2012), 'Pantomime justice: a cultural criminological analysis of "life stage dissolution"', *Crime Media Culture*, 8(2), 213–229, DOI:10.1177/1741659012444443.

Hayward, K. and Hobbs, D. (2007), 'Beyond the binge in "Booze Britain": market-led liminalization and the spectacle of binge drinking', *The British Journal of Sociology*, 58(3), 437–456, DOI:10.1111/j.1468-4446.2007.00159.x.

Health and Social Care Information Centre (2012), *Statistics on alcohol: England, 2012*. Leeds: HSCIC.

Heath, D. (1999), 'Drinking and pleasure across cultures', in Peele, S. and Grant, M. (eds) *Alcohol and pleasure: a health perspective*, New York: Taylor and Francis, pp. 61–72.

Heath, J. and Potter, A. (2006), *The rebel sell: how the counter culture became consumer culture*, Chichester: Capstone.

Hebdige, D. (1988), *Subculture: the meaning of style*, New York: Routledge.

Held, D., McGrew, A., Goldblatt, D. and Perraton, J. (1999), *Global transformations*, Cambridge: Polity Press.

Herd, D. (2005), 'Changes in the prevalence of alcohol use in rap song lyrics, 1979–97', *Addiction*, 100, 1258–1269.

Hobbs, D. (1988), *Doing the business: entrepreneurship, the working class and detectives in the East End of London*, Oxford: Clarendon.

Hobbs, D., Hadfield, P., Lister, S. and Winlow, S. (2003), *Bouncers: violence and governance in the night-time economy*, USA: Oxford University Press.

Hobbs, D., Lister, S., Hadfield, P., Winlow, S. and Hall, S. (2000), 'Receiving shadows: governance and liminality in the night-time economy', *British Journal of Sociology*, 51(4), 701–717.

Hobbs, D. and May, T. (1993), *Interpreting the field: accounts of ethnography*, Oxford, US: Clarendon Press.

Hobsbawm, E. J. (1976), *The age of capital, 1848–1975*, London: Abacus.

Hobsbawm, E. J. (1996), *Age of extremes: the short twentieth century, 1914–1991*, London: Abacus.

Hockey, J., Robinson, V. and Hall, A. (2010), 'Chronologising adulthood/ configuring masculinity', in Burnett, J. (ed.) *Contemporary adulthood: calendars, cartographies and constructions*, Basingstoke: Palgrave, pp. 88–104.

Holdaway, S. (1982), '"An inside job": a case study of covert research on the police', in *Social research ethics: an examination of the merits of covert participant observation*, pp. 59–79.

Hollands, R. (1995), *Friday night, Saturday night: youth cultural identification in the post-industrial city*. Newcastle: Newcastle University.

Hollands, R. (2002), 'Divisions in the dark: youth cultures, transitions and segmented consumption spaces in the night-time economy', *Journal of Youth Studies*, 5(2), 153–171.

Holt, D. B. (2004), *How brands become icons: the principles of cultural branding*, Harvard: Harvard Business Press.

Holt, M. P. (2006), *Alcohol: a social and cultural history*, New York: Berg Publishers.

Home Office (2000), '*Time for Reform: proposals for the modernisation of our licensing laws*', London: HMSO.

Home Office (2012) *The Government's alcohol strategy*. London: HM Government

Jackson, M. C., Hastings, G., Wheeler, C., Eadie, D. and MacKintosh, A. M. (2000), 'Marketing alcohol to young people: implications for industry regulation and research policy', *Addiction*, 95, 12(suppl. 4), 597–608.

James, O. (2007), *Affluenza: how to be successful and stay sane*, London: Vermilion.

Jameson, F. (1991), *Postmodernism, or, the cultural logic of late capitalism*, Durham: Duke University Press.

Jameson, F. (1998), *The cultural turn: selected writings on the postmodern, 1983–1998*, London: Verso Books.

Jarvinen, M. and Gundelach, P. (2007), 'Teenage drinking, symbolic capital and distinction', *Journal of Youth Studies*, 10(1), 55–71.

Jayne, M., Holloway, S. L. and Valentine, G. (2006), 'Drunk and disorderly: alcohol, urban life and public space', *Progress in Human Geography*, 30(4), 451.

Jayne, M., Valentine, G. and Holloway, S. L. (2008), 'Fluid boundaries: British binge drinking and European civility: alcohol and the production and consumption of public space', *Space and Polity*, 12(1), 81–100.

Jayne, M., Valentine, G. and Holloway, S. L. (2010), Emotional, embodied and affective geographies of alcohol, drinking and drunkenness, *Transactions of the Institute of British Geographers*, 35(4), 540–554.

Jernigan, D. and O'Hara, J. (2004), 'Alcohol advertising and promotion', in National Research Council Institute of Medicine, *Reducing underage drinking: A collective responsibility* pp. 625–653.

Jessop, B. (1997), 'Capitalism and its future: remarks on regulation, government and governance', *Review of International Political Economy*, vol. 4, no. 3, 561–581.

Johnson, T. (1972), Professions and Power, London: Macmillan.Jones, A. (2013), '"26 Pubs a Week Closing" but Hopes Rise for Future'. Available online at http://www.independent.co.uk/life-style/food-and-drink/news/26-pubs-a-week-closing-but-hopes-rise-for-future-8605795.html [accessed December 18, 2013].

Jones, G. (1995), *Leaving home*, Buckingham: Oxford University Press.

Keen, S. (2011), *Debunking Economics*, London: Zed Books.

Kelly, J. (1990), *Leisure identities and interactions*, London: Associated University Presses.

Klein, N. (2000), *No Logo*. London: Picador.

Klein, N. (2008), *The shock doctrine: the rise of disaster capitalism*, London: Penguin.

Kumar, K. (1995), *From post-industrial to post-modern society: new theories of the contemporary world*, Oxford: Wiley-Blackwell.

Lacan, J. (1992), *The ethics of psychoanalysis*, translated by Dennis Porter, New York: Norton.

Lacan, J. (2001), *Ecrits: the first complete edition in English*, New York: Norton.

Lasch, C. (1979), *The culture of Narcissism*, London: Norton.

Lasch, C. (1985), *The minimal self: psychic survival in troubled times*, London: Norton.

Lash, S. and Lury, C. (2007), *Global culture industry: the mediation of things*, Cambridge: Polity Press.

Lash, S. and Urry, J. (1987), *The end of organized capitalism*, Cambridge: Polity Press.

Lee, M. (1993), *Consumer culture reborn: the cultural politics of consumption.* New York: Routledge.

Lee, N. (2001), *Childhood and society*, Buckingham: Oxford University Press.

Liebow, E. (1967), *Tally's corner: a study of Negro streetcorner men*, Boston: Little, Brown and Co.

Lipset, S. M. and Bendix, R. (1992), *Social mobility in industrial society*, New York: Transaction Publishers.

Lloyd, A. (2012), 'Working to live, not living to work: work, leisure and youth identity among call centre workers in North-East England', *Current Sociology*, 60(5), 619–635.

Lloyd, A. (2013), *Labour markets and identity on the post-industrial assembly line*, Farnham: Ashgate.

Lodziak, C. (1995), *Manipulating needs: capitalism and culture*, London: Pluto Press.

Lovatt, A. (1996), 'The ecstasy of urban regeneration: regulation of the night-time economy in the transition to a post-Fordist city', in O'Connor, J. and Wynne, D. (eds) *From the margins to the centre: cultural production and consumption in the post-modern city*, Aldershot: Arena.

Lyon, D. (1999), *Postmodernity: concepts in social thought*, Minneapolis: University of Minnesota Press.

MacAndrew, C. and Edgerton, R. (1969), *Drunken comportment: a social explanation*, Chicago: Aldine.

MacDonald, R. R. and Marsh, J. J. (2005), *Disconnected youth? Growing up in Britain's poor neighbourhoods*, Basingstoke: Palgrave Macmillan.

Maggs, J. and Schulenberg, J. (2004), 'Trajectories of alcohol use during the transition to adulthood', *Alcohol Research & Health*, 28(4), 195–201.

Malbon, B. (1998) 'Clubbing: Consumption, Identity, and the Spatial Practices of Every-night Life', in T. Skelton and G. Valentine, *Cool places: geographies of youth cultures*, pp. 266–86. London: Routledge.

Malbon, B. (1999), *Clubbing: dancing, ecstasy and vitality*, London: Routledge.

Marazzi, C. (2011), *The violence of financial capitalism*, Los Angeles: Semiotext(e) Inc.

Marx, K. (1975), *Collected Works*, vol. 3. London: Lawrence & Wishart.

Matza, D. (1990), *Delinquency and drift*, New York: Wiley.

McCreanor, T., Greenaway, A., Barnes, H. M., Borell, S. and Gregory, A. (2005), 'Youth identity formation and contemporary alcohol marketing', *Critical Public Health*, 15(3), 251–262, DOI:10.1080/09581590500372345.

McGowan, T. (2004), *The end of dissatisfaction: Jacques Lacan and the emerging society of enjoyment*, Albany: State University of New York Press.

Measham, F. (2004), 'The decline of ecstasy, the rise of "binge" drinking and the persistence of pleasure', *Probation Journal*, 51(4), 309.

Measham, F. (2008), 'The turning tides of intoxication: young people's drinking in Britain in the 2000s', *Health Education*, 108(3), 207–222, DOI:10.1108/09654280810867088.

Measham, F. and Brain, K. (2005), '"Binge" drinking, British alcohol policy and the new culture of intoxication', *Crime, Media, Culture*, 1(3), 262.

Miles, S. (1998), *Consumerism: as a way of life*, London: Sage.

Miles, S. (2000), *Youth lifestyles in a changing world*, Buckingham: Open University Press.

Millon, T. (2004), *Personality disorders in modern life*, New Jersey: Wiley.

Minton, A. (2009), *Ground control: fear and happiness in the 21st century city*. London: Penguin.

Mirowski, P. (2013), *Never let a serious crisis go to waste: How neoliberalism survived the financial meltdown*. Verso Books.

Montgomery, J. (1998), 'Making a city: urbanity, vitality and urban design', *Journal of Urban Design*, 3(1), 93–116.

Moore, L., Smith, C. and Catford, J. (1994), 'Binge drinking: prevalence, patterns and policy', *Health Education Research*, 9(4), 497.

Morch, S. (1997), 'Youth and activity theory', in Bynner, J., Chisholm, L. and Furlong, A. (eds) *Youth, citizenship and social change in a European context*, Aldershot: Ashgate.

Morris, R. J. (1990), *Class, sect, and party: the making of the British middle class: Leeds, 1820–1850*, Manchester: Manchester University Press.

Mort, F. (1989), 'The politics of consumption', in Hall, S. and Jaques, M. (eds) *New Times*, London: Lawrence & Wishart.

Murgraff, V., Parrott, A. and Bennet, P. (1999), Risky single occasion drinking amongst young people, *Alcohol and Alcoholism*, 34(19), 3–14.

Murji, K. (1998), *Policing drugs*, Aldershot: Ashgate.

Neitzsche, F. (1994), *Thus spake Zarathustra*, Oxford: Oxford University Press.

Nicoletti, C. and Tanturri, M. L. (2008), 'Differences in delaying motherhood across European countries: empirical evidence from the ECHP', *European Journal of Population/Revue europÈenne de DÈmographie*, 24(2), 157–183.

O'Brien, L. and Harris, F. (1991), *Retailing: shopping, society, space*. London: Fulton.

O'Connor, J. and Wynne, D. (1995) 'From the margins to the centre', in: P. Sulkunen (ed.) *Constructing the new consumer society*, Oxford: Blackwell.

O'Connor, J. and Wynne, D. (1996), *From the margins to the centre: cultural production and consumption in the post-industrial city*, Arena.

Office for National Statistics (2013a), 'General lifestyle survey, 2011'. Available online at http://www.ons.gov.uk/ons/rel/ghs/general-lifestyle-survey/2011/index.html [accessed May 2].

Office for National Statistics (2013b), 'Appendix Tables' in 'Crime statistics, focus on: violent crime and sexual offences, 2011/12', Table 4.12.

Office for National Statistics (2013c), 'General lifestyle survey, 2011'. Available online at http://www.ons.gov.uk/ons/rel/household-income/middle-income-households/1977---2011-12/sty-middle-income-households.html [accessed December 3].

Pakulski, J. and Waters, M. (1996), *The death of class*, London: Sage.

Parker, B. J. (1998), 'Exploring life themes and myths in alcohol advertisements through a meaning-based model of advertising experiences', *Journal of Advertising*, 27(1), 97–112.

Plant, M., Singel, E. and Stockwell, T. (eds) (1997), 'Alcohol: minimising the harm: what works?', London: Free Association Books Limited.

Plant, M. (2004), 'The alcohol harm reduction strategy for England', *British Medical Journal*, 328(905), 7445.

Plant, M. A. and Plant, M. (2006), *Binge Britain: alcohol and the national response*, Oxford: Oxford University Press.

Polsky, N. (1971), *Hustlers, beats, and others*, Harmondsworth: Pelican.

Presdee, M. (2000), *Cultural criminology and the carnival of crime*, London: Routledge.

Prime Minister's Strategy Unit (2004), *Alcohol harm reduction strategy for England*. Home Office.

Punch, S. (2002), 'Research with children: the same or different from research with adults?' *Childhood*, 9(3), 321–341.

Punch taverns website (2013), Available online at http://www.punchtavernsplc.com/Punch [accessed February 3, 2013].

Reiner, R. (2007), *Law and order: an honest citizen's guide to crime and control*, Cambridge: Polity Press.

Reynolds, S. (1998), 'Rave culture: living dream or living death?' in Redhead, S., Wynne, D. and O'Connor, J, *The Clubcultures Reader*, Blackwell, Oxford, pp. 84–93.

Ritzer, G. (1998), *The McDonaldization thesis: explorations and extensions*, London: Sage Publications.

Roberts, K. (1978), *Contemporary society and the growth of leisure*, Longman: London.

Roberts, K. (1981), *Leisure*, London: Addison-Wesley Longman Limited.

Rojek, C. (1989), *Leisure for leisure: critical essays*, Basingstoke: Macmillan.

Rojek, C. (1999), 'Deviant leisure: the dark side of free-time activity', *Leisure Studies: Prospects for the twenty-first century*, 81–96.

Rosen, C. (2007), 'Virtual friendship and the new narcissism', *The New Atlantis*, 17(1): 15–31.

Rosenhan, D. L. (1974), 'On being sane in insane places', *Clinical Social Work Journal*, 2(4), 237–256.

Reuters (2010), Available online at http://uk.reuters.com/article/2010/02/08/uk-beer-idUKTRE6173IZ20100208 [accessed 20/12/2012].

Sack, R. D. (1992), *Place, modernity, and the consumer's world: a relational framework for geographical analysis*, Baltimore: Johns Hopkins University Press.

Savage, M., Barlow J., Dickens, P. and Fielding, T. (1992), *Property, Bureaucracy and Culture: middle class formation in contemporary Britain*, London: Routledge.

Savage, M., Devine, F., Cunningham, N., Taylor, M., Li, Y., Hjelbrekke, J., Le Roux, B., Friedman, S. and Miles, A. (2013), 'A new model of social class? Findings from the BBC's Great British Class survey experiment', Sociology, 47(2), April, 219–250.

Seaman, P. and Ikegwuonu, T. (2010), 'Drinking to belong: understanding young adults' alcohol use within social networks', York: Joseph Rowntree Foundation.

Simmel, G. (1903), 'The metropolis and mental life', in Lin, J. and Mele, C. (2013)(eds) The *Urban Sociology Reader*, Oxford: Routledge, 23–31.

Simmel, G. (1921) 'The sociological significance of the stranger' in Park, R and Burgess, E., *Introduction to the science of sociology*. Chicago: Chicago University Press, 322–327

Skelton, T. and Valentine, G. (1998), *Cool places: geographies of youth cultures*, London: Routledge.

Smith, L. and Foxcroft, D. (2009), 'Drinking in the UK: an exploration of trends', York: Joseph Rowntree Foundation.

Smith, O. (2012), 'Easy money', in Winlow, S. and Atkinson, R. *New directions in crime and deviancy*, Routledge.

Southwood, I. (2010), *Non-stop inertia*, Winchester: Zero Books.

Spracklen, K. (2011), 'Dreaming of drams: authenticity in Scottish whisky tourism as an expression of unresolved Habermasian rationalities', *Leisure Studies*, 30(1), 99–116.

Spracklen, K., Laurencic, J. and Kenyon, A. (2013), '"Mine's a pint of bitter": performativity, gender, class and representations of authenticity in real-ale tourism', *Tourist Studies*, 13(3), 304–321.

Stacey, M. (1960), *Tradition and change: a study of Banbury*, London: Oxford University Press.

Standing, G. (2011), *The precariat: the new dangerous class*, London: Bloomsbury.

Stiglitz, J. E. (2010), *Freefall: America, free markets, and the sinking of the world economy*, London: WW Norton.

Szmigin, I., Griffin, C., Mistral, W., Bengry-Howell, A., Weale, L. and Hackley, C. (2008), 'Re-framing "binge drinking" as calculated hedonism: empirical evidence from the UK', *International Journal of Drug Policy*, 19(5), 359–366.

Tanner, J. L. and Arnett J. J. (2009), 'The emergence of "emerging adulthood": the new life stage between adolescence and young adulthood', in Furlong A. (ed.) *Handbook of Youth and Young Adulthood*, New York: Routledge, pp. 39–48.

Taylor, I. (1999), *Crime in context: a critical criminology of market societies*, London: Polity Press.

Thurnell-Read, T. and Parker, A. (2008), 'Men, masculinities and firefighting: occupational identity, shop-floor culture and organisational change', *Emotion, Space and Society*, 1(2), 127–134.

Tomsen, S. (1997), 'A top night: social protest, masculinity and the culture of drinking violence', *British Journal of Criminology*, 37(1), 90.

Turner, V. W. (1975), *Dramas, fields, and metaphors: symbolic action in human society*, New York: Cornell University Press.

Tweedie (2006), Available online at http://www.telegraph.co.uk/news/uknews/1517460/100000-a-year-but-we-are-still-working-class.html [accessed 02/03/2014].

Van den Hoonaard, W. C. (2002), *Walking the tightrope: ethical issues for qualitative researchers*. Toronto: University of Toronto Press.

Van Moorst, H. (1982), 'Leisure and social theory', *Leisure Studies*, 1(2), 157–169.

Vaughan, B. (2002), 'The punitive consequences of consumer culture', *Punishment & Society*, 4(2), 195.

Veblen, T. (1994), *The theory of the leisure class*, USA: Oxford University Press.

Virilio, P. (2005), *The information bomb*, Verso Books, London.

Warde, A. (1992), 'Notes on the relationship between production and consumption', in Burrows, R. and Marsh, C. (eds) *Consumption and class: divisions and change*, London: Macmillan.

Weber, M. (1930), *The protestant ethic and the spirit of capitalism*, Los Angeles, California: Roxbury Publishing Corporation.

Whitbread homepage (2013), Available online at: http://www.whitbread.co.uk/homepage.html [accessed February 22, 2013].

Whyte, W. F. (1959), *Street corner society: the social structure of an Italian slum*, Harvard, Chicago: University of Chicago Press.

Whyte, W. H. (1956), *The organization man*, New York: Simon and Schuster.

Whyte, W. H. (1988), *City: rediscovering the center*, New York: Anchor.

Wiles, R., Charled, V., Crow, G. and Heath, S. (2006), 'Informed consent and the research process', *Paper presented at the ESRC Research Methods Festival, Oxford, July 2, 2004*. Available online at http://www.sociology.soton.ac.uk/Proj/Informed_Consent/methsfest%20.rtf [accessed 11/09/2013].

Williams, T. (1990), *The cocaine kids: the inside story of a teenage drug ring*, New York: Da Capo Press.

Willis, P. E. (1977), *Learning to labour*, Fansborough: Saxon House.

Willmott, P. and Young, M. (1973), *The symmetrical family*, New York: Pantheon Books.

Winlow, S. (2001), *Badfellas*, Oxford: Berg.

Winlow, S. and Hall, S. (2006), *Violent night*, Oxford: Berg.

Winlow, S. and Hall, S. (2009), 'Living for the weekend: youth identities in north-east England', *Ethnography*, 10(1), 91.

Winlow, S. and Hall, S. (2013), *Rethinking social exclusion: the end of the social*, London: Sage.

Wright, L. (1999), 'Young people and alcohol: what 11 to 24 year olds know, think and do', London: Health Education Authority.

Wright, O. (2013), 'For the first time in a century, today's middle-class children will be 'worse off than their parents', *The Independent*. Available online at http://www.independent.co.uk/news/uk/home-news/for-the-first-time-in-a-century-todays-middleclass-children-will-be-worse-off-than-their-parents-8877657.html [accessed December 15, 2013].

Wyn, J. and White, R. (1997), *Rethinking youth*. London: Sage.

Young, J. (1999), *The exclusive society: social exclusion, crime and difference in late modernity*, London: Sage.

Young, J. (2004), 'Voodoo criminology and the numbers game', in Ferrell. J., Hayward, K., Morrison, W., and Presdee, M. (eds) *Cultural criminology unleashed*, London: Glasshouse Press.

Žižek, S. (1989), *The sublime object of ideology*, London: Verso Books.

Žižek, S. (1991), *For they know not what they do: enjoyment as a political factor*, London: Verso.

Žižek, S. (1997), *The plague of fantasies*, New York: Verso Books.

Žižek, S. (1999), *The ticklish subject: the absent centre of political ontology*, New York: Verso Books.

Žižek, S. (2002a). *For they know not what they do: Enjoyment as a political factor*. Verso.

Žižek, S. (2002b), *Welcome to the desert of the real!: five essays on 11 September and related dates*, London: Verso Books.

Žižek, S. (2006), *The parallax view*, Cambridge: MIT Press.

Žižek, S. (2008), *Violence: six sideways reflections*, USA: Picador.

Žižek, S. (2009), *First as tragedy, then as farce*, London: Verso Books.

Žižek, S. (2010), *Living in the end times*, London: Verso Books.

Zukin, S. (1995), *The Cultures of Cities*. Oxford: Blackwell.

Zukin, S. (1998), 'Urban lifestyles: diversity and standardisation in spaces of consumption', *Urban Studies*, 35(5), 825–839.

Index

Printed and bound by CPI Group (UK) Ltd, Croydon, CR0 4YY